CULTURE and DOMINATION

CULTURE and DOMINATION

JOHN BRENKMAN

CORNELL UNIVERSITY PRESS

ITHACA AND LONDON

A portion of Chapter 4 was published under the title
"The Concrete Utopia of Poetry: Blake's 'A Poison Tree' "
in *Lyric Poetry: Beyond New Criticism*, ed. Chaviva Hošek
and Patricia Parker (Ithaca: Cornell University Press, 1985),
copyright © 1985 by Cornell University Press.

First published 1987 by Cornell University Press.

International Standard Book Number 0-8014-1457-1
Library of Congress Catalog Card Number 87-47543

Printed in the United States of America

*Librarians: Library of Congress cataloging information
appears on the last page of the book.*

*The paper in this book is acid-free and meets the guidelines for
permanence and durability of the Committee on Production Guidelines
for Book Longevity of the Council on Library Resources.*

Contents

Preface

I have written *Culture and Domination* in the conviction that the most valuable literary criticism contributes to social criticism. That conviction has given shape to an inquiry into the relations between cultural interpretation and social theory.

Culture does not stand above or apart from the many other activities and relationships that make up a society, including the socially organized forms of domination, exploitation, and power pervasive in our own society and its history. Granted, cultural practices foster social solidarity and collective identity. But that does not keep them from participating in social divisions and exclusions. Granted, culture is a site of reciprocal relationships and mutual understandings. But these achievements are not inevitable; they do not belong to culture categorically. Indeed, whether conceived as spirit, consciousness, superstructure, or the symbolic, culture is not a realm unto itself or a separate domain. Guided by that premise, I have sought to ask a two-sided question concerning culture and society:

How are social relations of domination inscribed within cultural practices, including the production and reception of art and literature, which are often held to embody the ideal or normative conception of culture?

And, conversely, how are a society's coercive, nonreciprocal relations organized—and contested—through symbolizations as well as institutions, moral relations as well as economic ones, discourse and consent as well as force and threat?

The search for a theoretical framework supple enough to respond to both questions led me to develop an immanent critique of hermeneutics, Marxism, and psychoanalysis. Each of these theoretical fields has produced concepts and procedures crucial to socially critical interpretations of cultural practices. Each has also, however, been inhibited from carrying through that task by its own premises and self-understandings.

Hermeneutics follows out the consequences of its basic insight that theory and interpretation are activities belonging to the culture they attempt to understand. Interpreters are thoroughly embedded in, and their capacities for understanding are preformed by, the very tradition they interpret. Traditional hermeneutics places this notion within a problematic that renders it complicit with traditionalism and rehabilitated prejudice. Hans-Georg Gadamer, for example, remains impervious to the ways in which coercive and nonreciprocal relationships within a society shape its culture. Having denied a connection between culture and domination, he then asserts that the Western cultural tradition already genuinely embodies the ideal of uncoerced, reciprocal understanding. In combination those premises lend Gadamerian hermeneutics to the legitimation of domination. Traditional hermeneutics actively constructs a cultural tradition in the guise of a unified realm of meanings and values separated from social relations of domination and power.

The insight into interpreters' embeddedness in traditions needs to be placed within an altogether different problematic. For cultural heritages in the modern world are plural, not monolithic and unified. They intersect and clash according to the complex circumstances surrounding the institutional and symbolic formation of interrelated social groups. The heritage of modern culture has indeed to be actively constructed. As a consequence, we have not only conflicting interpretations and valuations of specific texts but also competing constructions of tradition. When interpreters seek to recover, preserve, or reconstruct cultural heritages, they enter into the politically charged conflicts of interpretation—the wars of persuasion—that characterize modern culture.

Marxism revamps cultural theory by interrogating what the early Frankfurt School called the "affirmative character" of the Western cultural tradition. Culture becomes an alibi for domination and tacitly affirms the social order when it sets itself above the social struggles of contemporary history. The Western tradition at the same time supplies the philosophical and aesthetic values underlying critical social theory itself. Culture seems at once affirmative and critical. The researches of

Western Marxism—from Georg Lukács, the Frankfurt School, and Walter Benjamin through phenomenological Marxism and, more recently, Jürgen Habermas—attempt to capture this ambiguity felt at the heart of the Western cultural tradition. But Marxism's own commitment to the notion that culture is a domain apart hampers these researches. Marx inaugurated his paradigm of cultural theory by abandoning the view of culture as a complex set of material-social practices and replacing it with a view of culture as a realm of representations—"consciousness" as opposed to "real activity," a symbolic domain separated from, but controlled by, an economic domain. According to one tendency within Marxism, culture is an instrument of social domination; according to another, it transcends domination and prefigures its end. Both tendencies share the assumption that culture is a symbolic domain whose meaning and value, as a whole, are determined in relation to the economy.

The paradigm of the economy and the symbolic has to be supplanted, as does the choice between the instrumental and transcendent views of culture. For culture cannot be evaluated categorically. Specific cultural practices contain an interplay of ideological and utopian elements. A major premise drawn from posthistoricist hermeneutics is needed to keep the interpretation of ideology and utopia from slipping back into the original dichotomy. A text's meaning is not fixed once and for all, because it is determined by the situation of the interpreters as well as that of the text. Meaning therefore varies in time and changes with each distinct configuration of production- and reception-contexts. Marxism contributes to this problematic an understanding of the social and political character of these contexts. We must also, however, recognize that ideology and utopia are as contextual and as variable as any other sorts of meanings and valuations. This recognition precludes appeal to a transcendent perspective, be it that of universal interests, of "history" projected as the narrative of class struggles, or of the structure of "society" viewed as a totality. Interpreters have to distinguish the ideological and the utopian without any predetermined, independently grounded standpoint. Arguing from values and for new valuations, they have to make their interpretations persuasive through moral-political argumentation.

Psychoanalysis, in contrast to Marxism, does provide a model for an interpretive process in which critique proceeds contextually without reference to a meaning-securing "totality." And, in contrast to traditional hermeneutics, it is fully capable of envisioning the negative, distorting side of formative processes of education and culture. From Freud to Jacques Lacan, psychoanalysis lets us glimpse the stakes involved when interpreters actually approach those points at which their embeddedness in the discourse of others proves to have been formative of their identity, their desires and anxieties, their fantasies and cognitions. The analysand is indeed a plausible figure for the modern cultural interpreter or literary critic. What makes psychoanalysis relevant to hermeneutics is its attention to the formation of the subject in the "discourse of the Other." What makes it relevant to socially critical hermeneutics is its practice of a dialogue designed to transform participants' relation to their own history and their own discourse.

The social categories underpinning the specific concerns of psychoanalysis have to be made explicit to develop the relation between psychoanalysis and critical hermeneutics. Freud retreats from such a reflection by couching an entire range of social and cultural, institutional and symbolic processes in terms of the "psyche" or the "psychic apparatus." Lacan shifts the Freudian paradigm from intrapsychic mechanisms to intersubjective relations, and from quasi-biological instincts to language, partially opening psychoanalysis to cultural theory. The latent social content of basic Freudian categories—such as fantasy and play, pleasure and reality, the death drive—sustain a covert critique of reification in capitalist civilization. Other psychoanalytic categories, however, such as those Freud develops into a psychology of love, are covertly modeled on male fantasy and reproduce an entire set of social relations and cultural forms linking heterosexual intimacy and male dominance. Psychoanalysis must remain an object as well as a resource of critical hermeneutics so long as the social relations and cultural formations within which psychoanalysis is itself situated are obscured.

Culture and Domination is divided into three parts of two chapters each. The parts essentially correspond to the three theoretical fields— hermeneutics, Marxism, and psychoanalysis—from which I have tried to build the theoretical framework of socially critical hermeneutics. In counterpoint to the central theoretical discussions of Marxism and psychoanalysis I have presented interpretations of Blake's writings of the 1790s (Chapter 4) and Goethe's *Sorrows of Young Werther* (Chapter 6). My motivation has several aspects. To begin with, I have dealt with the utopian in Blake's poetry and the ideological strands of Goethe's novel as a response to the theoretical challenge I have made in my critique of Marxism. Moreover, both authors, writing in the latter part of the eighteenth century, belong to the period that, according to the Frankfurt School theorists, consolidated a specifically bourgeois form of affirmative culture. I have tested out aspects of that historical scheme in these chapters and questioned the underlying conceptions of literary form and of cultural interpretation. Blake and Goethe have also proved relevant to my attempts to underscore the extent to which Marxism and psychoanalysis are themselves part of cultural processes in which literature plays a formative role. And, finally, I have tried in these chapters of literary criticism to make good on my claims about the political and ideological significance of conflicts of interpretation. I have presented my reading of Blake in polemic with Harold Bloom and E. P. Thompson. And I have looked at Goethe in light of the interpretations of Schiller, Freud, and Lukács. It is my hope that the Blake and Goethe discussions demonstrate how interpretations can be socially critical without invoking a transcendental perspective, and how interpreters become caught up in a kind of transformative process when they become critical of their own formative cultural traditions. It is then that meanings and values are refashioned in the very process of being understood.

The writing of this book has spanned the two universities and two cities in which I have taught and lived since first conceiving the project. In Madison, I enjoyed an intellectual-political environment in which my work was encouraged and shaped by many collaborations and discussions. I am especially grateful to David Bathrick, Serafina Bathrick, Philip Bishop, Timothy Cole, Christine Holmlund, Jean Lind-Brenkman, Diane Waldman, and Philip Wexler. At the earliest stages of writing, I also received important suggestions from Stanley Aronowitz, Fredric Jameson, and Oskar Negt.

I have completed the book since coming to Northwestern University and am extremely grateful to Hugo Achugar, Nancy Fraser, Gerald Graff, Carla Kaplan, Thomas McCarthy, and Michael Warner for their comments and criticisms. Their suggestions have been invaluable. And I want finally to thank Jonathan Arac for reading every version of the manuscript with such care and insight.

JOHN BRENKMAN

Chicago/Madison

Part One

CRITICAL VERSUS TRADITIONAL HERMENEUTICS

I

Interpreting Affirmative Culture

The Critique of Affirmative Culture

"There is no document of civilization," wrote Walter Benjamin, "which is not at the same time a document of barbarism."[1]

This awareness is difficult to sustain. It introduces a moment of pain into the most refined moments of aesthetic pleasure. It bears witness to the violence and the residues of violence embedded within the most peaceful philosophical reflections. Yet Benjamin was not succumbing to some kind of moral fatigue when he advanced this thesis, nor is it the expression of an unhappy consciousness. To the contrary, it expresses a restless consciousness, one that senses in every work of culture the fact and the effects of social domination. At the same time, this restlessness, this critical attitude toward what is sometimes experienced as the "realm of freedom" and the very place of human meanings and values, also includes the hope of liberating the human capacity for thought and expression—a capacity that is promised or realized in still distorted and threatened ways in those forms of activity we call culture, art and literature, philosophy and science.

Benjamin made his statement in an unforgiving account of the cultural tradition as the consciousness of meaning which the victors in every great social upheaval have imposed upon the vanquished and upon posterity. The assertion brings to the question of culture Marx's

[1]Walter Benjamin, "Theses on the Philosophy of History," in *Illuminations,* trans. Harry Zohn (New York: Schocken, 1969), p. 256.

3

notion that humanity is still living its prehistory. Marx meant that the history of humanity is not yet human history. Even though the social world is the result of human activity, it continues to evolve independently of collectively formed human intent. History remains, in Marx's sense of the term, "accidental." Human history is still a "natural" history though there has formed within it the consciousness of the *possibility* of making natural history into human history. For Marx, such a consciousness was forming in the workers' movements of the nineteenth century insofar as the development of capitalism provoked its wage laborers to see through the veil of this natural history and discover that humanity makes its world of society and culture through its transformations of nature, that is, by its own labor. Marx considered the whole historical—or prehistorical—process to have been set in motion by the emergence of class societies. The social division of labor, most fundamentally in the division of manual and mental labor, had caused the material production of the conditions of life and the symbolic production of meanings and values to devolve onto different groups or classes, instituting within society organized power or domination. Benjamin turned this reflection onto the question of culture and the works of civilization in which the course of prehistory is documented. The preserved and validated monuments of Western culture are not only the achieved expression of meanings and values and a resource of potential means of expression for civilization; they also carry the imprint of the violence and forced labor which has made their creation possible.

The violence that founded and continues through our social history is also a violence against consciousness. Domination is a human act that tends to appear to human beings themselves as a mere fact of life. It is a violence that disguises itself as the order of society and the stability of meanings and values. Benjamin sought the links between the critique of society and the interpretation of culture because he recognized that these two modes of understanding depend on one another. The reading of a text, just as much as a cognition of social reality, catches us up within a historical process that can appear congealed in the order of established facts and achieved meanings or become the dynamic confrontation of memory and hope with the world as it is. I thus take Benjamin's notion that civilization and barbarism are interwoven in our cultural traditions and experiences as a challenge to cultural studies to develop interpretive and theoretical questions in relation to and as part of an ongoing critique of society.

This challenge has animated the social and aesthetic researches of the Frankfurt School from the earliest essays of Herbert Marcuse, T. W. Adorno, and Max Horkheimer down to the most recent work of Jürgen Habermas. It has also figured—sometimes as negative counterpoint, sometimes as shared project—in the phenomenological tradition from Husserl and Heidegger to such diverse thinkers as Maurice Merleau-Ponty, Karel Kosík, Paul Ricoeur, and Hans-Georg Gadamer. It is this latter tradition which has developed an extensive reflection on the theory and procedures of cultural interpretation, or hermeneutics, just as the neo-Marxist reflection of the Frankfurt School has insistently pushed the question of culture to the center of social theory and, conversely, demanded that the interpretive preservation and transmission of cultural traditions be linked to the critique of contemporary society.

By way of introducing my project in this work, I will devote this chapter and the following to some watersheds in the various antagonisms and collaborations between these two intellectual traditions— the early Frankfurt School and Husserl; Merleau-Ponty and Kosík; and Gadamer and Habermas—in order to pose again the question of the interrelation of critical social theory and cultural interpretation. My aim is to assess the tasks of what might be called the critical theory of culture, echoing the Frankfurt School's designation of its project as the critical theory of society, and, just as centrally, the tasks and procedures of a socially critical hermeneutics. Common to the critical theorists and the phenomenologists has been a recognition that the "theory of culture" is a self-reflective endeavor. Far from being a purely objective posture of knowledge which can take up "culture" or individual works as its object, theory is always already and inescapably a part of culture. Every theoretical conception of culture is itself a form of cultural activity, and, by the same token, every concrete act of interpretation will not only be implicated in the background of cultural practices which has formed the interpreters but will also develop or counter the implicit self-conception of that cultural background. In this sense, interpretations are caught up in a process of self-understanding or self-misunderstanding even as they engage an object or text to be understood. As we will see, such processes of hermeneutical self-understanding/self-misunderstanding are also bound up with the conflicting self-understandings of a society that is divided by its institutionalized relations of domination, coercion, and exploitation.

In a 1937 essay entitled "The Affirmative Character of Culture,"

Marcuse attempted to show that the prevailing conception and experience of culture, originating in Greek philosophy and culminating in bourgeois thought and art by the end of the eighteenth century, place "culture" outside the relations of social domination. He argued that the philosophical heritage of Western thought, beginning with Plato, inaugurated the idea of culture—art, literature, and philosophy or theory itself—as a realm *separated* from the factual domain of social life and material necessity. "Insofar as philosophy is concerned with man's [*sic*] happiness—and the theory of classical antiquity held it to be the highest good—it cannot find it in the established material organization of life. That is why it must transcend this order's facticity."[2] The "higher good" of the philosopher's own pursuit of knowledge becomes the model for the growing idea that culture is the transcendent realm of those meanings and values not realized in the actual life of society as a whole.

Marcuse then suggests that this separation of idea from reality, of culture from the material realm of production, has an ambiguous history. On the one hand, it gives the idealist philosophical tradition an essentially critical attitude toward society, in that society is always implicitly condemned as a lower order or unfulfilled or incomplete mode of existence. On the other hand, bourgeois society will transmute this tension between the real and the ideal, the transitory and the permanent, the material and the meaningful, into a fixed separation between an outer world of ugly fact and an inner world of harmony called the soul. The very satisfactions that the inner world provides—be they spiritual, intellectual, or aesthetic—become justifications for the outer world as it is. Culture becomes "affirmative." The higher value attributed to the soul, thought, and art becomes the apology for reality rather than an implicit condemnation of it.

This change in the experience and understanding of culture occurs in the name of the bourgeoisie's claim that the separated realm of meaning and value is universal and valid for all. With the bourgeoisie there

> emerges the thesis of the universality and universal validity of "culture." With good conscience, the theory of antiquity had expressed the fact that most men [*sic*] spent their lives providing for necessities while a smaller number devoted themselves to enjoyment and truth. Although

[2]Herbert Marcuse, "The Affirmative Character of Culture," in *Negations*, trans. Jeremy J. Shapiro (Boston: Beacon, 1968), p. 89.

the fact has not changed, the good conscience has disappeared. Free competition places individuals in the relation of buyers and sellers of labor power. The pure abstractness to which men are reduced in their social relations extends as well to intercourse with ideas.... Just as each individual's relation to the market is immediate (without his personal qualities and needs being relevant except as commodities), so his relations to God, to beauty, to goodness, and to truth are relations of immediacy. As abstract beings, all men are supposed to participate equally in these values.[3]

The ambiguity Marcuse discerns in affirmative culture has corresponding effects on critical theory itself. On the one hand, critical theory condemns the bourgeois claim to universality on the grounds that it falsifies the real conditions of class society, namely, that the cultivation of the so-called inner world remains a privilege and an alibi of those who are not compelled to produce the material necessities of social life and, second, that the claimed universality and equality of bourgeois culture are therefore a merely abstract identification on the part of individuals with universal "Man." On the other hand, it is precisely because bourgeois culture contains this *claim* to universality that the space for the critical theory of class society opens in the first place. Without the falsifiable claim to universality and equality there would be nothing more than the "good conscience" of the ancients. Marcuse's attempt to recover the socially critical element of affirmative culture which he here attributes to ancient philosophy is motivated by the bad conscience of bourgeois culture.

Indeed, the Frankfurt School theorists are exemplars of virtually the last generation of European intellectuals whose own formation (*Bildung*) was thoroughly organized by the intellectual and aesthetic education of affirmative culture. As is so vividly evident in the rhetoric of their writings, their own socially critical attitude is an aggressive expression of just this bad conscience of the bourgeoisie. The resulting ambiguity manifests itself theoretically in the fine line dividing two possible forms of the immanent critique of bourgeois culture. To what extent do the Frankfurt School's researches represent a critical moment or potential *within* affirmative culture, to what extent a critique *of* affirmative culture? The question does not admit of a ready answer, for it tends to be raised anew in nearly every strand of these theorists' work. At the most general level the question concerns how to turn the

[3]Ibid., pp. 93–94.

claim to universality intrinsic to bourgeois culture back against the affirmative character of that culture.

There are two particular aspects of the Frankfurt School's approach to the question which I want to single out here: first, their tendency to accept some variant of the notion that culture is a "realm" held apart from the material production of social life; and second, their tendency to thematize social critique in terms of the opposition between fact and essence. Both tendencies find a condensed representation in Marcuse's picture of the bourgeois form of life, a picture that also reflects something of the Frankfurt theorists' self-understanding of their own cultural formation and social existence. According to Marcuse, the bourgeois form of life splits the individual's life into two realms. Practical existence is lived as the sheer submission to external fact and to the forces of the marketplace, while an inner life takes the shape of an autonomous realm of intellectual and aesthetic experiences whose significance lies precisely in their disconnection from "mere fact." As alibi for domination and as abstract illusion of universality, the placing of thought and art in a separate realm gives bourgeois culture its affirmative character. However, the autonomy of thought and art vis-à-vis the instrumental tasks of carrying out the imperatives of the capitalist marketplace makes this realm at the same time appear, to the critical theorists themselves, as both a refuge from capitalist social relations and a standpoint for critique itself.

In the course of this work I will return to several problems related to the ambiguous conception of culture as a separated realm: the autonomy or, alternatively, the relative autonomy of "culture"; the use of the term "culture" to refer either broadly to forms of life or narrowly to canonical traditions of Western philosophy and art; the aesthetic and psychoanalytic problems posed by the Frankfurt School's conception of the splitting of the bourgeois subject; and so on. But for now, it is the thematization of social critique in terms of the opposition of fact and essence that I want to look at. Not only does this question engage the basic self-understanding of critical theory, but it will also permit us to juxtapose the neo-Marxist and phenemenological traditions as regards their different conceptions of cultural interpretation.

The distinction between fact and essence was the conceptual cornerstone of Horkheimer's programmatic essay "Traditional and Critical Theory"[4] and established the basic themes of the early Frankfurt

[4]Max Horkheimer, "Traditional and Critical Theory," in *Critical Theory: Selected Essays*, trans. Matthew J. O'Connell (New York: Seabury, 1972), pp. 188–252.

School's account of the relation between the tradition of Western philosophy insofar as it has been part of affirmative culture and the tradition of social theory which leads from Hegel through Marx to the Frankfurt School itself. Horkheimer defined critical theory as against traditional theory in terms of two antagonistic ways of relating knowledge to fact. According to Horkheimer, traditional theory, especially in its development from Descartes to Kant, considers fact a mere *given*, a datum, in opposition to which the transcendent truth of theory is an ideality or essence. Critical theory considers facts to be the social *product*—the result or effect—of the activities of human beings as those activities are organized by the historical form of society. The paradigm or model for the latter view is Marx's analysis of commodities. In the capitalist mode of production, activity or labor appears as a commodity, that is, an object exchanged in the marketplace according to its abstract, economically designated value; although this "appearance" is lived and real, it nonetheless conceals the "essence" of labor, namely, that it is the activity which produces all other commodities. In its true essence, labor is activity and productive of the material conditions of social life; in its real appearance, labor is a commodified object like any other. With this model in mind, Horkheimer drew his distinction between traditional and critical theory. Traditional theory posits an essence which lies in a transcendent realm of thought (pure theory); critical theory considers social reality to be the product of social processes whose essence or truth is in turn concealed behind this product's facticity. For Horkheimer, as for Marcuse, the fate of the distinction between essence and fact had become doubtful in the dialectic of bourgeois culture. On the one hand, the distinction became a means of accommodating thought to reality, and, on the other, it reflected the historically real but false character of capitalism itself. Critical theory therefore saw itself as the genuine inheritor of idealism's original project insofar as it sought to establish the claims of truth *against* reality.

Marcuse renewed Horkheimer's line of argument in his study of Hegel, *Reason and Revolution,* and provided a narrative to explain how philosophy had to become social theory in Hegel and ultimately critical social theory in Marx. At issue is the preservation of the normative or critical force of reason. According to Marcuse, the concept of reason which the idealist tradition had evolved from Plato to Kant carried within it a call for freedom. Reason represented the power of human consciousness to apprehend reality and truth without external coercion. Marcuse argues that across the eighteenth and nineteenth centuries this connection between freedom and reason was increasingly undermined by the development of capitalism. Reason became more and more associated with technical rationality in the sense of the scientific mastery or control of nature. "Modern rationalism, as a result, had a tendency to pattern individual as well as social life on the model of nature. . . . The human world was presented as governed by objective laws, analogous to or even identical with the laws of nature, and society was set forth as an objective entity more or less unyielding to subjective desires and goals. Men [sic] believed their relations to each other to result from objective laws that operate with the necessity of natural laws, and their freedom to consist in adapting their private existence to necessity."[5] The connection between reason and freedom begins to dissolve as freedom becomes adaptability to objective laws that are themselves but the integration of human reason into the self-functioning processes of capitalist production. Reason loses its normative force. "The more reason triumphed in technology and natural science, the more reluctantly did it call for freedom in man's social life."[6] Part and parcel of the disjoining of reason and freedom is a philosophical concept of reason which expresses the split between an inner and outer realm characteristic of affirmative culture more generally. "The representative philosophers of the middle class (particularly Leibniz, Kant, and Fichte) reconciled their philosophical rationalism with the flagrant irrationality of the prevailing social relations, and inverted human reason and freedom so that they became ramparts of the isolated soul or mind, internal phenomena quite compatible with external realities, even if these contradicted reason and freedom."[7]

It was Hegel, Marcuse argues, who sought to counteract this separation of reason from reality, of freedom from history. To do so he had to transform philosophy into social theory. For Hegel, reason is something that realizes itself in society and its institutions. In place of the stagnant contradiction between thought and reality, the Hegelian dialectic views reason and social reality as joined together, though contradictorily. This "resulted in the dissolution of the harmonious world of fixed objects posited by common sense and in the recognition that the truth philosophy sought was a totality of pervasive contra-

---

[5]Herbert Marcuse, *Reason and Revolution: Hegel and the Rise of Social Theory* (Boston: Beacon, 1960), pp. 255–256.

[6]Ibid., p. 256.

[7]Ibid.

dictions."[8] Hegel turned philosophy into social theory in order to preserve or recover the relation between philosophical thought and a historically dynamic reality. For Marcuse, this endeavor was limited to the extent that the bourgeois society of Hegel's time was limited; the concepts "stopped where the content stopped, that is, in the state that governed civil society, while the ideas and values that pointed beyond this social system were stowed away in the realm of Absolute Mind, in the system of dialectical philosophy."[9]

Marcuse's narrative then places Marx as the thinker who turned Hegelian social theory into *critical* social theory. In Marx, theory itself discovers that the unity of reason and freedom requires a practical, rather than only a theoretical, negation of existing social reality. The normative power of reason can be preserved only by becoming revolutionary. Critical theory thereby allies itself with those forces, tendencies, and movements in society which point toward a transformed reality and toward a society in which freedom would be grounded in the rational, collectively exercised control over the processes of producing material life. Whereas bourgeois thought defined freedom as the individual's rational adaptation to a reality that was historically constituted but perceived as natural necessity, Marx saw the historical necessity of transforming society in order that human freedom could be realized in the rationality of collective praxis. The Frankfurt School theorists thus understood their own intellectual heritage as the process through which philosophy's traditional commitment to reason became a commitment to the social transformation of capitalism.

A contrastive thematization of the crisis of reason in European culture was worked out, more or less contemporaneously, by Edmund Husserl. The contrast is striking and sets the stage for later avatars of the exchange between critical theory and phenomenology. The Frankfurt School looked to grasp social and political developments in categories drawn from a philosophical tradition they shared with Husserl—that of Plato, Descartes, and Kant—but at the same time pursued an immanent critique of that tradition's inherence in the structure of class societies. As Husserl assessed the dissolution of the connection between reason and freedom, he sought to restore philosophy to its "original" tasks and to place it once again firmly within the separated sphere of affirmative culture. With Husserl, in other words,

[8]Ibid.
[9]Ibid., p. 257.

traditional theory reasserts the autonomy of ideas with respect to social developments. It radicalizes the separation of philosophical reason and empirical reality. Husserl understood this project as a renewal of philosophy's struggle against the fragmentation and technologicization of modern knowledges and as a reassertion of the primacy of the *Geisteswissenschaften* against positivism and the ascendency of the natural sciences as a model of knowledge. Those two themes, which at times resonate with the Frankfurt School's "critique of instrumental reason," will emerge again later in Gadamer's philosophical hermeneutics.

In a 1935 lecture, "Philosophy and the Crisis of European Man," Husserl pictures himself and his philosophical project threatened and embattled in the face of the growing influence of the natural sciences. He rejects the notion that the true model of scientific knowledge lies in the procedures of natural science and at the same time eschews any pure separation of the sciences of nature and the sciences of spirit. He argues for the centrality of the human sciences on the grounds that every act of understanding, including those within the domain of the natural sciences, is itself a human or cultural or "spiritual" act that cannot adequately understand itself according to the same procedures by which it understands nature: "Obviously, too, it is forgotten that natural science (like all sciences as such) is a title for spiritual activities, those of natural scientists in cooperation with each other; as such these activities belong, as do all spiritual occurrences, to the realm of a science of spirit (*Geisteswissenschaft*)."[10] It is this forgetting of the conditions of knowledge which for Husserl is the source of the crisis he is addressing. The date of his lecture alone, however, makes it impossible to ignore that this plea for a restoration of the project of European reason is made in the context of the rise of fascism. Husserl concludes his lecture with a sense of alarm that cannot be easily dissociated from the surrounding political reality: "The reason for the downfall of a rational culture does not lie in the essence of rationalism itself but only in its exteriorization, its absorption in 'naturalism' and 'objectivism.' The crisis of European existence can end in only one of two ways: in the ruin of a Europe alienated from its rational sense of life, fallen into a barbarian hatred of spirit; or in the rebirth of Europe from the spirit of philosophy, through a heroism of reason that will definitively overcome naturalism."[11]

[10]Edmund Husserl, "Philosophy and the Crisis of European Man," in *Phenomenology and the Crisis of Philosophy*, trans. Quentin Lauer (New York: Harper, 1965), p. 154.
[11]Ibid., pp. 191–192.

The crisis of reason which Husserl laid at the feet of objectivism and naturalism Horkheimer and Adorno attributed to fascism. They saw in fascism the capacity of capitalist society to fuse irrationalism in the cultural and ideological realm with an increasing technical rationality in production and in the bureaucratic administration of a militarized society, including its communications and public sphere. A revival of the "spirit of philosophy" hardly seemed an adequate response to this historical development. At the same time, the Frankfurt School saw that the Marxist tradition could no longer confidently maintain that proletarian revolution was the only, or the "historically necessary," process by which bourgeois society, along with its ideologies, its philosophy, its politics, and its cultural heritage, could be negated and transformed; fascism itself negated and transformed bourgeois society in a revolution that left the exploitative social and economic structure of capitalism intact. Horkheimer and Adorno's response to this situation was to undertake a series of reflections, culminating in their *Dialectic of Enlightenment,* on the intellectual and cultural as well as political traditions of bourgeois society in a renewed effort to link an immanent critique of those traditions and a socialist transformation of capitalism.

Husserl, on the other hand, never related the dominance of technical rationality to the evolving organization of capitalism. From the viewpoint of a philosophy that laid claim to being a "rigorous science" on account of a radical separation of ideas from empirical reality, it was unthinkable to derive the predicament of philosophy from a historical social process. Thus Husserl thematized the "exteriorization of rationalism" as a "forgetting" of the spiritual grounding of reason rather than as the evolution of new social, economic, and political structures. To overcome such forgetfulness would require repairing the lineage of Descartes and Kant and radicalizing the concept of transcendental consciousness. The exteriorization of reason was to be countered by a renewed and more complete interiorization of reason; through the phenomenological procedures of "meditation" and "bracketing," consciousness would intuit ideas in their pure ideality without reference to an external world, others, or even one's own body. In order for the human subject to become self-constituting—that is, free in a radical sense—philosophy had, according to Husserl, to recover the attitude of transcendental consciousness and the autonomy of ideas. It is in this form that Husserl made his call to renew philosophy's place within affirmative culture.

From the viewpoint of the Frankfurt School theorists, such a stance could only deepen the impasse. The affirmative character of bourgeois culture had relegated philosophy in the tradition of Descartes and Kant to preserving the normative force of reason and its link to human freedom while leaving the rationalization of social and economic life to the nonnormative imperatives of capitalist accumulation. Husserl's program for traditional theory could not help but capitulate to this same trend even as he denounced it. The Kantian distinction, revived and radicalized by Husserl, between the transcendental ego as site of philosophical reflection and the empirical ego as the instrumental agency of the self in the external world was, for Horkheimer and Adorno, an expression rather than resolution of the dilemma of modern rationality:

> Kant's concepts are ambiguous. As the transcendental, supraindividual self, reason comprises the idea of a free, human social life in which men [sic] organize themselves as the universal subject and overcome the conflict between pure and empirical reason in the conscious solidarity of the whole. This represents the idea of true universality: utopia. At the same time, however, reason constitutes the court of judgment of calculation, which adjusts the world for the ends of self-preservation and recognizes no function other than the preparation of the object from mere sensory material in order to make it the material of subjugation. The true nature of schematism . . . is ultimately revealed in contemporary science as the interest of industrial society.[12]

For Horkheimer and Adorno, the normative concept of universal reason and the socially critical potential of the essence/fact distinction are threatened as soon as Kant attributes "essence" to the autonomous, a priori structure of understanding. He thereby merely adduces the philosophical analogue of capitalist production. The latter treats reality—nature and society reduced to "fact"—as a neutral field of objects upon which the subject acts following the abstract economic imperative of realizing values, whether in the form of wages or profits. The appearance of an autonomous ego and of a priori structures of understanding derives in this sense from the subject's economic activity as it is framed and prescribed by the capitalist organization of production. At this point, the original distinction between essence and fact collapses, for the transcendental ego, which is supposed to be the bearer of the

---

[12]Max Horkheimer and Theodor W. Adorno, *Dialectic of Enlightenment,* trans. John Cumming (New York: Seabury, 1972), pp. 83–84.

essential and of universal reason, turns out to be the (unacknowledged) representation of the empirical ego shaped by the historical form of society. In the aphoristic thesis of *Dialectic of Enlightenment,* "the burgher, in the successive forms of slaveowner, free entrepreneur, and administrator is the logical subject of the Enlightenment."[13]

With this thesis, however, Horkheimer and Adorno approach an impasse all their own. They had started with a critique of bourgeois philosophy and culture. According to that critique, the development of modern capitalism has increasingly subordinated knowledge to capital and integrated scientific consciousness so thoroughly into the production of economic values that the tension still felt by Kant between instrumental reason and those forms of rationality he associated with pure reason, moral autonomy, and aesthetic judgment has been lost. As Habermas has recently argued, Horkheimer and Adorno then took this thesis further. First of all, under the rubric of the "critique of instrumental reason," they turned the distinction between instrumental and universal reason into a straightforward dichotomy; all individual and collective processes of "self-preservation" became associated with the demise of universal reason, that is, the utopian aspect of "true universality" contained in Kant's conception of pure reason. Second, no longer keeping to the historically precise meaning that Lukács had given to the term "reification," they generalized "instrumental reason" to mean the capacity of the human subject to represent, conceptualize, and make use of objects. They came to the view that instrumental reason was, in Habermas's words, "the mechanism that produces the reification of consciousness in the anthropological foundations of the history of the species, in the form of existence of a species that has to reproduce itself through labor."[14] Horkheimer and Adorno had thus rethematized the control of nature for human purposes; it no longer figured as the hidden essence of social life as it did in their work of the 1930s, but rather emerged as a subjugation or domination of nature in the same sense we speak of the social domination of human beings.

Habermas describes the outcome of this line of thought in the following summary of *Dialectic of Enlightenment:*

---

[13]Ibid., p. 83.
[14]Jürgen Habermas, *The Theory of Communicative Action,* vol 1: *Reason and the Rationalization of Society,* trans. Thomas McCarthy (Boston: Beacon, 1984), p. 379.

Lukács used the concept of reification to describe that peculiar compulsion to assimilate interhuman relations (and subjectivity) to the world of things, which comes about when social actions are no longer coordinated through values, norms, or linguistic understanding, but through the medium of exchange value. Horkheimer and Adorno detach the concept not only from the special historical context of the rise of the capitalist economic system but from the dimension of interhuman relations altogether; and they generalize it temporally (over the entire history of the species) and substantively (the same logic of domination is imputed to both cognition in the service of self-preservation and the repression of instinctual nature). This double generalization of the concept of reification leads to a concept of instrumental reason that shifts the primordial history of subjectivity and the self-formative process of ego identity into an encompassing historico-philosophical perspective.[15]

The immanent critique of the project of idealist philosophy, insofar as it gave ambivalent expression to the affirmative character of bourgeois culture and culminated in conceptions of the transcendental ego, arrives here at its impasse. Having counterposed in absolute terms a reason that serves the aims of "self-preservation" and a reason that would seek the "truth," and having made the former the driving force of civilization as a whole, Horkheimer and Adorno narrow the resources of social and cultural critique to the supposed upsurge of the noninstrumentalized, resistant energies of "nature" (the external world, the body, the unconscious). By their own account, however, this countermovement to instrumental reason is impervious to conceptualization or discursive thought. It can expressively indict the prevailing social order, but it cannot generate categories of social analysis. "As the placeholder for [the] primordial reason that was diverted from the intention of truth, Horkheimer and Adorno nominate a capacity, *mimesis,* about which they can speak only as they would about a piece of uncomprehended nature.... The paradox in which the critique of instrumental reason is entangled," argues Habermas, "consists then in this: Horkheimer and Adorno would have to put forth a *theory* of mimesis, which, according to their own ideas, is impossible."[16]

This bind results, Habermas argues, from the fact that Horkheimer and Adorno's immanent critique of their philosophical heritage did not break with the "paradigm of the philosophy of consciousness," that is, the conceptualization of social theory in terms of the relation be-

[15]Ibid., pp. 379–380.
[16]Ibid., p. 382.

tween a knowing/acting subject (whether the individual, a collectivity, or society as a whole) and an object to be known and acted upon (nature, others, the body). What is missed by the philosophy of consciousness is the notion that "the reproduction of social life is tied not only to the conditions of cognitive-instrumental dealings with external nature . . . and to the conditions of cognitive-strategic dealings of individuals and groups with one another" but also to "conditions of the intersubjectivity of understanding among participants in interaction."[17]

Habermas's "paradigm shift" in *The Theory of Communicative Action* from an immanent critique of the philosophy of consciousness to a communications theory of intersubjectivity attempts to retrieve a conception of the normative force of rationality without recourse to either the pure reason of a transcendental ego or "mimesis." The form of reason which is at once normative, thereby providing a standpoint for critical theory, and intrinsic to the processes by which societies reproduce themselves he calls *communicative rationality:*

> The phenomena in need of explication are no longer, in and of themselves, the knowledge and mastery of an objective nature, but the intersubjectivity of possible understanding and agreement—at both the interpersonal and intrapsychic levels. The focus of investigation thereby shifts from cognitive-instrumental rationality to communicative rationality. And what is paradigmatic for the latter is not the relation of a solitary subject to something in the objective world that can be represented and manipulated, but the intersubjective relation that speaking and acting subjects take up when they come to an understanding with one another about something. In doing so, communicative actors move in the medium of a natural language, draw upon culturally transmitted interpretations, and relate simultaneously to something in the one objective world, something in their common social world, and something in each one's subjective world. In contrast to *representation* or *cognition,* *coming to an understanding* requires the rider *uncoerced,* because the expression is meant to be used here as a normative concept.[18]

How might such an altered perspective affect the tasks of the socially critical hermeneutics of culture? It is toward that question that I am aiming. The question is tangential to Habermas's explicit concerns, but it is tacitly posed in two ways. First of all, his arguments for the paradigm shift suggest that the limitations of Horkheimer and Adorno's

[17]Ibid., p. 392.
[18]Ibid.

critical theory of society derive from their commitment to the immanent critique of affirmative culture as a foundation for critical theory. By implication we must in turn ask what altered form the critique of affirmative culture should take in the wake of the impasses Habermas exposes. Second, the view elaborated in *The Theory of Communicative Action* had its beginnings in the debate with Gadamer, in which Habermas, on the one hand, adopted much of Gadamerian hermeneutics in order to clarify the communicative dimension of social life, but, on the other hand, argued that hermeneutical experience and understanding had to be counterbalanced with a theoretically elaborated normative standpoint. The debate raises the question of the interrelation of hermeneutical processes and social critique within the domain of cultural interpretation as well as that of social analysis. I will turn to that debate in the next chapter, but first I want to trace the very different path taken by phenomenological Marxism, in particular in the work of Merleau-Ponty and Kosík, in its attempt to synthesize a philosophy of consciousness and a critical theory of society.

Praxis Philosophy and Traditional Hermeneutics

Phenomenological Marxism had to overcome the resistance that each of its theoretical traditions has to the basic problematic of the other. On the one hand, Husserl's tendency to center the structures of human consciousness on the transcendental ego had to be modulated into an alternative conception of consciousness in which the historical situatedness of human beings in social relations could be grasped as a fundamental dimension of consciousness itself. On the other hand, the tendency within Marxism to treat consciousness, including the expressions and symbolizations comprising "culture," as a simple reflex of "objective conditions" or as the reflection of class positions within the material realm of production had to be countered with a return to the early Marx's conception of "praxis" as the totality of activities by which human beings transform nature into a human world, that is, a world of meanings and consciousness as well as of technologies and economic forces. The first of these tasks finds exemplary expression in Merleau-Ponty's reassessment of the relation between philosophy and sociology and in his attempt to transcribe the Husserlian transcendental ego into a historically situated intersubjectivity. The second task underlies Kosík's *Dialectics of the Concrete;* following out the same premise adopted by Horkheimer and Adorno, namely, that the transformation of nature for human purposes is the deep-seated anthropological project of humanity, he arrived at an outcome which reverses their account of instrumental rationality, namely, the notion that the model of human praxis has the critical and utopian capacity to indict the social structures of capitalism—and state socialism—and provides the philosophical framework for directing the meanings and values of Western culture and art toward social transformation.

In an essay entitled "The Philosopher and Sociology," Merleau-Ponty challenges the separation of philosophy and sociology by questioning the moment at which each pretends to be able to do without the other. When sociology, taking social reality as its object, construes this reality as a purely external field of data, it forgets that a society is already an intersubjective field of human activities and meanings and, second, that the observing consciousness, the scientific subject, is already embedded within social reality, constituted by the intersubjectivity he or she must observe and understand. Afflicted with this forgetting, the social scientist "will pretend to approach social fact as if it were alien to him [sic], as if his study owed nothing to the experience which, as social subject, he has of intersubjectivity."[19] While this criticism of the self-understanding of the social sciences carries forward the motifs of Husserl's work, Merleau-Ponty also argues that the phenomenological philosopher had fallen into a similar trap. By reducing historical reality to mere empirical data, to mere facticity, Husserl attempted to lodge truth in an ideal sphere wholly separated from history. The later Husserl also developed the idea that transcendental subjectivity is intersubjectivity, especially in *The Crisis of European Science and Transcendental Phenomenology*.[20] Merleau-Ponty turns this idea against the postulate of a transcendental ego, even though Husserl himself intended the concept to affirm the universality of the transcendental standpoint. "Now if the transcendental is intersubjective," Merleau-Ponty asks, "how can the borders of the transcendental and the empirical help becoming indistinct? For along with the other person, all the other person sees of me—all my facticity—is reintegrated into subjectivity, or at leasted posited as an indispensible element of its definition. Thus the transcendental descends into history."[21]

[19]Maurice Merleau-Ponty, "The Philosopher and Sociology," in *Signs*, trans. Richard C. McCleary (Evanston: Northwestern University Press, 1964), p. 99.
[20]Edmund Husserl, *The Crisis of European Science and Transcendental Phenomenology: An Introduction to Phenomenological Philosophy*, trans. David Carr (Evanston: Northwestern University Press, 1970), pp. 182 ff.
[21]Merleau-Ponty, "The Philosopher and Sociology," p. 107.

Merleau-Ponty thus interrupts the path taken by Husserl in his efforts to secure a refuge for pure reason. The beginning of truth does not lie in the pursuit of "pure *theoria*" and the effort "to build theoretical knowledge upon theoretical knowledge *in infinitum*" from the philosopher's privileged position as "disinterested spectator, overseer of the world."[22] The category of truth, Merleau-Ponty asserts, must be freed from the separation of fact and essence. These are not hierarchically "layered" but implicated in one another. Neither a transcendental phenomenology that reserves truth for the ideal sphere nor a social science that construes society as sheer fact takes account of the intersubjective conditions of both knowledge and reality. Truth is situational and historical:

> Since we are all hemmed in by history, it is up to us to understand that whatever truth we may have is to be gotten not in spite of but through our historical inherence. Superficially considered, our inherence destroys all truth; considered radically, it founds a new idea of truth. As long as I cling to the ideal of an absolute spectator, of knowledge with no point of view, I can see my situation as nothing but a source of error. But if I have once recognized that through it I am grafted onto every action and knowledge which can have meaning for me, and that step by step it contains everything that can *exist* for me, then my contact with the social in the finitude of my situation is revealed to me as the point of origin of all truth, including scientific truth.[23]

Even though Merleau-Ponty reconceptualizes society as intersubjective reality, he continues to restrict the definition of intersubjectivity to the interrelation of consciousnesses. But social reality is also constituted through the interchange and coordination of *activities* among the members of society. In *Dialectics of the Concrete,* Kosík attempts to incorporate this notion into a new synthesis of the philosophy of the subject and Marxism. His premise derives from ideas expressed in Marx, particularly in such writings as the *Grundrisse* and the *Philosophical and Economic Manuscripts,* but also in *Capital.* According to this premise, subjectivity is human activity (praxis), and the "world" of human beings is produced through the practical transformation of nature into human reality. Kosík then extends the two-pronged critique found in Merleau-Ponty. He confronts Marxism's tendency to restrict social reality to "objective conditions" with the notion that human

[22]Ibid.
[23]Ibid., p. 109.

consciousness and being inhere in these conditions; at the same time, he develops an uncompromising critique of phenomenology's failure to incorporate a concept of praxis into its descriptions of being and consciousness.

The overcoming of the respective failures of phenomenology and Marxism and the synthesis of their separate problematics Kosík calls a *philosophy of labor*. Transcendental phenomenology failed to connect the self-constituting power of subjectivity to the empirical existence of the historical world because it could not see in labor the active process by which humanity makes itself and its world. Nonetheless, only a philosophical, as opposed to political-economic, concept of labor overcomes the tendency of the social sciences proper to forget the intersubjective and constituting character of labor. Understood philosophically, economics "is not only the production of material goods; it is the totality of the process of producing and reproducing man [*sic*] as a socio-historical being."[24]

As with the reading of Marx first developed by Lukács and then the Frankfurt School, Kosík locates the mainspring of critical theory in the analysis of the commodity and the corresponding concepts of alienation and reification: "Marx's theory is a *critique* of economics" in the sense that it exposes "the *real movement of economic categories as a reified form of the social movement of people*. This critique *discovered that categories of the social movement of things are necessary and historically transient existential forms of the social movement of people*."[25] Kosík argues for a unified view of reality as the historical product of human activity on the basis of two theses: (1) "Economics is the production of material goods but also of social relations, of the context of this production." And, (2) "labor is both a transformation of nature and a realization of meanings in it."[26] In order to maintain that (*a*) the transformation of nature, (*b*) the realization of meanings, and (*c*) the production of social relations form a conceptual unity, Kosík, like Horkheimer and Adorno, has to evoke the distinction between essence and fact. Social reality is in "essence" the product of the totality of human praxis, but in "fact" it appears and is lived in the form of the class divisions and reification which make this very human activity

[24]Karel Kosík, *Dialectics of the Concrete: A Study on Problems of Man and World*, trans. Karel Kovanda with James Schmidt (Boston: Reidel, 1976), p. 115.
[25]Ibid., pp. 115–116.
[26]Ibid., p. 122.

function as a mere thing. The concept of labor as praxis thus acquires its critical and utopian valence in relation to the actual nature of labor in capitalist society. While labor is a (conceptually) integral element of the praxis that produces social life itself, labor in its capitalist form appears and is lived not as the active interchange of activities among human beings but rather as the movement of a relation between things insofar as the materials, the products, and the acts of labor are equally commodities.

As a consequence of the divergence between the empirical conception of labor as commodified exchange-value and the critical-utopian con-ception of labor as praxis, an internal tension affects the concepts of critical theory. When thematized, in terms of a distinction between essence and fact, this tension takes the following form: the concepts of critical theory strive at once to describe reality as it is and to posit the truth of this reality as its obstructed potential for transformation. Such a view Kosík shares with Horkheimer and Adorno. Accordingly, they consider the truth articulated by critical theory ultimately to be validated only outside the observation of existing reality; critical theory points toward a future in which its theoretical claims would be brought to realization through the transformation of society.[27] As we saw, Horkheimer and Adorno came to locate their reference point for this latent or obstructed "truth" in the so-called mimetic as opposed to instrumental relation to nature. Kosík, by contrast, continues to locate

[27]Horkheimer, for example, casts the problem in terms of the experiential standpoint and intellectual activity of the individual theorist: "Critical thinking is the function neither of the isolated individual nor of a sum-total of individuals. Its subject is rather a definite individual in his [sic] real relation to other individuals and groups, in his conflict with a particular class, and, finally, in the resultant web of relationships with the social totality and with nature. The subject is no mathematical point like the ego of bourgeois philosophy; his activity is the construction of the social present. Further-more, the thinking subject is not the place where knowledge and object coincide, nor consequently the starting-point for attaining absolute knowledge. Such an illusion about the thinking subject, under which idealism has lived since Descartes, is ideology in the strict sense, for in it the limited freedom of the bourgeois individual puts on the illusory form of perfect freedom and autonomy. As a matter of fact, however, in a society which is untransparent and without self-awareness the ego, whether active simply as thinker or active in other ways as well, is unsure of itself too. In reflection on man, subject and object are sundered; their identity lies in the future, not in the present. The method leading to such an identification may be called explanation in Cartesian language, but in genuinely critical thought explanation signifies not only a logical process but a concrete historical one as well. In the course of it both the social structure as a whole and the relation of the theoretician to society are altered, that is both the subject and the role of thought are changed." "Traditional and Critical Theory," pp. 210–211.

the normative or critical-utopian standpoint in the essential, or hypothetical, unity of human praxis.

In an effort to maintain the reference to the *unity* of human praxis while at the same time describing the actual *divisions* and *alienation* of that praxis in capitalist society, without thereby reducing the critical-utopian concept of praxis to a sheer abstraction, Kosík develops the notion that the realm of culture, particularly art, is an ongoing realization, on the symbolic level, of the unity of human praxis even as such unity is denied and obstructed by capitalist social relations. The cultural tradition—the documents of civilization—can, as preserved and transmitted, acquire the appearance of a unified culture. Marcuse's reflections, however, posed a question toward which he and the other Frankfurt School theorists remained ambivalent: is this apparent unity of Western culture the transcendent result, the symptom, or the alibi of the exploitative divisions of class society? Kosík is more sure in his 'response to this question, but to the detriment of the problem itself. He attributes to the modern world, and the twentieth century in particular, the capacity for active cultural memory, by which he means the ability to take up every earlier and distinctive cultural creation and integrate it into a developing realization of human nature. "Historical periods of human development," he argues in a polemic against historicism, "are not empty casts from which life would have evaporated *because of* mankind having reached higher forms of development. Rather they are continually incorporated into the present through praxis—the creative activity of mankind. This process of incorporation is at the same time a critique and an appreciation of the past. . . . Human history is an incessant totalization of the past, in the course of which human praxis incorporates and thus revives moments of the past."[28] Kosík's concept of praxis here risks losing its critical aspect. The notion that the cultural tradition is "an incessant totalization of the past" even under conditions of social exploitation and division is but a variant of the traditional theory of affirmative culture and the uncritical humanism which conceives culture as "Man's" developing realization of universal representations and meanings.

Such a recourse to traditional theory results from the fact that the very terms in which praxis philosophy frames its critical theory of society cannot be carried through to a critical theory of culture. In the case of Kosík, the thematics of a dialectic of the concrete as regards

[28]Kosík, p. 85.

the concept of labor presupposes a concept of art which is neither dialectical nor concrete. Evoking the Marxian distinction between the realms of "necessity" and "freedom," Kosík advances the following proposition: "Human doing is thus divided into two areas: in one it is performed under pressure of necessity and is called labor, in the other it is realized as free creation and is called art."[29] As it stands, the identification of labor with necessity and of art with freedom rigidifies the historical separation of labor and art and turns it into a universal opposition between matter and spirit.

Aware of the problem, Kosík proceeds to modify the proposition, but the modification applies to just one side of the opposition, namely, the designation of labor as the realm of necessity. Moreover, the qualification revives the essence/fact distinction in a way that replicates the original problem. Kosík argues that labor is *in fact* separated from the realm of freedom insofar as the division of labor causes this labor to be performed not merely under the pressure of natural necessity but under social constraint and coercion; those whose activity provides for the existence not only of themselves but of others labor in a state of human unfreedom. Kosík then argues that *in truth*—that is, from the standpoint of the postulated totality of human life as praxis—labor is at the same time what makes possible the "realm of freedom," including art: "labor is a human doing which *transcends* the realm of necessity *and forms within it* real prerequisites of human *freedom,* even without leaving it."[30]

This line of argument is indispensable to praxis philosophy's concept of labor, but it is also inconsistent and incomplete insofar as it cannot grant the same kind of two-sidedness to art and the existing "realm of freedom." There is no basis for presupposing that social domination figures in the production of art merely as the contingent historical condition which has made art as "free creation" possible. Or for presupposing that the divisions of society are merely external to the "work itself," leaving no imprint on its form and inner logic. Art, I will argue, constitutes itself *within* and *against* the forms of domination that organize the society in which the work is produced and the one in which it is received. Such a hypothesis would complete Kosík's challenge to any simple opposition between necessity and freedom and would insist that the contradiction between freedom and unfreedom is within art

[29]Ibid., p. 124.
[30]Ibid., p. 125.

just as much as within labor. But at that point, praxis philosophy loses its theoretically needed reference to art and culture as the domain in which social domination is already, though symbolically, transcended and in which, therefore, the project of human "self-realization" is prefigured as the unity of praxis. This impasse, however compelling praxis philosophy's conception of universal humanity may be, cannot, I think, be overcome.

The impasse also affects the hermeneutics of culture which praxis philosophy requires. For example, Kosík carries on an important, often persuasive polemic against historicism, especially Marxist historicism, but the terms of the critique are insufficient. He argues against dissolving forms of consciousness and forms of expression to the "social conditions" from which they arise:

> The contradiction between man [sic] and "conditions," the antinomy between an impotent consciousness and omnipotent "conditions," is an antagonism within "conditions" themselves and a split within man himself. Social being is not equivalent to conditions, circumstances, or to the economic factor, all of which, taken in isolation are deformations of that being. In certain phases of social development, man's being is cleft because the objective aspect of his being, without which he ceases to be man and turns into an idealistic vision, is separated from human subjectivity, activity, from his potentialities and possibilities.[31]

To follow through with this line of argument would again require that we abandon Kosík's assumption that art, as a fragment of praxis, is the sphere of consciousness and expression which already realizes itself "freely." The more adequate counterassumption is that every text or work within the tradition is affected by this antagonism within conditions and manifests this split within social being. A Marxist hermeneutics of culture has the task of discovering such a dialectic through the interpretation of the concrete forms of expression which comprise the tradition. Literature—but also philosophy—must be read in relation to the social situation of its creation without reducing the work's significance to "objective conditions" in the manner of historicism, but also without regarding these conditions, in a reductive manner, as external or purely contingent to the work's form and signification. It is just this task which, though it can be initially posed in the terms of praxis philosophy and phenomenological Marxism, cannot be resolved by them.

[31]Ibid., p. 70.

2

For a Critical
Hermeneutics

The Gadamer/Habermas Debate

The debate between Gadamer and Habermas refashioned the dialogue
between Marxism and hermeneutics. Initiated by Habermas's review
of *Truth and Method,* the debate established both a new set of shared
aims and questions and, in turn, a new ground of divergence and
dispute. Both participants had already criticized, or were in the process
of rethinking, key aspects of their respective theoretical traditions. Gadamer's entire project started from the notion that the transcendental
ego elaborated by Husserl was inadequate to a theory of linguistically
mediated understanding generally or of cultural interpretation specifically. Developing Heidegger's critique of transcendental phenomenology, Gadamer sought to replace the transcendental ego with a
conception of understanding as a historically situated, temporally dynamic intersubjectivity. Habermas was in the process of abandoning
the essence/fact distinction as a foundation of critical theory and was
seeking to replace Horkheimer and Adorno's critique of instrumental
reason with an alternative conception of social relations and interactions, one that would focus on the symbolically mediated, norm-
governed intersubjectivity of social reproduction. Moreover, Habermas
has repudiated the belief that praxis philosophy can provide a coherent
conception of contemporary Western societies and their potential for
transformation.[1] And Gadamer, of course, has maintained considerable

[1]"When Marx borrowed from Romanticism (through Hegel) the expressivist ideal

distance from the synthesizing endeavors of phenomenological or existential Marxisms.

I do not intend to present the Gadamer-Habermas debate comprehensively, or even primarily on its own terms. This has been done in several excellent commentaries that address the question posed by Habermas: Can the model of interpretive understanding developed by hermeneutics with regard to cultural traditions be generalized to the analysis of social institutions and processes of societal change?[2] My focus will be on the question that rather paradoxically falls through the cracks of the debate itself: What is required of a socially critical hermeneutics of culture?

In my view, Gadamer radically altered the self-understanding of what I am calling traditional hermeneutics. But he also restored its basic project and aim of constructing and interpreting cultural tradition in such a way as to assure that the validated meanings and values of that tradition appear to stand above the social relations of domination prevalent in the actual social world of text and interpreter. His work helps reveal, against the grain of its own intentions, the nature of that

---

of self-formation, transferred aesthetic productivity to the practical working life of the species, conceived social labor as the collective self-realization of the producers, and against this background, represented the activity of the modern wage-laborer at once as alienated and as the modern emancipatory force, he found himself faced with a series of difficulties. These difficulties cannot be overcome by anthropologically elucidating a concept of *Praxis* which relies on the wealth of its horizon of meaning within the history of ideas." Jürgen Habermas, "A Reply to My Critics," in *Habermas: Critical Debates,* ed. John B. Thompson and David Held (Cambridge: MIT Press, 1982), p. 224.

[2] Jürgen Habermas, "A Review of Gadamer's *Truth and Method,*" in *Understanding and Social Inquiry,* ed. Fred Dallmayr and Thomas McCarthy (South Bend, Ind.: Notre Dame University Press, 1977), pp. 335–363. The most extensive commentaries on the debate are the following: Albrecht Wellmer, *Critical Theory of Society,* trans. John Cumming (New York: Seabury, 1974), pp. 31–51; Paul Ricoeur, "Hermeneutics and the Critique of Ideology," *Hermeneutics and the Human Sciences,* ed. and trans. John B. Thompson (Cambridge: Cambridge University Press, 1981), pp. 63–100; Dieter Misgeld, "Critical Theory and Hermeneutics: The Debate between Habermas and Gadamer," in *On Critical Theory,* ed. John O'Neill (New York: Seabury, 1976), pp. 164–183; Thomas McCarthy, *The Critical Theory of Jürgen Habermas* (Cambridge: MIT Press, 1978), pp. 169–193; David Couzens Hoy, *The Critical Circle: Literature, History and Philosophical Hermeneutics* (Berkeley: University of California Press, 1978), pp. 117–130; Jack Mendelson, "The Habermas-Gadamer Debate," *New German Critique* 18 (Fall 1979), 44–73; Josef Bleicher, *Contemporary Hermeneutics: Hermeneutics as Method, Philosophy and Critique* (London: Routledge and Kegan Paul, 1980), pp. 203–209, 233–235; John B. Thompson, *Critical Hermeneutics: A Study in the Thought of Paul Ricoeur and Jürgen Habermas* (Cambridge: Cambridge University Press, 1981), pp. 66–68, 118–120, 163–170.

project, its basic suppositions, and the limits it imposes on processes of interpretation. This set of questions has remained of only oblique interest to Habermas. His approach, on the one hand, drew on Gadamerian theory to sketch out the communicative and hermeneutical dimension of social life and institutions and, on the other hand, criticized Gadamer's exclusion of the normative or critical-utopian standpoint required for a critical theory of society. Even as he tried to show the limits of hermeneutics in sociological and social-theoretical inquiry, he tended to leave aside, or even concede, the question of the adequacy of Gadamerian hermeneutics in the domain of cultural interpretation. My commentary on the debate will bear on that question, and propose alternatives to the conclusions of both Gadamer and Habermas.

There are several points on which Gadamer and Habermas agree and which decisively shift the terms of the relation between Marxism and hermeneutics. I will treat these general propositions as already established through various arguments made in the original debate and by later commentators. First, interpretation or interpretive understanding is an intersubjectivity embedded in and mediated by language and occurs along the entire continuum of communicative experiences, from so-called everyday conversation to the specialized interpretation of artworks. Second, understanding is the activity of historically situated interpreters and therefore is not grounded in either a transcendental ego or an objective, substantive framework of meaning. Third, the temporal or historical gap between interpreters and the texts they attempt to understand is productive of understanding rather than a mere obstacle to it. And, fourth, the hermeneutical process can be viewed, for analytical purposes at least, as involving three distinct moments: fore-understanding, by which Gadamer means the prestructured anticipation of meaning which every culturally formed interpreter brings to the encounter with an individual text; interpretation, by which is meant the understanding that is worked up in the course of the (hypothetical) dialogue with the text; and application, by which is meant the process in which the interpreter confirms the validity of the interpreted meaning of the text by bringing it to bear on his or her own life-context and -practice.

With the title *Truth and Method* Gadamer counterposed the "phenomenon of understanding" and the "methodological ideal of science" in an assertion, reminiscent of Husserl's, of the primacy and anteriority of hermeneutical experience to methodical research:

The phenomenon of understanding not only pervades all human relations to the world. It also has an independent validity within science and resists any attempt to change it into a method of science. The following investigation starts with the resistance within modern science against the universal claim of scientific method. It is concerned to seek that experience of truth that transcends the control of scientific method wherever it is to be found, and to inquire into its legitimacy. Hence the human sciences are joined with modes of experience which lie outside science: with the experiences of philosophy, of art, and of history itself. These are all modes of experience in which a truth is communicated that cannot be verified by the methodological means proper to science.[3]

The controversies provoked by this statement and the qualifications Gadamer has given to it have centered on such questions as the legitimacy of the Gadamerian determination of "truth," the status of his apparently rigid separation of truth and method, and the validity of the conception of science as having a different epistemological basis, as opposed to the traditional understanding of it, from the so-called human sciences.[4] Such questions will arise in Habermas's discussion of the relation between hermeneutics and social science.

As regards Gadamer's theory of cultural hermeneutics, there is, however, a different question to be raised. Gadamer's restoration of the traditional hermeneutics of culture does indeed claim to provide a model of the intersubjectivity of human understanding as such. It, therefore, purports to account for the necessarily shared, premethodological experiences that background all specific forms of inquiry within the human sciences, the social sciences, or the natural sciences. But what Gadamer presents as the universal conditions of the hermeneutics of tradition is in fact a constellation of particular interpretive commitments that are themselves quite inseparable from the methodological procedures in which they are elaborated. Gadamer's "truth" *is* a "method" even as it presents itself as the premethodological experience of all interpreters.

---

[3]Hans-Georg Gadamer, *Truth and Method*, trans. Garrett Barden and John Cumming (New York: Seabury, 1975), pp. xi-xii. Hereafter cited in the text as *TM*.

[4]On the philosophical and metatheoretical issues posed by Gadamer's discussion of science and hermeneutics, see in particular, Richard Rorty, *Philosophy and the Mirror of Nature* (Princeton: Princeton University Press, 1979), pp. 357–389; and the related debate in *The Review of Metaphysics* 34 (September 1980), which includes Hubert L. Dreyfus, "Holism and Hermeneutics," pp. 3–23; Charles Taylor, "Understanding in Human Science," pp. 25–38; Richard Rorty, "A Reply to Dreyfus and Taylor," pp. 39–46; and Rorty, Taylor, and Dreyfus, "A Discussion," pp. 47–55.

Gadamer has a theoretical—or, as we will see, ideological—commitment to a set of premises concerning the nature of cultural tradition: (1) The cultural tradition is a *universe of meaning* in the strong sense that the meaningfulness of transmitted texts is determined by the tradition as a whole just as the tradition as a whole is a unity comprised of the meaning of the texts transmitted within it. (2) The tradition derives its authoritativeness in the present from the power of transmitted texts to carry meaning forward in time without reference to or dependence upon the social context in which they were originally produced. (3) The tradition is renewed and reappropriated in every age through the application of an interpretively secured understanding which renders the tradition the sole and unified source of meaning for that age.

Now, these principles have to be actualized through a corresponding set of methodological procedures whose methodological character is at the same time denied: (1) Interpretations are regulated by the postulate of the unity of part/whole relations within individual transmitted texts and within the entirety of texts comprising the tradition. (2) The social genesis of the text is methodically bracketed on the grounds that the internal coherence of the text and its meanings can be separated from their original context. (3) The sociocultural context of contemporary reception is also methodically bracketed, assuring that the tradition will appear as the unified and valid source of meanings and values in the present.

Our first task, then, is to interrogate these three sets of commitments in order to specify the project of traditional hermeneutics.

(1) Gadamer's commitment to the notion that the cultural tradition is a universe of meaning is so pervasive in *Truth and Method* that it is a virtual axiom. So, too, is the methodological procedure which backs it up:

> What follows for understanding from the hermeneutic condition of belonging to a tradition? We remember here the hermeneutical rule that we must understand the whole in terms of the detail and the detail in terms of the whole.... The anticipation of meaning in which the whole is envisaged becomes explicit understanding in that the parts, that are determined by the whole, themselves also determine this whole.... It is also necessary for this expected meaning to be adjusted if the text calls for it. This means, then, that the expectation changes and that the text acquires the unity of a meaning from another expected meaning. Thus the movement of understanding is constantly from the whole to the part

and back to the whole. Our task is to extend in concentric circles the unity of the understood meaning. The harmony of all the details with the whole is the criterion of correct understanding. The failure to achieve this harmony means that understanding has failed. [*TM*, pp. 258–259]

The supposition that the resolution of part/whole relations into a unity is a condition of intelligibility and meaningfulness operates in three distinct registers of Gadamer's theory. It is, first of all, a supposition about the internal formal, semantic, or argumentative structure of a text; at this level, the so-called hermeneutical rule goes back to Schleiermacher and Dilthey and states that every interpretation must be guided by the intention of assembling the particular and partial significations of a text into an overarching meaning-structure that can lay claim to organizing the text as a whole. Second, Gadamer's axiom for the relation of text and tradition includes the notion that a tradition—as we will see, *the* tradition—is ultimately a univocal totality even though it undergoes changes in the course of time; accordingly, every text belonging to that tradition is by definition integral to its monological totality. And, third, the part/whole supposition informs Gadamer's account of Heidegger's "hermeneutical circle"; the process of understanding begins in the anticipation that the parts of a text will eventually constitute a "unity of meaning," proceeds through the incessant movement "from the whole to the part and back to the whole," until the interpreter arrives at either a successful, if approximate, completion of this unifying understanding or a discovery of a disjunction of part and whole, at which point, according to Gadamer, the interpreter experiences the unintelligibility of the text and seeks "to discover in what way it can be remedied" (*TM*, p. 261).

It will not be useful to interrogate the second and third of these suppositions until we see how they emerge from the larger pattern of Gadamer's argument. It is, however, obvious that they require the first supposition regarding the formal-semantic organization of individual works. And that supposition is open to considerable skepticism. Even if we limit ourselves to artworks, which tend to be Gadamer's paradigm for texts, and grant that all the elements of an artwork are internally related, such an assumption does not require us to conclude that this relatedness takes the form of the *unity* of part and whole. Nor does the fact that these internally related elements can be methodically assembled into a formal or semantic unity require us to concude that they must or should be in any given case. Interpretive procedures that yield such a unity are always susceptible to being questioned as to the selectiveness of their screening processes. The text does not supply adequate proof for a procedure; the interpreter's appeal to the "text itself" is always a necessary but never a sufficient grounds for justifying an interpretation. For the moment, then, Gadamer's invocation of the "hermeneutical rule" should be considered an unwarranted supposition about the nature of meaning and interpretation; it functions within a larger agenda of the traditional hermeneutics of culture.

(2) Gadamerian hermeneutics also entails a procedural commitment that methodically brackets the social genesis of the text. The methodological issue is, however, hidden in Gadamer's argumentation. He slides from a convincing critique of historicism to an alternative which suppresses questions still left open in the wake of that critique. Against the historicist premise that the real meaning of a text is the one that it must have had for its original audience and in its original context, Gadamer develops a critique that he then wrongly assumes lays to rest the interpretive problems posed by the culturally transmitted text's historical inherence in a society different from our own. At issue is how to construe the following thesis, which caps Gadamer's call for an alternative to historicism:

> Every age has to understand a transmitted text in its own way, for the text is part of the whole of the tradition in which the age takes an objective interest and in which it seeks to understand itself. The real meaning of a text, as it speaks to the interpreter, does not depend on the contingencies of the author and whom he [*sic*] originally wrote for. It is certainly not identical with them, for it is always partly determined by the historical situation of the interpreter and hence by the objective course of history. [*TM*, p. 263]

Gadamer arrives at this thesis through a two-pronged criticism of historicism—or what he sometimes calls "historical hermeneutics"—directed against (*a*) its failure to recognize the impact of the aesthetic dimension of cultural reception and (*b*) its self-misunderstanding regarding the conditions of possibility of all interpretation, including its own.

(*a*) Artworks produced in the past have, for later interpreters, the force of a contemporaneous expression, as though the work were addressed to them across the gap of intervening time and societal change. Historicism diminishes or even denies this aspect of aesthetic experience insofar as it restricts interpretation to the restoration of the artwork's supposed original meaning. Gadamer's critique seeks to expand the cultural value of aesthetic interpretation by insisting that the interpretation of artistic traditions understand itself as an activity fully within, and productive of, contemporary culture. By the same token, the contemporaneous force of aesthetic experiences signals that the artwork's claim to validity reaches beyond its original context:

> The experience of art does not only understand a recognizable meaning, as historical hermeneutics does in its handling of texts. The work of art that says something confronts us itself.... [T]he experience of art is *experience* in a real sense and must master anew the task that experience involves: the task of integrating it into the whole of one's orientation to a world and one's own self-understanding. The language of art is constituted precisely by the fact that it speaks to the self-understanding of *every* person and it does this as ever present and by means of its own contemporaneousness.[5]

As an indictment of historicism's failure to recognize and incorporate aesthetic experience into its interpretive procedures, Gadamer's argument is unassailable. When it comes, however, to specifying how artworks manifest their contemporaneousness and their claim to universality, Gadamer commits himself to a particular, contestable conception of aesthetic experience in the guise of delineating the axiomatic elements of all such experiences. He slides from the notion that the artwork reaches beyond the social site of its genesis to the assertion that it "only in a limited way... retains its historical origin within itself" and so "reaches fundamentally beyond any historical confinement." And he slides from the notion that every reception context discovers new configurations of meaning in the artwork to the assertion that the artwork enjoys an "absolute contemporaneousness" and "offers itself... in an absolute presence."

These second-level assertions prejudge the consequences of the critique of historicism for interpretation. With them Gadamer cuts short another possible line of inquiry—one which would entertain the possibility that the opposition between an artwork's historical inherence in a past society and its expressive power in the present is an open, complex relation, rather than assuming that "historical confinement" and "contemporaneousness" are mutually exclusive. From this alter-

[5]Hans-Georg Gadamer, "Aesthetics and Hermeneutics," *Philosophical Hermeneutics*, ed. and trans. David E. Linge (Berkeley: University of California Press, 1976), pp. 101–102.

native standpoint, aesthetic experience provokes hermeneutical questions of a type Gadamer's commitments preclude. Thus, for example:
How does an artwork bear within its formal and communicative structures the traces of its inherence in a set of social relations and practices?
How at the same time does it effect a break with its context, and how
do this break *and* that context become readable in the course of
aesthetic-hermeneutical experience? Assuming that the artwork thus
has a relative, as opposed to absolute, autonomy with respect to its
own society, and therefore with respect to our own, how is aesthetic
experience implicated in the historical continuities and discontinuities
between the social site of an artwork's genesis and the social site of
our reception of it?

None of these questions can be answered in advance of concrete acts
of interpretation. The particular standpoint Gadamer adopts against
historicism, however, eschews such questions from the outset and thus
belies his commitment to particular hermeneutical procedures—that is,
methods—which are destined to reconstruct an artwork's meaning in
a particular way. Specifically, these methods obliterate the traces of
the work's historical imbeddedness in a society, cast its contemporaneous power as the sign of art's absolute autonomy vis-à-vis society,
and thus construe the artwork's claim to universal validity as its
achievement of meanings whose continuity over time transcends the
discontinuities of societal change.

(*b*) Gadamer's other charge against historicism is that it is further
caught in an acute self-misunderstanding to the extent that it cannot
account for its own conditions of possibility. This problem Gadamer
illustrates with reference to the study of classical antiquity and the
notion of the classical. Historicism maintains that its object domain is
unaffected by the interests of modern interpreters themselves; that the
techniques of the historical-philological method are capable of dissolving such modern prejudices and recovering the real, original meaning of ancient texts; and that the concept of the classical can be
employed as a value-neutral category of periodization and stylistic
description. Historicism's commitment to these premises has, Gadamer
shows, precluded a reflection on "what constituted the real merit of
its favorite objects," that is, of the transmitted texts of classical antiquity.
The required self-criticism of historical hermeneutics takes its impetus
from the normative—as distinct from the periodizing or stylistic-
descriptive—content of the concept of the classical. Gadamer argues
that this normative element conditions the possibility of any study of

classical antiquity, whatever its methodological commitments or its self-understanding. For it is the normative standing of the texts of ancient culture that explains why these texts keep returning as an object of inquiry and knowledge. The mode of preservation and transmission which brings the classical text to its interpreters cannot be factored out of the intellectual and aesthetic interest that the text commands for its interpreters, including even the most strictly historicist philologists: "It is the general nature of tradition that only that of the past which is preserved offers the possibility of historical knowledge" (*TM*, p. 257). And such preservation inscribes the transmitted text with a contemporary cultural value for its interpreters.

Gadamer thus indicts, again persuasively, the self-misunderstanding that afflicts historicism. Its methodological commitments mask and deny the process by which its objects of inquiry emerge within a culturally evolved field of inquiry in the first place. Although Gadamer's alternative to historicism indeed avoids the latter's error, he does not acknowledge that this alternative still requires justification in comparison to other possible solutions to the historicist dilemma. Instead, he elevates his own hermeneutical commitments to the status of the necessarily shared experience of all interpreters of the classical. He slides from the notion that the mode of preserving-transmitting the classical is an integral element of the interpretive process, prestructuring any particular act of interpretation, to the assertion that the classical text is immune from any historicizing critique which would measure the distance between the classical text and the standpoint of its interpreters: "The classical is what resists historical criticism because its historical dominion, the binding power of its validity that is preserved and handed down, precedes all historical reflection and continues through it" (*TM*, p. 255).

What is the mode of the preservation-transmission of the classical? What form do the binding power and preserved validity of the classical take? Gadamer draws his own view from a description, in itself illuminating, of the way in which Renaissance humanism and then German classicism appropriated and validated the monuments of classical antiquity. Key to this mode of preservation-transmission was a form of cultural time-consciousness in which cultural meaning and value appeared emphatically retrospective as well as normative: "It is an awareness of decline and distance that gives birth to the classical norm. . . . Every 'new humanism' shares, with the first and oldest, the awareness of being directly committed to its model which, as something past, is unattainable yet present. Thus there culminates in the classical a general character of historical being, preservation among the ruins of time" (*TM*, pp. 256–257). Without acknowledging the need for further argumentation or justification, Gadamer then assumes that the authentic time-consciousness of all cultural meaning and value follows the pattern of this appropriation of the classical in the so-called high periods of Western culture, and that authentic cultural reception is always and necessarily organized around models that are normative yet retrospective, unattainable yet present, lost yet binding.

Gadamer thus slides from the notion that every interpretation of transmitted texts is affected by the prestructuring influence of their preservation-transmission to two very different, never justified conclusions: first, that there has been and is but one valid mode of preservation-transmission intrinsic to Western culture, the emphatically retrospective-normative mode; and, second, that the prestructuring influence of that mode can never be fundamentally challenged or altered in the process of interpretation itself. It is only on the basis of these assumptions that Gadamer can presuppose that his particular hermeneutical commitments are the premethodological, shared condition of all interpreters, and so secure the claim that the texts preserved-transmitted in the retrospective-normative mode are themselves immune from historicizing critique.

Gadamer has, in sum, construed the communicative power of artworks as their "timelessness" and cast the retrospective-normative appropriation of the classical as the model for cultural time-consciousness generally. He can then mesh two conceptions, which are not otherwise necessarily linked, regarding the interaction between tradition and interpretation. He can hold to the posthistoricist notion that "every age" appropriates tradition anew "in its own way," while at the same time rehabilitating the antihistoricizing notion that the whole of cultural meaning in the present resides in the authority of the cultural productions of the past.

The conjunction of these notions informs Gadamer's celebrated concept of the "historical fusion" between tradition and interpretation:

> Does this kind of historical fusion of the past with the present that characterizes what is classical, ultimately lie at the base of the whole historical attitude as its effective substratum? Whereas romantic hermeneutics had taken human nature as the unhistorical substratum of its theory of understanding and hence had freed the connatural interpreter from all historical limitations, the self-criticism of historical conscious-

ness leads finally to seeing historical movement not only in process, but also in understanding itself. Understanding is not to be thought of so much as an action of one's subjectivity, but as the placing of oneself within a process of tradition, in which past and present are fused. This is what must be expressed in hermeneutical theory, which is far too dominated by the idea of a process, a method. [*TM*, p. 258]

This passage reveals the self-misunderstanding of Gadamerian hermeneutics. Gadamer slides from the notion that the historical movement of traditions animates, rather than inhibiting, understanding to the supposition that this historical movement necessarily takes the form of cultural continuity. According to that supposition, the cultural tradition appears, from the vantage point of each age, as a realm of internally unified, historically continuous meanings and values. In other words, Gadamer considers it axiomatic that those meanings and values which appear continuous and unified across the whole of the tradition—and only those meanings and values—are valid and binding for the present. But is this really axiomatic? On the contrary, the Western cultural tradition acquires this appearance of unity and continuity only as the result of the sort of second-level postulations Gadamer makes, specifically, the timelessness of artworks and the universality of the retrospective-normative mode of reception. "Historical fusion" of the kind Gadamer evokes above is not the premethodological experience lying "at the base of the whole historical attitude as its effective substratum," but rather is the *product* of specific hermeneutical commitments and procedures.

To make "classical" texts and "timeless" artworks the core around which the cultural tradition can appear as a unified whole is to *construct* a tradition. Gadamerian hermeneutics misunderstands its constructed tradition as *the* cultural tradition. It likewise denies that its own hermeneutical commitments are procedural and methodological. The constructed tradition of Gadamerian hermeneutics depends upon interpretive procedures which, to summarize my account thus far, subsume part-whole relations under the principle of semantic-discursive unity; screen out the traces of an artwork's historical inherence in a set of social relations and practices; transform the artwork's claim to universality into the interpreter's presupposition that the artwork always already embodies universal validity; and render the classic text or artwork immune from historicizing critique.

(3) The posthistoricist-antihistoricizing view that the cultural tradition possesses internal unity, historical continuity, and universal va-

lidity ultimately requires a third procedural commitment. Gadamerian hermeneutics methodically brackets the sociocultural context of reception. Gadamer, it is true, initially grants that interpretations are affected by two vectors of determination: on the one hand, the effective mode of preservation-transmission of the tradition in question; and, on the other hand, the "historical situation of the interpreter and hence... the totality of the objective course of history." I have already criticized his restrictive account of the first of these vectors of determination. As for the second, Gadamer proceeds to empty the "historical situation of the interpreter" of all specificity. Most often this shows indirectly, especially in the unperturbed self-assurance with which he designates the historical situation of contemporary interpreters as "our age" and refers to all potential interpreters in contemporary society as an undifferentiated "we" unmarked by class, race, or gender and unaffected by any concrete social interests or ideological commitments. At this level, the methodical bracketing of the sociocultural context of reception amounts to the tacit foreclosure of any reflection on the cultural differences and social conflicts which animate the community of interpreters.

The bracketing procedure is more explicitly announced in *Truth and Method* with regard to the creations of contemporary culture:

> Everyone knows that curious impotence of our judgment where the distance in time has not given us sure criteria. Thus the judgment of contemporary works of art is desperately uncertain for the scientific consciousness. Obviously we approach such creations with the prejudices we are not in control of, presuppositions that have too great an influence over us for us to know about them; these can give to contemporary creations an extra resonance that does not correspond to their true content and their true significance. Only when all their relations to the present time have faded away can their real nature appear, so that the understanding of what is said in them can claim to be authoritative and universal. [*TM*, p. 265]

Why assess the "extra resonance" of contemporary artworks as noise, uncontrolled prejudice, and confusion? As regards the specific problem of the relationship between new art and tradition, Gadamer displays a cultural conservatism even more rigid than that of, say, T. S. Eliot, whose famous dictum in "Tradition and the Individual Talent" made partisanship toward particular trends in contemporary literature the motive for revaluations and new appropriations of tradition. But there is something more at stake in the passage just quoted. I take Gadamer's reference to contemporary artworks to be a kind of synecdoche for the entire continuum of cultural practices and symbolic expressions in "our age." The discourses, expressive forms, and artworks of contemporary culture have an extra resonance because they determine the context of cultural reception in the present. They are, moreover, sites of conflict among the *competing* self-interpretations of "our age." It is this conflict of interpretations which Gadamer characterizes as polyphonous noise.

Conceptually, his position appears contradictory: on the one hand, he insists that "every age" interprets cultural tradition in a distinct, innovative manner because its own interests and reception-capacities are historically situated; on the other hand, he removes any reflection on the concrete elements of that historical situatedness from the interpretive process. Strategically, however, this double gesture is perfectly coherent. It permits Gadamer to mute the unsettled, unsettling dialogue among the conflicting self-interpretations of the present and thus to position the constructed tradition as the univocal source of legitimate meanings and values for our own era. The monologue of tradition can thus eclipse the dialogical plurality of contemporary culture. And the methodically constructed universe of meanings and values can be set above the social conflicts and competing ideologies within contemporary society, just as the texts and artworks of the constructed tradition have been methodically detached from their historical situatedness in earlier societies. The cultural tradition can ultimately be counted on to fill the present with authoritative meanings and values.

The procedure just outlined is the basis for Gadamer's tendency, criticized at length by Habermas, to promote an altogether one-sided conception of "application," that is, the moment in the hermeneutical process when the meanings and values articulated in the transmitted-interpreted text are accepted as valid for the present and hence "applied" to the life-context of the interpreters. In a recent coda to the original debate, Habermas has argued that Gadamer's conception of application does not square with the latter's own premise that interpreter and text are related in the manner of partners, albeit hypothetical, in a dialogue or conversation:

Gadamer endangers his fundamental hermeneutical insight because hidden behind his preferred model of philological concern with canonical texts lies the really problematic case of the *dogmatic interpretation of sacred scriptures*. Only against this background is he able to analyze interpretation exclusively along the lines of *application*. . . . Philosophical hermeneutics rightly asserts an internal connection between questions of meaning and questions of validity. To understand a symbolic expression means to know under what conditions its validity claim would have to be accepted; but it does *not* mean assenting to its validity claim without regard to context.[6]

Habermas is, of course, disputing the use of the classical texts of the cultural tradition or the sacred texts of religious communities as the model for understanding in the social sciences. My concern is that we not concede that the Gadamerian paradigm adequately describes the hermeneutics of the cultural tradition, even when narrowly conceived as the canonical texts of so-called high culture. At stake is Gadamer's assertion that the cultural tradition has authority in a manner parallel to that which he ascribes to the law or sacred texts in his account of legal and biblical hermeneutics:

Hermeneutics in the sphere of literary criticism and the historical sciences is not "knowledge as domination," ie an appropriation as a "taking possession of," but rather a subordination to the text's claims to dominate our minds. Of this, however, legal and theological hermeneutics are the true model. To interpret the law's will or the promises of God is clearly not a form of domination, but of service. They are interpretations—which includes application—in the service of what is considered valid. Our thesis is that historical hermeneutics also has a task of application to perform, because it too serves the validity of meaning, in that it explicitly and consciously bridges the gap in time that separates the interpreter from the text and overcomes the alienation of meaning that the text has undergone. [*TM*, p. 278]

In order to accord this form of authority to the cultural tradition on analogy with his conception of legal and theological interpretation, Gadamer has again to presuppose that the (constructed) tradition's unity and universality inform the premethodological experience of cultural preservation-transmission-understanding. Such was his first line of defense against Habermas's original critique: "the *Geisteswissenschaften* were the starting point of my analysis in *Truth and Method* precisely because they related to experiences that have nothing to do with method and science but lie beyond science—like the experience

---

[6]Habermas, *Theory of Communicative Action*, vol 1. *Reason and the Rationalization of Society*, trans. Thomas McCarthy (Boston: Beacon, 1984), pp. 135–136.

of art and the experience of culture that bears the imprint of its historical tradition. The hermeneutical experience as it is operative in all these cases is not in itself the object of methodical alienation but is directed against alienation."[7] As I have argued, Gadamer's view of art and culture does not describe an experience "prior to all methodical alienation." It is itself the product of a complex of methodical procedures. And that complex yields Gadamer's conception of cultural authority and hermeneutical application.

As can be seen by summarizing the three sets of hermeneutical commitments we have discussed, they forge in their combination the methodical procedures required for such a conception. First, the interpretation of texts proceeds methodically on the presupposition that the interaction of part and whole, whether within individual texts or in the relation of text and tradition, is a relation of unity; as a consequence, the interpretively constructed tradition acquires the appearance of a univocal totality of meanings and values. Second, the methodical bracketing of the social genesis of the transmitted text dissolves the distinction between meaningfulness and validity; interpretation thereby constructs meanings that appear detached from the social relations and practices out of which the text was originally produced, and hence lends those meanings an aura of continuity. Third, the methodical bracketing of the sociocultural context of reception completes the fusion of meaningfulness and validity; having abstracted itself from the conflict of interpretations and self-interpretations in contemporary culture, Gadamerian hermeneutics finally renders its constructed tradition the sole, therefore authoritative source of meanings and values and thus assents to that tradition's validity claims without regard to context. By means of these procedures, however, the hermeneutical circle is rendered tautological. And the conception of application comes to rest on a pair of false equations: first, that *estrangement* from a text's meaning equals *nonunderstanding;* and, second, that *understanding* equals *appropriation* and *application.* Gadamer has slid from the notions that the interpreter's relation to historically distant texts is a mix of "familiarity" and "strangeness," and that interpretation passes through the question of a text's meaning in order to confront the question of its validity, to the very different assertion that overcoming estrangement or alienation in the process of

---

[7]Gadamer, "On the Scope and Function of Hermeneutical Reflection," *Philosophical Hermeneutics*, p. 26.

understanding implacably terminates in the interpreter's acceptance of the text's claims to validity.

Gadamer's conception of application crowns the project of what I am calling the traditional, as opposed to critical, hermeneutics of culture. It gives cultural tradition the appearance of a universe of meanings and values that exists apart from social conflicts and struggles. Gadamerian procedures operationalize two essential presuppositions of traditional hermeneutics: that of a monological universe of meaning and value which is valid for "our age," and that of a unified social community of which the interpreters-purveyors of the cultural tradition are the legitimate representatives, a community to which the tradition they construct is "applicable" as its source of meanings and values, that is, as its legitimate self-interpretation. Gadamer thereby has provided the methodical procedures and the theoretical self-understanding for a hermeneutics that preserves-transmits what Marcuse calls "affirmative culture."

Let us reprise Marcuse's critique of affirmative culture in light of our critique of Gadamer's traditional hermeneutics. According to Marcuse, the bourgeoisie was the first social class in Western history to claim—and to have to claim—that its own cultural productions, in particular the symbolic representations and expressive forms embodied in its artworks, were universally valid, in the sense that they gave expression to meanings and values binding for all classes in the society. It had further to claim that its own cultural productions were continuous with all valid, that is, validated, culture preserved from the past. Since the claims to universality had to be squared with the fact of social inequalities and exploitation, a permanent tension afflicts bourgeois culture. The progressive moment contained in the claim to universality expected from cultural creations, whether past or present, collapses into a corresponding regressive moment, namely, the affirmation that the cultural creations of the bourgeoisie and the appropriated-validated monuments of the cultural tradition actually fulfill this claim and embody an achieved universality independent of the forms of domination prevalent in society. Marcuse further argued that the illusory fulfillment of the claim to universality anchored an experience—I would say an interpretively organized, procedurally secured experience—of culture as a sphere separated from social and political relations and belonging to the inner life of individuals.

Truth and Method is the *belated clarification* of this class project. The need for clarification Gadamer himself thematizes along two lines:

on the one hand, it is necessary to correct the self-misunderstandings that disturb previous hermeneutical theory, particularly romantic hermeneutics and historicist hermeneutics; and, on the other hand, it is necessary to revive the centrality of the hermeneutical experience of self-understanding against the tendency of modernity, according to Gadamer's diagnosis, to subordinate such self-understanding to the imperatives of scientific knowledge and technological mastery. I, however, see the Gadamerian clarification as belated, or anachronistic, insofar as it responds to another crisis which is never thematized by Gadamer, namely, the fact that the social function of the *Geisteswissenschaften* as conceived by the whole of traditional hermeneutics— romantic, historicist, *and* philosophical—has been thrown into doubt by the dissolution of the bourgeoisie as a culturally coherent class. The Gadamerian project is in effect an effort to restore bourgeois culture in the absence of a bourgeoisie.

Such belatedness hardly renders Gadamer's traditional hermeneutics defunct; he indeed succeeds in articulating what is arguably the theoretical self-understanding of the prevalent types of research in the humanities today. Nonetheless, the belated, defensive posture of traditional hermeneutics in contemporary society should alert us that a socially critical hermeneutics cannot rest with the Gadamerian project, despite its occasional appearance of going against the grain of social and cultural tendencies that critical theory too needs to diagnose. Nor can a critical hermeneutics presuppose that a simple negation of such categories as cultural continuity or univocal meaning will suffice as a *socially* critical theory of culture.[8] As we will now see, Habermas's

---

[8]The latter position has been especially apparent in literary critics who have tried to derive categories of social and cultural critique from Jacques Derrida's "deconstruction of metaphysics." See, for example, Michael Ryan, *Marxism and Deconstruction* (Baltimore: Johns Hopkins University Press, 1982). A disturbing example of the opposite position has recently come from an otherwise astute commentator on the Frankfurt School, Martin Jay, in his essay, "Hierarchy and the Humanities: The Radical Implications of a Conservative Idea," *Telos* 62 (Winter 1984–1985), 131–144. That Jay sets up Ryan's book as the strawman for his own argument dramatizes the extent to which the anachronistic defense of the Western cultural tradition and undifferentiated, totalizing critiques of that tradition are but mirror images of one another. Rather than addressing the methodological and institutional problems to be faced by a socially critical, transvaluating interpretation of the Western cultural tradition, Jay sees only the need "to make the case for the ambivalent virtues of hierarchy" in disciplines such as literature and intellectual history. Despite the disclaimer that he seeks "to 'refunction,'" in Brecht's sense, rather than defend the value of cultural hierarchy," his rhetoric and conceptual categories betray a discomfort with the dialectical project of preserving

position in the debate with Gadamer inaugurated a socially critical assessment of traditional hermeneutics but did not altogether clear the path toward a socially critical hermeneutics of culture. The ambiguities in Habermas's argument will, I hope, illuminate that task.

Conflicts of Interpretation

The Gadamer-Habermas debate came to turn on the question of the relation between interpretive understanding modeled on the appropriation of tradition and explanatory understanding modeled on the critique of society. Habermas argued that a limitation of social inquiry to the former abandoned critique in favor of tradition and subordinated reason to the "rehabilitated" authority of prejudice. Gadamer countered that Habermas's call for a form of "critical reflection" based on transcendental norms not bound to tradition was a dangerous abstraction which recapitulated the Enlightenment's prejudices and its antithesis between reason and authority. Behind these sharply contrasted positions lay two unsolved questions. How could Gadamer's conceptions of tradition and of the linguisticality of understanding encompass the sort of social criticism Habermas sought to secure theoretically? And, on the other hand, how could Habermas establish some Archimedian point of "critical reflection" outside historically situated, culturally evolved norms?

---

expressive forms of the cultural tradition by means of their critique. Instead, he seeks to "redress the balance" supposedly upset by "what has now become a widespread complaint" against "cultural elitism"; this "complaint" is especially audible to Jay in "the crescendo of criticism directed against 'white, male, heterosexual' culture by those who fall outside its categories." His plea for cultural discrimination confuses questions of aesthetic valuation—In which artworks are the expressive capacities of art at a given historical moment most fully realized? How are such expressive capacities made available for, or constrained from, expressing generalizable interests and needs in a particular society?—and of cultural validity—What meanings and values articulated in our artistic and intellectual traditions should be carried forward into the present?—with an altogether different question of cultural hierarchy which he vaguely defines as "our capacity to make distinctions of quality and rank." At best, this confusion leaves hopelessly obscure what Jay means by "higher" in his assertion that "the exact content of what we privilege as higher than other aspects of our cultural experience must constantly be rethought and challenged." At worst, it makes common cause with the intellectual currents and institutional forces that would delegitimate the rethinking and the challenge posed by just those critical trends that by examining the Western cultural tradition's inherence in structures of social domination and in ethnocentric, racist, and androcentric structures of meaning, question whether that tradition as preserved-transmitted in the humanities fulfills its claim to universality.

For my purposes, the crucial element in Habermas's objections to Gadamerian hermeneutics lies in the following formulation regarding the question of the linguistically mediated character of intersubjectivity:

> It makes good sense to conceive of language as a kind of metainstitution on which all social institutions are dependent; for social action is constituted only in ordinary language communication. But this metainstitution of language as tradition is evidently dependent in turn on social processes that are not reducible to normative relationships. Language is *also* a medium of domination and social power; it serves to legitimate relations of organized force. Insofar as the legitimations do not articulate the power relations whose institutionalization they make possible, insofar as these relations merely manifest themselves in the legitimations, language is *also* ideological. Here it is a question not of deceptions within a language but of deception with language as such. Hermeneutic experience that encounters this dependency of the symbolic framework on actual conditions changes into critique of ideology.[9]

This passage fundamentally challenges Gadamer's notion that the linguisticality of the hermeneutical experience assures that the understanding of tradition in itself guarantees the truth of tradition. But two problems also arise from Habermas's formulation. First, what is meant by "actual conditions" as against the "symbolic framework" of tradition? And, second, what does it mean for "hermeneutic experience" to *change into* "critique of ideology"?

Habermas goes on to clarify the first point but in the process employs an equivocal opposition between "linguistic infrastructure" and "the constraint of reality":

> The linguistic infrastructure of a society is part of a complex that, however symbolically mediated, is also constituted by the constraint of reality—by the constraint of outer nature that enters into procedures for technical mastery and by the constraint of inner nature reflected in the repressive character of social power relations. These two categories of constraint are not only the object of interpretations; behind the back of language, they also affect the very grammatical rules according to which we interpret the world. *Social actions can only be comprehended in an objective framework that is constituted conjointly by language, labor, and domination.* . . . Such a reference system can no longer leave tradition undetermined as the all-encompassing.[10]

[9]Habermas, "Gadamer's *Truth and Method*," p. 360.
[10]Ibid., p. 361.

The problem I want to pose is not so much why a critical sociology of the system of labor and relations of domination in a society cannot be contained within the Gadamerian model of the appropriation of tradition. On that issue Habermas is quite persuasive. It is the second of the questions asked above that needs to be examined if we are to carry Habermas's criticisms of Gadamer back into the arena of cultural theory. Why does Habermas accept so much of Gadamer's conception of cultural tradition that he has to place the moment of critique outside hermeneutics: "hermeneutic experience changes into critique of ideology"?

At issue is how to proceed once one accepts Habermas's claim that cultural symbolizations and representations can "serve to legitimate relations of organized force." This claim asks us to specify how an exploitative system of labor and social relations of domination leave their imprint on the forms of linguistically mediated intersubjectivity which comprise culture. There are two options. According to the first, cultural creations are so enmeshed in the social relations of domination—of the society in which they were produced and of the society in which they are preserved-transmitted—that "hermeneutic experience" is permeated with historically situated conflicts between forms of domination and struggles for freedom, forms of exploitation and struggles for justice, forms of subordination and struggles for equality. In this view, the cultural work and its interpretation are—in ways yet to be formulated—*internally* affected by the clash between the legitimation and the critique of domination. It is this option which I will eventually argue should orient the critical hermeneutics of culture. The second option is the one Habermas develops here and in several later writings. According to this second option, cultural creations and traditions are two-tiered: on one level, they elaborate the essential linguisticality of human intersubjectivity and understanding into concrete, contingent "forms of life," while on another level their communicative capacity is susceptible of being "exploited... for the legitimation of domination."[11]

It is this two-tiered conception of cultural traditions which leads Habermas to make the critique of ideology *external* to hermeneutical experience; cultural traditions are preserved-transmitted by herme-

---

[11] Jürgen Habermas, "Walter Benjamin: Consciousness-Raising or Rescuing Critique," *Philosophical-Political Profiles*, trans. Frederick G. Lawrence (Cambridge: MIT Press, 1983), p. 158.

neutical understanding in just the Gadamerian sense, while the instrumentalization of culture as legitimation of domination is, separately, the object of critique. These dichotomies fit with a theme developed in Habermas's social theory as a whole, according to which capitalist modernization has distorted "forms of life" by means of an "erosion" or "devaluation of their traditional substance."[12] The programmatic implication of this diagnosis is that the critical theory of culture ought to foster the preservation-transmission of traditions against the eroding effects of capitalist modernization, while simultaneously criticizing the ideological instrumentalization of culture. That such a program is doomed to bifurcate into incompatible moments is evident in the fact that Habermas's 1970 essay on Gadamer has to assert the primacy of critique over preservation, while his 1972 essay on Benjamin reverses the valuation and sets the task of preserving-transmitting traditions above the critique of ideology. In my view, such problems arise because the two-tiered conception of cultural tradition is in itself flawed. By not granting that social relations of domination leave their imprint on the very forms and semantic contents of cultural symbolizations and representations, Habermas cannot make critique internal to processes of cultural preservation-transmission. Moreover, his diagnosis of the effects of capitalist modernization on cultural traditions neglects, fully as much as Gadamer's, the fact that it is a condition of modern culture that traditions or heritages henceforth have to be constructed, and that

---

[12]For a decisive critique of Habermas's opposition between *system* and *lifeworld* and the concomitant theme of the "colonization of the lifeworld," see Nancy Fraser, "What's Critical about Critical Theory? The Case of Habermas and Gender," *New German Critique* 35 (Spring/Summer 1985), 97–131. Fraser argues that "even in late capitalism the norms and meanings of gender identity continue to channel the influence of the lifeworld onto systems. These norms continue to structure the state-regulated economy, as the persistence, indeed exacerbation, of labor force segmentation according to sex shows. And these norms also structure state administration, as the gender segmentation of U.S. and European social-welfare systems shows. Thus, it is not the case that in late-capitalism 'system intrusions' detach life-contexts from 'value-orientations *per se.*' On the contrary, welfare capitalism simply uses other means to uphold the familiar 'normatively-secured consensus' concerning male dominance and female subordination. But Habermas' theory overlooks this counter-motion from lifeworld to system. Thus, it posits the evil of welfare capitalism as the evil of a general and indiscriminate reification. So it fails to account for the fact that it is disproportionately women who suffer the effects of bureaucratization and monetarization. And for the fact that, viewed structurally, bureaucratization and monetarization are, among other things, instruments of women's subordination."

the competing constructions of tradition involve ideologically relevant conflicts of interpretation.

With these problems in mind, let us examine the shortcomings of Gadamer's response to Habermas's separation of hermeneutical experience and critique of ideology. Gadamer retorts that the understanding of social relations of production and domination, that is, of labor and power, is in no way external to hermeneutics. He argues that understanding such "actual conditions" or "constraints of reality" is, just as much as the understanding of cultural tradition, a linguistically mediated activity. The critique of ideology is, he concludes, never external to the hermeneutics of cultural tradition. But this counterargument rings hollow, for nowhere does Gadamer in fact make such an analysis of social relations or such a critique of ideology internal to the hermeneutics of tradition. Indeed, his effort to recuperate the critique of ideology within his hermeneutical framework reveals that his notion of ideology has no resemblance to the neo-Marxist problematic invoked by Habermas. In the Marxian conception, ideology is, in Adorno's phrase, *"socially necessary* false consciousness" or, in Habermas's, "the dogmatism of *life-practices."* Gadamer, by contrast, conceives ideology merely as subjective error, that is, as a misinterpretation of the world: "there is no societal reality, with all its concrete forces, that does not bring itself to representation in a consciousness that is linguistically articulated. Reality does not happen 'behind the back' of language; it happens rather behind the back of those who live in the subjective opinion that they have understood 'the world' (or can no longer understand it); that is, reality happens precisely within language."[13] With this formulation, Gadamer simply sidesteps Habermas's initial, very precise definition of the ideological dimension of cultural forms and traditions; what is at stake are not misinterpretations of the world, but rather world-interpretations that serve "to legitimate relations of organized force" through discourses that "do not articulate the power relations whose institutionalization they make possible" but let "these relations merely manifest themselves in the legitimations."

The Gadamer-Habermas debate here leaves us at an impasse as regards the question of a socially critical hermeneutics. Gadamer's argument culminates in an evasion of the problem aimed at in Habermas's notion of critique of ideology. And Habermas adduces an aporetic program for critical theory by separating the hermeneutical preserva-

---

[13]Gadamer, "On the Scope and Function of Hermeneutical Reflection," p. 35.

tion-transmission of cultural tradition from the critique of the ideological use of culture to legitimate domination. To get beyond this
impasse requires that Habermas's position on the interrelation of traditions and critique be modified in two directions.

The first modification has been argued most compellingly by Jack
Mendelson in his excellent account of the debate as a whole. Mendelson
seeks to recast the relation between traditions and the normative standpoint required for critique so as to overcome the lurking sense in
Habermas's arguments that the normative standpoint is external to the
traditions in which the critical theorist and his or her addressees are
steeped.

Since Mendelson frames the problem of norms with respect to the
theory of communication that Habermas has developed in the wake
of the debate with Gadamer, a brief excursus on Habermas's general
conceptions is in order.[14] Habermas argues that certain ideal norms
are built into the pragmatics of communication, that is, language in
use among participants in an interaction. Participants in discourse tacitly pledge themselves to provide justifications for their utterances if
called upon to do so. A challenge or test of an utterance might aim at
whether it is true, whether it is just, or whether it is sincere. On the
one hand, then, Habermas attempts to account for language's capacity
for error, unjustness, or (self-)deception and, on the other hand, to
characterize the pragmatics of linguistically mediated interactions as
susceptible to a critical interrogation to which the participants themselves are tacitly pledged.

It follows, furthermore, that another normative reference point is
tacit in communicative-social interaction, namely, that all potential
participants in a discourse—that is, all those whose interests might be
affected by the actions decided upon, arrived at, or justified through
the discourse—have an equal chance of participating in it on a par
with others. This formulation gives Habermas the normative basis from
which a critical theory of society can study and evaluate social relations
and institutions. Institutions become criticizable once it can be shown
that they, for example, structurally preempt a social group's partici-

[14]The relevant essays by Habermas are the following: "Toward a Theory of Communicative Competence," in *Recent Sociology*, no. 2, ed. Hans Peter Dreitzel (New
York: Macmillan, 1970), pp. 114–148; "Some Distinctions in Universal Pragmatics,"
Theory and Society 3 (1976), 156–167; "What Is Universal Pragmatics?" *Communication and the Evolution of Society*, trans. Thomas McCarthy (Boston: Beacon, 1979),
pp. 1–68; and "Reply to My Critics," pp. 269–274.

pation on a par with others in such discursively mediated interactions. Such institutions distort communication by making discourse, in its pragmatic and/or semantic component, structure legitimations for relations of domination. Rather than false consciousness in the traditional sense, one is dealing with the systematically distorted discursive practices that regulate social relations of production and power. The norm against which such systematically distorted communication can be evaluated is what Habermas calls the "ideal speech situation."

Habermas has called his postulation of the ideal speech situation a *"weak* transcendentalism" in the sense that this ideal norm represents a purely formal-procedural rationality as opposed to some substantive conception of reason. Mendelson calls attention to a second aspect of Habermas's "weak transcendentalism" as well; since the ideal speech situation is merely the tacit norm of rationality in the pragmatics of discourse, the norm is activated only situationally in accordance with historically specific conflicts between actual social institutions and members of a society who are potential participants in communicative action. Consequently, the knowledges developed in social-theoretical critique have a merely hypothetical validity relative to the current and potential self-understandings and actions of the social groups or movements addressed by the critique.

Mendelson rightly insists on this aspect of Habermas's position against Gadamer's claims that Habermas fosters a terrorism of reason. Critical theory "must ultimately prove itself by guiding interpretations in which addressees recognize themselves. In this sense, even the theoretical aspects of critique cannot be completely grounded theoretically, but retain a contingent, hypothetical status which can only be redeemed by reentering the life-process of society and contributing to successful processes of enlightenment."[15] Mendelson nonetheless remains concerned that Habermas has overdrawn the distinction between normative ideals in critical theory and the historically contigent, tradition-bound lifeworld of the addressees, and, therefore, has undermined just this link between theory and practice: "While in a sense the ideal of rational consensus may be immanent in language *per se* and not simply an external standard, in most societies it is bound to remain unarticulated in the actual culture. It becomes politically relevant as an ideal to be consciously striven for only in societies which have begun to approach it on the level of their own cultural traditions."[16]

[15]Mendelson, "The Habermas-Gadamer Debate," p. 63.
[16]Ibid., pp. 72–73.

A second modification of Habermas's view is needed to overcome the separation of critique from cultural traditions and hermeneutical experiences. But this modification cuts the other way. As I have already suggested, missing from Habermas's conception of culture and tradition is the recognition that the social relations objectified in the framework of labor (the institutionalization of the mastery of nature) and power (the institutionalization of domination) internally affect cultural practices and traditions. The critical theory of culture, just as much as that of society, requires a tighter weave between hermeneutical experience and social critique.

Let me propose the following working hypothesis as a way of overcoming the deficiency in Habermas's conception: Culture comprises the symbolizations, representations, and expressive forms through which a collectivity secures its identity and solidarity at the same time that it relates itself to nature and differentiates itself from other collectivities with which it has relations of interdependence, whether cooperative or antagonistic. Social relations of domination are thus inscribed within and symbolized by cultural practices and traditions. And, by the same token, the conflict between the legitimation of domination and the resistance or opposition to domination is woven into the hermeneutical experiences through which cultural practices and traditions are produced, received, and preserved-transmitted. Let us also add two clarifications. First, modern societies include a plurality of collectivities in this sense, including those defined by class, race and ethnicity, and gender. And, second, individuals in modern societies are likewise members of several interlaced collectivities, so that their social identities are formed by and their discursive participation occurs within several potentially conflicting cultural practices/traditions at once. As a consequence the cultural practices of modern societies elaborate a multilayered dialectic of identity and difference, of solidarity and struggle, of possible community and actual social conflict.

From this perspective, the question of Gadamer's foreclosure of critique can be reframed. At what level do we make reference to the normative standard of the so-called ideal speech situation? Habermas engaged Gadamer at the metatheoretical level, and there the normative standpoint in question is simply missing from Gadamer's discourse. In the debate, Gadamer in turn gave reasons for his rejection of that normative standpoint. I want now to locate Gadamer's foreclosure of critique not at the level of his metatheoretical concepts but at the level of the pragmatics or action of his discourse on culture. I have criticized

Gadamer on the grounds that he tends to misrepresent his procedural and interpretive commitments as the theoretically required self-understanding of the *Geisteswissenschaften*. There is a further reason for opposing this tendency. For it is a small step from the theoretical misrepresentation in question to a dogmatic stance that would simply rule out-of-order several current controversies in the humanities.

The cultural tradition to which Gadamer is committed has increasingly been subject to challenges which would relativize that tradition and dispute the claim that it embodies the universal meanings and values of "Man." These challenges most often come from historical, anthropological, and literary researches that have taken their impetus directly or indirectly from the political and cultural self-consciousness of oppressed groups in the Third World as well as the First World. Such researches no longer take for granted the prevailing mode(s) of cultural preservation-transmission—and of cultural omission-exclusion. Moreover, they question not only the class character but also the ethnocentric and androcentric particularity of the meanings and values which traditional hermeneutics claims are universal. Also opened to dispute has been the construction of the archive of cultural studies, including the question of the discursive contexts or intertextual matrix in relation to which so-called canonical texts should be interpreted.

Disputes regarding the relativized or universalized standing of a cultural tradition; competing conceptions and processes of cultural preservation-transmission; debate over the construction of the archive of cultural interpretation—all these areas of controversy have become stakes in humanistic research. None of these controversies can be settled by appeal to some theoretically required self-understanding of the *Geisteswissenschaften*. Those who share Gadamer's particular procedural-interpretive commitments are obliged to provide reasons for their claims concerning the universality of the cultural tradition they construct; the value of the modes of preservation-transmission/omission-exclusion on which that constructed tradition depends; and the privilege accorded an archive built around artworks and classical texts that have been set apart from the discursive practices and cultural representations of the societies in which they were produced.

These commitments do not find their justification at the level of "truth" independent of "method," any more than they arise from universal process of understanding independent of particular, contestable social interests. When traditional hermeneutics attempts to exempt its commitments from argumentation and justification, it congeals a dogmatic stance aimed at preempting, or disqualifying, the hermeneutical projects of its opponents in the very debate in which it does not want to engage. Gadamer's discourse does this by retreating behind a theory of "the hermeneutical experience"; others do it by rigidly limiting humanistic study to the so-called canon.[17] Either way, the discourse of traditional hermeneutics falls short of the formal-procedural rationality immanent in the pragmatics of its discourse; it violates the pledge to give reasons for claims that are open to argument.

Moreover, as Habermas's communication theory is meant to show, such a systematic distortion of the speech situation betrays an insti-

---

[17]Consider "To Reclaim a Legacy," the report on the humanities in higher education issued by the National Endowment for the Humanities in 1984, and authored by its chairperson, William J. Bennett, shortly before his appointment as secretary of education for the Reagan administration. For the text of the report, see the *Chronicle of Higher Education*, November 28, 1984, pp. 16–21.

According to Bennett's conception of the humanities, the cultural tradition is unquestionably the archive of canonical texts and comprises a stable substance of knowledge and values to be acquired through authoritative instruction and transmitted intact from one generation to the next. When proffered by the head of the agency that funds considerable research and curriculum development in the humanities, even clichés acquire the force of a threat: "Properly taught, the humanities bring together the perenniel questions of human life with the greatest works of history, literature, philosophy, and art. Unless the humanities are taught in this way, there is little reason to offer them." The fact that many doing research and teaching in the humanities today do not share his assumptions or follow his blueprint does not lead Bennett to engage his opponents in debate or acknowledge their right to contend with views like his own in the contemporary university. Instead, he levels a broad, intellectually vacuous attack on the "relativism" and "scepticism" that he is convinced, despite the lack of any evidence, are the real cause of declining enrollments in the humanities.

"Relativism" and "scepticism" are Bennett's consistent code-words for all approaches that do not rehearse some version of the Arnoldian dictum about "the best that has been. . . ." It is not hard to imagine a list of offenders: Ricoeur, with his notion of the conflict of interpretations; Gadamer, with his theory of the context-dependent character of meaning and interpretation; deconstruction; Foucault's archaeology of knowledge and genealogy of power-knowledge regimes; history "from below"; neo-Marxism; feminism; Third World studies—all these theoretical positions and fields of inquiry deviate from Bennett's hermeneutic and pedagogic norms. Yet he does not feel compelled to address any of them on their own ground. Indeed, since he steadfastly pretends that his own view contains no ideological commitments or contestable values, he fashions his indictment of the N.E.H.'s newly constructed enemy in the following terms: "The study group was alarmed by the tendency of some humanities professors to present their subjects in a tendentious, ideological manner. Sometimes the humanities are used as if they were the handmaidens of ideology, subordinated to particular prejudices and valued or rejected on the basis of their relation to a certain social stance."

tutional structuring of power. The educational system and the cultural public sphere in our society are the institutionally secured space in which *conflicts of interpretation* occur. In political terms, demands for democratization require that these institutions secure the openness of cultural interpretation and admit the plurality of conflicting processes of cultural preservation-transmission and hence of possible avenues of cultural transformation. It is just this openness and this plurality which Gadamerian hermeneutics, discursively and institutionally, would foreclose. The foreclosure of critique is, therefore, a part of the discursive-institutional *action* of traditional hermeneutics as well as an element in its conceptual, metatheoretical stance.

This line of argument against Gadamer also cuts back against the grain of Habermas's program for the critical theory of culture. For Habermas concedes too much to Gadamer's conception of the hermeneutics of cultural tradition. Consequently, he states the limits to traditional hermeneutics in a way that yields the bifurcated conception of interpretation and critique, rather than a conception of socially critical hermeneutics: "The objectivity of a 'happening of tradition' that is made up of symbolic meaning is not objective enough. Hermeneutics comes up against the walls of the traditional framework from the inside, as it were. As soon as these boundaries have been experienced and recognized, cultural traditions can no longer be posed as absolute. . . . Hermeneutic experience that encounters [the] dependency of the symbolic framework on actual conditions changes into critique of ideology."[18] Hermeneutics bangs against the inner walls of tradition only so long as cultural tradition is constructed in the form of a monological realm of unified meanings and values whose very validity depends upon their separation from the social relations of their production- and reception-contexts. Such a construct, I have argued, describes not the hermeneutical experience as such but a particular, procedurally elaborated, methodically secured tradition. The interpretive situation looks quite different from the perspective of the alternative hypotheses I have proposed. If the clash between the legitimation and the contestation of domination is internal to expressive forms themselves; if cultural traditions in the modern world are plural, often conflicting, rather than singular and monological; and, finally, if the competing constructions of cultural traditions, whether culture is viewed in the broadest terms as "forms of life" or in the narrowest as

---

[18]Habermas, "Gadamer's *Truth and Method*," p. 360.

the classical-centered canon, reflect ideologically charged, politically relevant conflicts of interpretation—then hermeneutical experience is always already caught up within social systems of labor and social relations of domination. Since the happening of traditions does not have the sort of objectivity Gadamer imputes to culture, critical hermeneutics does not need quite the kind of objectivity Habermas imputes to the notion of critique. Interpretation need not "change into" critique. Rather, interpretations are socially critical or socially uncritical according to the commitments they develop with regard to the symbolic and social struggles between the legitimation and the contestation of domination.

Viewed against the backdrop of the Gadamer-Habermas debate, the point of departure for a socially critical hermeneutics should, on the one hand, expect a less grounding, more relativized tradition than Gadamer's and, on the other, require an even weaker transcendentalism than Habermas's. Gadamer vitiates his general insight into the historically contingent and situated status of interpretation by developing a set of procedures which construct *the* cultural tradition as, after all, a universe of meanings and values. As we question and abandon that construction, we recognize that a condition of modern culture is that indeed all effective heritages have to be constructed, and that the dialogues provoked by this necessity are not encompassed within any monological horizon. Habermas, on the other hand, began by acknowledging the ambivalence of expressive forms—namely, that they develop forms of life through symbolically mediated interactions that hold the promise of uncoerced mutual understanding and mutual recognition, but at the same time may be instruments of the legitimation of domination. Rather than dichotomizing this ambivalence, we must develop interpretive procedures which can account for the ways that the dialectic of legitimation and contestation internally structures expressive forms. By the same token, the conflict of interpretations provides a different perspective on the problem of the normative standpoints from which critique is conducted.

Habermas seems to me right to insist that the social critic-theorist make explicit the tacit formal-procedural norms of rationality which belong to the actual communicative context of society and from the vantage point of which that same context can be criticized and the critique justified via argumentation. And I have already suggested how such an argumentation might develop with regard to the dogmatic implications of Gadamerian hermeneutics and its institutional intervention. The negative-critical reference to the ideal speech situation guides the *procedures* of the critical theory of society and culture. However, the *motive* and the *leverage* of critique come, on the one hand, from the interpreters' inherence in and commitments to "the struggles and wishes of the age," and, on the other hand, from the structuration of the expressive forms being interpreted insofar as they are internally affected by the struggles and wishes of their age and ours. I allude here to the definition Marx once gave of critical theory or what he at the time called critical philosophy, namely, that it is "the self-clarification of the struggles and wishes of the age."[19] In drawing upon and departing from the reflections of Gadamer and Habermas, I have tried to flesh out the hermeneutical and discursive aspects of such a definition of critical theory.

[19]Karl Marx, letter to Ruge, September 1843, in *Early Writings*, trans. Rodney Livingstone and Gregor Benton (New York: Vintage, 1975), p. 209.

Part Two

MARXISM AND THE PROBLEM OF CULTURE

3

The Economy and
the Symbolic

The Inaugural Paradigm of Marxist Cultural Theory

Nowhere did Marx advance a developed reflection on culture and cultural interpretation. Nowhere did he even provide an extensive discussion of the concept of culture. Nonetheless, his fragmentary comments on the "realm of necessity" and the "realm of freedom," his more systematically elaborated notion that the social division of labor was inaugurated historically in the separation of manual and mental labor, and his and Engels's first significant elaborations of the concept of ideology have together provided far more than just clues to Marx's thinking about culture. Indeed, the concepts of realm of necessity/realm of freedom, the social division of manual and mental labor, and ideology are the guiding threads of cultural theory and interpretation in the Marxist tradition. From Marx's writings it is possible to construct what I consider the inaugural paradigm of Marxist cultural theory—a paradigm whose value, in my view, persists because of its ability to raise theoretical problems and define interpretive tasks that have not been adequately treated "outside" Marxism, but whose flaws, on the other hand, are so intrinsic to the paradigm itself as to raise, in turn, basic questions about its continuing validity and vitality.

Culture—in the sense of forms of learning, science, philosophy and theology, art and literature—Marx took to be specialized forms of activity which have historically been engendered and developed within class societies. He turned his attention from the outset to the general social conditions that have made the pursuit of such specialized activities possible and therefore made them a part of the organization of society as a whole. Refusing the notion that culture is the manifestation of a self-generating human spirit, he looked at cultural practices as an aspect of the social development of wealth indissociable from the whole process of creating wealth, including the material processes of human labor:

> In relation to the whole of society, the creation of *disposable time* is then also creation of time for the production of science, art, etc. The course of social development is by no means that because one individual has satisfied his [*sic*] need he then proceeds to create a superfluity for himself; but rather because one individual or class of individuals is forced to work more than is required for the satisfaction of its needs—because *surplus labor* is on one side, therefore not-labor and surplus wealth are posited on the other.[1]

"Free time" is the social good whose production and distribution enable the pursuit of those activities that in turn create a society's intellectual and artistic wealth. In class societies free time is distributed unequally. Not only do laboring classes receive a smaller share of it, but moreover it is because they devote more time to laboring than is required to provide for their own material needs that free time and therefore intellectual and artistic wealth are created. Surplus labor falls upon one social grouping, surplus wealth belongs to another.

Marx finishes his note in the *Grundrisse* on "disposable time" and culture with a comment that exhibits his at once critical and utopian perspective on the social division of laboring and nonlaboring classes, surplus labor and surplus wealth: "In reality the development of wealth exists only in these opposites [*Gegensätze*]: in potentiality, its development is the possibility of the suspension of these opposites."[2] The utopian possibility or potentiality evoked here is radically egalitarian. Marx envisions a society in which those who create the surplus wealth would not be confronted by that wealth in the guise of an opposing class and its privileged possessions, a class materially advantaged and empowered through the very activities made possible by its appropriation of free time—but rather would encounter free time and the intellectual and artistic wealth created within it as *their own*. Marx saw

[1] Karl Marx, *Grundrisse: Foundations of the Critique of Political Economy*, trans. Martin Nicolaus (New York: Vintage, 1973), p. 401 n.
[2] Ibid.

no theoretical or political need to spell out how an egalitarian society might distribute free time. Nor did he see the need to reflect on the politics of culture in the interval between class societies and classless society. These questions had no urgency for him, presumably because of his own political expectations of imminent social revolution.

For us it is different. The efficient repressiveness of "cultural policy" in the Soviet bloc and the failures and consequences of the Cultural Revolution led by Mao Zedong have challenged Marxists to address anew questions of cultural freedoms, the distribution of the means of communication, and the development of egalitarian forms of learning and expression. From our own particular perspective in the West, the survival of capitalism has made the interval between class and classless society the persisting field of political and cultural struggle, not a brief interlude between two sharply separated epochs. To discover the relevance of the Marxian paradigm of cultural theory requires, first, that we sharpen, and modify, its self-understanding. To begin with, I will argue that the value of Marx's theoretical discourse is its *critical-utopian* value; it does not preside over a punctual event—the Revolution—dividing two epochs, but is itself situated between the development of wealth it criticizes and the development of wealth it advocates. As a part of the intellectual wealth of its own society, this theoretical discourse is an instance of the very process Marx neglects: namely, a cultural practice taking place within and against the culture of a class society and therefore within and against the existing development of wealth. And surely it cannot be the only such counterpractice! We must acknowledge that what Marx called the "actual" and "potential" development of wealth are not punctually separated by an event in history but in some sense exist within the same changing social space.

We need, then, to clarify how it is that cultural practices are a part of the political struggles over the development of social wealth. Marx's own clarification advanced in the third volume of *Capital* is significant but partial. It will point us toward a fuller critique of the inaugural paradigm. There Marx expresses the difference between class and classless society in terms of two distinct forms of the relation between a "realm of necessity" and a "realm of freedom":

> In fact, the realm of freedom actually begins only where labor which is determined by necessity and mundane considerations ceases; thus in the very nature of things it lies beyond the sphere of actual material pro-

duction. Just as the savage must wrestle with Nature to satisfy his [*sic*] wants, to maintain and reproduce life, so must civilized man, and he must do so in all social formations and under all possible modes of production. With his development, this realm of physical necessity expands as a result of his wants; but at the same time, the forces of production which satisfy these wants also increase. Freedom in this field can only consist in socialized man, the associated producers, rationally regulating their interchange with Nature, bringing it under their common control, instead of being ruled by it as by the blind forces of Nature; and achieving this with the least expenditure of energy and under conditions favorable to, and worthy of, their human nature. But it nonetheless still remains a realm of necessity. Beyond it begins that development of human energy which is an end in itself, the true realm of freedom, which, however, can blossom forth only with this realm of necessity as its basis.[3]

Marx has here redrawn the distinction made in the *Grundrisse* between class and classless society by now counterposing the actual relation between the realm of necessity and the realm of freedom and their potential relation. The counterpositioning is, however, clearer than the definitions of the various realms, in particular the two opposing realms of freedom. The actual realm of necessity is itself unfree, in the sense that it structures the relations among individuals and groups according to a nonreciprocal, coercive interdependence of laboring and nonlaboring classes; because the material interchange with nature is organized through such nonreciprocal social relations, that interchange has the force not merely of physical necessity but also of a blind power ruling human beings. Against this unfree realm of necessity Marx counterposes the vision of an egalitarian realm of necessity in which "the associated producers," that is, all the members of society insofar as they must necessarily satisfy their wants through the material interchange with nature, would "rationally [regulate] their interchange with Nature, bringing it under their common control, instead of being ruled by it as by the blind forces of Nature; and achieving this with the least expenditure of energy and under conditions favorable to, and worthy of, their human nature." To this egalitarian realm of necessity would correspond what Marx emphatically calls "the *true* realm of freedom," which he defines as the sphere of activity in which would unfold "that development of human energy which is an end in itself." The force of the final phrase in the passage quoted above: "the true realm of freedom

[3]Karl Marx, *Capital*, vol. 3 (New York: International Publishers, 1967), p. 820.

...can blossom forth only with this realm of necessity as its basis," seems to make two statements: first, that the true realm of freedom can emerge only from an egalitarian as opposed to an unfree, class-divided realm of necessity; and second, that, in keeping with the general import of the whole paragraph, no realm of freedom exists except insofar as the material preconditions for it have been fulfilled within the realm of necessity, namely, the freedom from physical want and the creation of free time. Marx condenses these two statements again as he concludes the discussion of the true realm of freedom: "The shortening of the working day is its basic prerequisite."[4]

There remain several questions, because Marx is much more precise in defining and contrasting the opposing realms of necessity than the realms of freedom. What does he mean by the development of human activity which is *an end in itself?* And what then is the force of the phrase "true realm of freedom," especially since its critical-utopian valence has to define, on the rebound, the existing realm of freedom? Is the latter, which Marx himself would have defined as the culture of class societies and understood quite narrowly as the Western cultural tradition, then to be considered "untrue," "false," "illusory," "deceptive," and in what sense?

The idea of human capacities and activities developing as ends-in-themselves is a nodal point in the relation of Marxian theory to the cultural tradition in question. For not only has this idea been produced within that cultural tradition, it has also been the normative principle of that culture's conception of itself, especially in Greek philosophy, in Renaissance humanism, and in the thought of middle-class German intellectuals in the half-century just preceding Marx. Let us juxtapose Schiller and Marx, since in Schiller we can see both the ideal of *Kultur* that Marx draws upon and the cultural self-conception he criticizes.

Writing in 1795, Schiller despairs of the ability of the German middle class to lead a political revolution as had their French counterparts. He can glimpse the "possibility...of honouring Man [*sic*] at last as an end in himself and making true freedom the basis of political association. Vain hope! The *moral* possibility is wanting and the favourable moment finds an apathetic generation."[5] Considering the terrain of politics barred, Schiller proposes to redirect the general pro-

---

[4]Ibid.
[5]Friedrich Schiller, *On the Aesthetic Education of Man in a Series of Letters*, trans. Reginald Snell (New York: Frederick Ungar, 1965), p. 35.

cess of human emancipation and self-realization into what he called the aesthetic education. The cultivation of feeling and reason is thereby disconnected from direct political action and social change. The "task of culture" takes precedence:

> The more multiform the cultivation of the sensibility is..., the more potentiality does Man [sic] develop within himself...; and the more freedom the reason gains..., the more does he create outside himself. Thus his culture [Kultur] will consist of two things: first, providing the receptive faculty with the most multifarious contacts with the world, and as regards feeling, pushing passivity to its fullest extent; secondly, securing for the determining faculty the fullest independence from the receptive, and as regards reason, pushing activity to its fullest extent. Where both qualities are united, Man will combine the greatest fullness of existence with the utmost self-dependence and freedom, and instead of abandoning himself to the world he will rather draw it into himself with the whole infinity of its phenomena, and subject it to the unity of his reason.[6]

In Schiller's conception of the aesthetic education, culture is an end-in-itself in two distinct senses. First of all, the sensibility and activity it cultivates are not instruments of power; they are not means of subordinating one human being to another. Even as he states this meaning of the normative principle of culture, however, Schiller also treats the aesthetic education as more than the compensatory substitute for, or anticipation of, politically wrought freedoms; instead, he ultimately declares that it is superior to them, not only detached from power relations but separated from politics altogether: "If in the *dynamic* state of rights man [sic] encounters man as force and restricts his activity, if in the *ethical* state of duties he opposes him with the majesty of law and fetters his will, in the sphere of cultivated society, in the *aesthetic* state, he need appear to him only as a shape, confront him only as an object of free play. *To grant freedom by means of freedom* is the fundamental law of this kingdom."[7] The second sense in which culture is an end-in-itself is its separation from, and superiority to, the whole realm of necessity: "for Art is a daughter of Freedom, and must receive her commission from the needs of spirits, not from the exigency of matter. But today Necessity is master, and bends a degraded humanity beneath its tyrannous yoke. *Utility* is the great idol of the age,

[6]Ibid., p. 69.
[7]Ibid., p. 137.

to which all powers must do service and all talents swear allegiance."[8] Its repudiation of possessive individualism aside, Schiller's identification of culture with spirit over and above matter belongs to the tradition reaching back to Plato's notion that a bed made by a craftsman-slave was an inferior copy of the idea of the bed contemplated by the citizen-philosopher.

When Marx takes over the ideal of human activities that are ends-in-themselves, he responds to both meanings incorporated in Schiller's concept. He preserves the normative principle of an activity not entangled in the exercise of power, in the sense of subordination and domination. And he contests the ideal of culture as a realm independent of material social life. By insisting that there can be no realm of freedom except on the basis of society's realm of necessity, Marx disputes the claim that any aspect of culture, including art and aesthetic education, arises from spiritual as opposed to material conditions. That argument, however, touches only the material preconditions of culture. Marx went further by insisting that so long as the realm of freedom does not have its basis in an egalitarian realm of necessity, so long as it arises from social relations of inequality and domination, it cannot realize its aim of a human cultivation that is an end-in-itself. With that argument Marx discovered the socially critical value in the humanist ideal of culture. He used it to indict the social relations of capitalism and to put in question the claim of aesthetic education or *Kultur* to fulfill its own aims without a transformation of society as a whole. As we have already seen, this form of the indictment of capitalism and the interrogation of bourgeois culture through an immanent critique of Western cultural ideals culminates in Marcuse's analysis of the "affirmative character" of culture.

Now, Marx's earlier writings sketched a very different line of argument against the separation of cultural from material processes. In the *Economic and Philosophical Manuscripts* of 1844, he had obviously already formed the intention of turning the self-conception of the Western cultural tradition against the intellectual acceptance and legitimation of capitalist society. But there his approach to "cultural development" centers on its practices, not merely on its self-conception. And his critique starts from an alternative account of artistic capacities and aesthetic education, one which establishes that they are themselves instances of social and material processes, and that the individuals who

[8]Ibid., p. 26.

directly engage in practices of artistic production and aesthetic reception do so as socially formed beings:

> Let us look at the question in its subjective aspect: only music can awaken the musical sense in man [*sic*] and the most beautiful music has *no* sense for the unmusical ear, because my object can only be the confirmation of one of my essential powers, i.e., can only be for me in so far as my essential power exists for me as a subjective attribute.... In the same way, and for the same reasons, the *senses* of social man are *different* from those of non-social man. Only through the objectively unfolded wealth of human nature can the wealth of subjective human sensitivity— a musical ear, an eye for beauty of form, in short, *senses* capable of human gratification—be either cultivated or created. For not only the five senses, but also the so-called spiritual senses, the practical senses (will, love, etc.), in a word, the *human* sense, the humanity of the senses— all these come into being only through the existence of *their* objects, through *humanized* nature. The *cultivation* of the five senses is the work of all previous history.[9]

Sifted and restated, this passage makes the following arguments: (1) Artistic productions can be received only through senses that are educated for such products, and, conversely, the education of the senses develops only from contact and experience with such products. (2) This interplay between artistic production and aesthetic receptivity is a *material* process, in the sense that it works with and works on natural phenomena and physical life; and it is a *social* process, in the sense that it is through the interaction of individuals, including the coordinated effects of activities separated in space and time, that the capacity for artistic production and aesthetic reception develops, in the form of

---

[9]Karl Marx, *Early Writings*, ed. Quinton Hoare and trans. Rodney Livingstone and Gregor Benton (New York: Vintage, 1975), p. 353. I am not concerned with the limitations of the philosophical idiom Marx uses in this passage, in particular, the subject/object framework and the postulate of "essential human powers." The line of argument I want to identify does not ultimately depend on that idiom and can be restated in other terms. There is one clarification—regarding the equivocal use of the term "objective"— which should bring the import of Marx's argument into focus. "Objective" can refer, on the one hand, to material objects, including (or especially) those which have been fashioned, crafted, or manufactured by human beings; and, on the other hand, it can refer to processes or skills that individuals acquire only as the result of the coordinated activities and productions of many human beings over extended periods of time. Thus, a piano or the sounds that it emits are "objective" in the first sense, while the ability to play music on the piano or to hear it as music is "objective" in the second sense. In what follows, I redesignate the latter as *material-social practices*.

artistic instruments, forms, conventions, techniques, and so on. (3) Artistic production, artworks, and aesthetic reception are thus inter-related elements in a complex of *material-social practices* that link interchanges with nature to interactions among individuals.

On the basis of this alternative conception of cultural wealth, Marx then attempts to make persuasive a revaluation of values. One can even think of his argument as an appeal specifically to other intellectuals who, having undergone a similar cultural-intellectual formation, esteem their society's "cultural development" because it represents for them activity that is an end-in-itself, uncoerced and uncoercive, and because it embodies a highly valued form of human wealth. If this wealth of culture results from the material-social practices of human beings in association with one another, then what justifies, Marx is asking, a denigrating view of the industrial and manual production of life's ne-cessities? For is not industrial production, like art, also a complex of material-social practices performed by human beings in association for the satisfaction of their socially evolved needs?[10] Along the same lines Marx challenges the valuation that opposes culture to necessity; it is not the realm of necessity which inhibits human development but the restraining, impoverishing organization of that realm by private prop-erty and capital. Marx announces this countervaluation with hyper-bole: "Private property has made us so stupid and one-sided that an object is only *ours* when we have it. . . . [A]*ll* the physical and intellectual senses have been replaced by the simple estrangement of *all* these senses—the sense of *having*."[11]

I am insisting on that aspect of Marx's argument which articulates a conflict of values because that is how the entire discussion of art enters into the *Economic and Philosophical Manuscripts*. Marx ad-vocates a new valuation of society, industry, and science through a reassessment of values already associated with culture, art, and aes-thetic capacity. The argument addresses whoever recognizes in "cul-tural development" sensuous enrichment, uncoerced activity, and humanly esteemed wealth, and asks them to imagine the potential

---

[10]I do not think that Marx can be charged here, as he sometimes rightly is, with viewing industrial labor on the model of craft, thus making it easier, and falsely so, to assimilate labor by analogy to art. A metaphysics of work is not at issue here. Rather, Marx is suggesting that both industry and art, as forms of material-social practice, can be valued according to their capacity to be uncoerced activity and reciprocal interactions among those participating and enrichments of human life.

[11]Marx, *Early Writings*, pp. 351–352.

extension, even expansion, of just those values throughout a "fully developed" society:

> Just as in its initial stages society is presented with all the material for this *cultural development* through the movement of *private property* and of its wealth and poverty—both material and intellectual wealth and poverty—so the society that is *fully developed* produces man [*sic*] in all the richness of his being, the *rich* man who is *profoundly and abundantly endowed with all the senses,* as its constant reality. It can be seen how subjectivism and objectivism, spiritualism and materialism, activity and passivity [*Leiden*], lose their antithetical character, and hence their existence as such antitheses, only in the social condition; it can be seen how the resolution of the *theoretical* antitheses themselves is possible *only* in a *practical* way, only through the practical energy of man, and how their resolution is for that reason by no means a problem of knowledge, but a *real* problem of life, a problem which *philosophy* was unable to solve precisely because it treated it as a *purely* theoretical problem.[12]

Read as a response, indeed a virtually direct one, to Schiller's hope that *Kultur* would lead to an emancipation of the senses and of reason, and to their reconciliation, the above passage manifests the *critical-utopian* register of Marxian discourse. Its argument evokes the normative principle expressed in Schiller—the uncoerced and uncoercive activity pursued by associated human beings for their own enrichment—and shifts it over onto the organization of industrial capitalist society as a whole. The utopian expectations regarding *Kultur* are transformed into a critique of capitalism and a utopian expectation about a radically egalitarian industrial society.

In this critical-utopian register, Marx's is an *enthymemic* discourse: it argues from values to conclusions about reality; it advocates action within the reality so understood; and it promotes new values to orient that action and change those real circumstances. Obviously, however, this is not the only way to read the passage quoted above, nor is the critical-utopian the only register of Marx's discourse. The unpublished *Manuscripts* also performs in a philosophical-scientific register, and lays claim to being an *epistemic* discourse: it argues from a philosophically grounded account of the historical movement of society as a whole and identifies the political actions Marx supports as the completion of a process already in motion. Faced with the contrast between the two registers voiced in the *Manuscripts,* one might prefer one over

[12]Ibid., p. 354.

the other—the epistemic discourse for its promise of a systematic account of the social totality, the enthymemic for its rhetorical strategies of persuasion—or one might attempt to explicate their compatibility or seek to synthesize them differently. It seems to me, however, that the contrasting registers actually indicate a significant ambivalence, even confusion in the Marxian discourse. For the arguments made about culture along these two discursive paths lead in the end to very different, irreconcilable theoretical and interpretive outcomes. By mapping this divergence, we can clarify another of the problems posed by the inaugural paradigm of Marxist cultural theory, namely, how to specify the sense in which the culture of class society is not a *"true realm of freedom."*

In the epistemic discourse, Marx contrasts capitalism and communism via three arguments that will remain, through changing terminologies and theoretical refinements, cornerstones of his later work.

(*a*) In every historical epoch, human life is social activity and social existence. The material interchange with nature and structured social interaction are two sides of the same process; nature, labor, and interhuman relationships are the interconnected moments in this process. Marx stated this position a few years later in the following terms: "In production, men [*sic*] not only act on nature but also on one another. They produce only by co-operating in a certain way and mutually exchanging their activities. In order to produce, they enter into definite connections and relations with one another and only within these connections and relations does their action on nature, does production, take place."[13]

(*b*) Contrasted with this *social* process is *private property,* which gives production as defined above a particular historical shape. In capitalist society, private property achieves its most evolved form: the means of production (land, tools, machinery) become privately owned; the capacity to work (labor power) becomes something the individual worker "owns" in the sense that he or she must sell it to a capitalist in order to live; and the surplus wealth generated by labor takes the form of movable property appropriated by the capitalist (profit), to become once again capital to buy raw materials, the means of production, and the worker's labor power. Marx thus analyzed capitalism in terms of the conceptual polarity between the private and the social:

[13]Karl Marx, "Wage Labor and Capital," in Karl Marx and Frederick Engels, *Selected Works* (New York: International Publishers, 1968), p. 81.

whereas production is intrinsically social, capitalism organizes this social process into a series of private economic relationships. That organization of the social in the form of the private he called
"estrangement." Lucio Colletti has described the crux of Marx's position in the *Manuscripts* as the thesis that capital is an "estranged
social relation": "Marx envisages the process of estrangement as oc-
curring in three directions or dimensions at the same time: (1) as the
estrangement of the worker from the material, objective product of his
[*sic*] work; (2) as the estrangement of his work-activity itself (he does
not belong to himself at work, but to whomever he has sold his day's
work-activity [to]); (3) lastly, as estrangement from other men, that is
from the owner of the means of production and of the use to which
his labour-power is put."[14]

(*c*) Having construed capitalism as the estrangement of intrinsically
social human existence, Marx then argues that communism, as the
abolition of private property, is (to be) the overcoming of that estrangement and the achievement of human relationships free of the
coercion, inequalities, and poverty which capitalism generates and on
which it depends: "*Communism is the positive supersession of private
property as human self-estrangement,* and hence the true *appropriation*
of the *human* essence through and for man [*sic*]; it is the complete
restoration of man to himself as a *social,* i.e., human, being, a restoration which has become conscious and takes place within the entire
wealth of previous periods of development."[15]

The epistemic discourse thus describes the social injustices of capitalism as elements of its estrangement of social life, and the eradication
of those injustices as the overcoming of that estrangement. Unlike the
enthymemic discourse, it does not argue from values—what is just and
unjust—but rather from what claims to be an account of the *objective
movement* of the social totality. That is, its inner organization and its
historical momentum. So, too, when the question of culture is taken

[14]Lucio Colletti, "Introduction," to Marx, *Early Writings*, p. 52. I concur with Colletti's general position that this line of argument in the *Manuscripts* is conceptually
continuous with the later development of the theory of wage labor in *Capital*, as against
the Althusserian notion of an "epistemological break" separating the earlier and the
later work. The distinction that I have made between the enthymemic and epistemic
discourses of Marx further suggests that the "mature" Marx continued to derive basic
conceptions from the early works, though I am critical of just that strand which leads
to a rhetoric of knowledge as opposed to values.

[15]Marx, *Early Writings*, p. 348.

up by the epistemic discourse, art and aesthetic education become aspects of estrangement:

> for man [sic], moving in the realm of estrangement, was only capable of conceiving the general [as opposed to the objective] existence of man— religion, or history in its abstract and universal form of politics, art, literature, etc.—as the reality of man's essential powers and as *man's species-activity*.[16]

If this statement simply expressed Marx's ongoing polemic against idealist historiography, it would be unobjectionable. He is certainly right to indict the tendency to equate the history of humanity with the "history . . . of politics, art, literature, etc.," and to charge that such a conception of history is "abstract and universal," in that it suppresses both the concrete social relationships in history and, more specifically, the history of laboring classes and popular masses. That is, however, not all that Marx is saying. He is also saying that "politics, art, literature, etc.," are themselves the abstraction and universalization of human history. It is this proposition which is wholly at odds with his own reconceptualization of art and culture as a complex of material-social practices. The proposition is, on the other hand, wholly consistent with the philosophical-scientific register of the *Manuscripts*, and spawns the conception of culture which will eventually fit the base/ superstructure model.

The shift from culture as material-social practice to culture as superstructure is particularly visible in the following passage. Marx's model of private property as the estrangement of social relations compels him to restrict the sense in which cultural practices are material-social practices by qualifying them as merely *"particular* modes of production" in opposition to the supposedly "general" mode of production, and then to alter the conception of culture yet further by designating it as "consciousness" in a context where consciousness is set in opposition to real activity:

> Religion, the family, the state, law, morality, science, art, etc. are only *particular* modes of production and therefore come under [the] general law [of private property]. The positive supersession of *private property*, as the appropriation of *human* life, is therefore the positive supersession of all estrangement, and the return of man [sic] from religion, the family,

---

[16]Ibid., p. 354.

the state, etc., to his *human*, i.e. *social* existence. Religious estrangement as such takes place only in the sphere of *consciousness*, of man's inner life, but economic estrangement is that of *real* life—its supersession therefore embraces both aspects.[17]

If culture is consciousness in this sense of a second-order estrangement from social activity and social existence and is thus based on a first-order estrangement of "real," "material," "sensuous," "practical" activity, it cannot be a complex of material-social practices. The epistemic and enthymemic discourses here diverge. The former specifies that the culture of class society is not a *"true* realm of freedom" in the sense that it is a realm of illusory, because estranged, consciousness.

In the enthymemic discourse, Marx's line of argument—as I have reconstructed it—first proposes a conception of aesthetic education, and of culture, as a complex of material-social practices; and, second, advocates a new valuation of material-social practices generally, challenging the prevailing dichotomous, hierarchical valuations of art and industry. If both art and industry are complexes of material-social practices, that is, historically evolved forms of activity in which interchanges with nature are linked to interactions among socialized individuals, we cannot specify the interrelationships between these two areas of practice, art and industry, "culture" and "production," until the concept of material-social practice has been adequately elaborated. It is this elaboration that Marx's epistemic discourse cuts off. To pursue it, therefore, requires us to make explicit a series of propositions which remain oblique or latent in the text of the 1844 *Manuscripts.* Of the three propositions below, the first two follow more or less directly from arguments Marx does make and the way in which he makes them, while the third is absent from the text; it follows from the first two but directly contradicts the conclusions drawn in the epistemic discourse.

(*a*) Material-social practices can be evaluated according to whether they are (to take only examples found in Marx) coercive or uncoercive, exploitative or reciprocal, impoverishing or enriching. These are categories of cultural and/or political valuation. The specific values that are operative within, or applicable to, a particular set of practices are historically variable and contextual. The valuation of practices does not have, and need not have, a scientific or even a philosophical foundation (as Marx's own form of argumentation illustrates).

[17]Ibid., p. 349.

(*b*) Because material-social practices are *interactions which incorporate values and value-interpretations,* the participants in them have a capacity for valuating and revaluating their own practices. As participants, they accept and apply values and moreover have a potential capacity to displace values from one practice to another or give rise to new valuations. (It is in just this manner that the Marxian discourse relates to the intellectual-cultural tradition within which and against which it forms: it applies and displaces the political-cultural valuations of *Kultur* in an effort to alter the dominant valuations not only of culture but of society.)

(*c*) The valuating-revaluating capacity of the participants prevents us from presupposing that any particular material-social practice is *intrinsically* uncoercive or reciprocal or enriching, since the very understanding of coercion, reciprocity, or wealth can change: values and value-interpretations are historically variable. By the same token, every material-social practice is potentially politicizable, that is, can become the site of conflicting valuations and of struggle among the participants. An already accepted value can be applied critically to the practice, or the very understanding of the practice can come into question through a displacement of values or a new valuation. Even though the potential for conflict may be latent for extended periods of time, even for the entire historical duration of a given practice, there is no theoretical basis for claiming that any practice can be in principle immune from dissension among its participants.

The cultural problematic that can be developed along these lines leads us to extend Marx's criticism of the Schillerian tradition and ultimately to reject Marx's own position as expressed in his epistemic discourse. It is first of all not possible to valuate a culture whole-cloth, in the sense of the culture of an entire society or a historically specific "realm of freedom." As a complex of material-social practices, culture is not a "realm" in any rigorous sense. Schiller could present it as such because he considered cultural practices the *unique* space in which human activity is realized as an end-in-itself. Art and aesthetic education were for him, accordingly, intrinsically uncoercive, reciprocal, and enriching. Marx too attempts to valuate culture as a whole, and categorically, when he argues that it is the manifestation of the consciousness which arises from the estrangement of "real," "material" social relations. Had he carried through his own insight that cultural practices themselves are material and social, he would have had to reach a different conclusion. For cultural practices are permeated with social relations and are an aspect of social relations. We cannot distinguish "industry" and "art," "production" and "culture," on the basis of a categorization and valuation of culture as illusory, estranged consciousness. It can no longer be a question of the relation between (estranged) practices and (illusory) consciousness or between real social relations and their distorted reflection. It is, rather, a question of the relations among differently situated, differently deployed sets of material-social practices. As Raymond Williams has astutely remarked, in an argument that applies to Marx's own discourse as well as to many strands of Marxism, the problem with the base/superstructure model is

> that it was never materialist enough. . . . What is most often suppressed is the direct material production of "politics." Yet any ruling class devotes a significant part of material production to establishing a political order. The social and political order which maintains a capitalist market, like the social and political struggles which created it, is necessarily a material production. From castles and palaces and churches to prisons and workhouses and schools; from weapons of war to a controlled press: any ruling class, in variable ways though always materially, produces a social and political order. These are never superstructural activities. . . . The complexity of this process is especially remarkable in advanced capitalist societies, where it is wholly beside the point to isolate "production" and "industry" from the comparably material production of "defence," "law and order," "welfare," "entertainment," and "public opinion." In failing to grasp the material character of the production of a social and political order, this specialized (and bourgeois) materialism failed also, but even more conspicuously, to understand the material character of the production of a cultural order.[18]

As the range of institutions and activities enumerated by Williams indicates, the material-social practices of capitalist society do not divide into categories of base and superstructure. Nor do they permit a rigorous separation of "realms" of production, politics, and culture.

Marx tends to make just this separation when he categorizes and valuates culture as a whole. And the specific way in which productive, political, and cultural processes are separated from one another in the distinction between the realm of necessity and the realm of freedom goes to the heart of the shortcomings of the inaugural paradigm of

---

[18]Raymond Williams, *Marxism and Literature* (New York: Oxford University Press, 1977), pp. 92–93.

cultural theory. The problem centers on the several meanings of the term "freedom," which need first to be disentangled and then related to one another anew. The basic meaning is "disposable time," as in the notion that the realm of freedom is made up of those activities individuals pursue when released from participation in, let us say for the moment, the direct production of the necessities of life. As Williams's argument suggests, however, this definition can make only the roughest distinction between "necessary" and "disposable" time. Material resources and social time have to be devoted, especially in modern societies, to securing the political and social conditions of the production of life necessities. Such resources and time are by no means unnecessary as opposed to necessary, purely intellectual as opposed to material, or pursued freely as opposed to instrumentally.

The second meaning, related to the first, has posed yet other kinds of problems. As we have seen, Marcuse argued that the exemption from manual labor, that is, the appropriation of "disposable time," gave rise to the Western tradition's ideal of freedom as the capability of cultivating activities for their own sake, but he in turn argued, quite persuasively, that this very ideal has tended to imbue the traditional concept of culture with its fundamental illusions or, as I would prefer to say, its self-misunderstandings. In reconceptualizing culture as material-social practices, we cannot prejudge how such self-misunderstandings come into play in a cultural practice, or how a particular practice embodies or contests a prevailing form of cultural self-misunderstanding. These rather are questions open to interpretation and inflected by specific historical contexts and political exigencies. The primary fault of the base/superstructure model is precisely that it presupposes that cultural practices are always ultimately determined by the epochal self-misunderstanding of a class, whether this determination is conceived as estrangement, ideology, or false consciousness.

It is the third sense of the term "freedom" which most needs to be redefined and allocated a different theoretical place. This is the political sense of the term. It poses questions as to the ways in which a cultural practice is—or is not—coercive and nonreciprocal. Marx did not sharply distinguish this sense from the other two, because he assumed that cultural practices, from everyday learning processes and interactions to science, art, and literature, would *become* uncoercive in the wake of, indeed, as the result of, an egalitarian reorganization of the realm of necessity. When he speaks of a "true realm of freedom" he apparently means a sphere of activities which is, *all at once,* formed through an egalitarian distribution of free time; devoted to activities which are ends-in-themselves; and productive of uncoercive and un-coerced forms of interaction and knowledge. What is the interrelation among these three senses of freedom, linked, respectively, to produc-tion, culture, and politics? As a condensation of Marx's enthymemic discourse, the threefold definition of the true realm of freedom is a utopian image with considerable critical force. As a thesis within the epistemic discourse, however, it establishes a thoroughly questionable chain of determinations: activity as an end-in-itself will follow from the egalitarian distribution of free time and will (consequently) be uncoercive and reciprocal activity. On this view, the political sense of freedom never figures *directly* in the valuation of culture. The coercion or noncoercion, nonreciprocity or reciprocity, of cultural practices is determined externally—by social relations, which are increasingly for Marx separated from cultural practices as such and defined as relations of production.

It is this exclusion of the political from the cultural which gives the base/superstructure model its premise: namely, that the organization of the realm of necessity as a whole determines the organization of the realm of freedom as a whole. Prior to an egalitarian reorganization of "production," the political dimension of cultural practices is deemed irrelevant, because they manifest only a consciousness estranged from "real practice"; afterward, the political dimension is presumed superseded because cultural practices cease being estranged conscious-ness and become instead ends-in-themselves. In neither class society nor classless society do specifically political forms of freedom and un-freedom have a place within cultural practices. The political dimension can, however, no longer be made external to "culture," or "culture" made secondary to "production," once both production and culture are viewed as sets of material-social practices. Coerciveness and non-coerciveness, nonreciprocity and reciprocity, have to be raised as in-terpretive and theoretical questions about cultural practices themselves, just as those practices are in reality sites of interpretive conflicts and political struggles. Questions of domination and power—of social re-lations and political relations—cannot be separated from culture. They are internal, not external, to its practices.

The Eclipsing of Politics and Culture in Marxism

Marx's inaugural paradigm of cultural theory removes the specifically political dimension from cultural practices and at the same time projects culture as a special domain of activity and experience separated from, yet ultimately determined by, "production."[19] Such an outcome congeals cultural theory into the base/superstructure model and its variants. While Marxist cultural critics have always struggled against the confinements of this model, it has continued to haunt cultural interpretation and theory within the whole Marxist tradition. But it is not only cultural theory in the relatively specialized sense of the term that has suffered from Marx's twofold tendency to narrow the scope of culture within his general social theory and to elide the political from the analysis of material-social practices. This tendency has also had the effect of minimizing the significance of culture and politics in the formation of social antagonisms and political struggles. This effect already shows in *The German Ideology*, where the separation of culture and the elision of the political become constituents of—determining by their absence—the theoretical space in which Marx and Engels attempt to account for the formation of the nineteenth-century working class and the direction of its struggles within and against capitalism. What is at stake in the congealing of the theoretical paradigm can be illustrated with reference to Marx and Engels's approach to two issues: (*a*) the forms of coercion and nonreciprocity imposed on workers by the capitalist organization of the material-social practices of "production"; and (*b*) the forms of association which Marx and Engels took to be evidence of the working class's anticipated historic role as agents of social revolution.

From coercive, nonreciprocal social relations to the
"fetter on production"

In developing the concept of material-social practices from Marx's early writings, I have emphasized how the participants have, at least latently, the capacity to valuate their practices as coercive and nonreciprocal. As regards the specific complex of practices grouped under the rubrics "industry" or "production," the following question can be posed: Under what conditions can a historically specific form of these material-social practices come to be valuated, by the participants engaged in them, as coercive and nonreciprocal to such a degree that, or under circumstances in which, those individuals acquire the aim of radically transforming those practices, the conditions under which they

---

[19]I will place scare-quotes around "production" to indicate the strict and indeed reductive sense of the processes of producing the material necessities of life.

are performed, and/or the social relations embedded in them? When Marx and Engels broach this question they frame it without giving any direct relevance to the processes of cultural valuation and the specifically political forms of organization required for such contestation. In place of the cultural and political processes through which a practice becomes visibly and unacceptably coercive and nonreciprocal for the participants, and therefore a site of antagonisms and struggles, they substitute the single process by which conditions of "production" become a constraint on "productivity." For the culturally shaped politial categories of coercion and nonreciprocity they substitute the socioeconomic category of a fetter on "production."

They do not, it is true, make this substitution all at once. It occurs only as the meaning of what they call "self-activity" moves more and more in the direction of the limited meaning of "productivity" and "productive forces." "Self-activity" is the term in *The German Ideology* which combines the materialist emphasis on individuals' real, practical activity with the normative principle of human activity as potentially an end-in-itself. According to Marx and Engels, the whole of individuals' material-social practices constitutes the capacities and means through which they "produce their material life and what is connected with it," including everything required for continuing that production. So long as the social relations in which those individuals actively participate ("forms of intercourse") are compatible with their own capacities for production ("productive forces"), they experience those conditions as essentially enabling: "The conditions under which individuals have intercourse with each other . . . are conditions appertaining to their individuality, in no way external to them; conditions under which these definite individuals, living under definite relationships, can alone produce their material life and what is connected with it, are thus the conditions of their self-activity and are produced by this self-activity."[20] So long as the "forms of intercourse" and the "productive forces" mesh, the material-social practices in which individuals participate do not appear to them only as the means for achieving some end but are also in themselves ends or purposes, that is, the self-activity of those individuals. Their material-social practices are simply their way of life, and the "conditions" for engaging in those practices establish something like the outer horizon of what

[20]Karl Marx and Frederick Engels, *The German Ideology*, ed. C. J. Arthur (New York: International Publishers, 1970), p. 87.

those individuals consider possible, at least as regards their social (and earthly) existence.

From this perspective Marx and Engels consider the evolution of society a sequence of specific "forms of intercourse" corresponding in each epoch to the degree of development of the "productive forces." They then attribute the transformations undergone by Western societies to phases in which the prevailing "forms of intercourse" cease to be the enabling condition of individuals' "productive" capacity and horizon of their way of life, but become instead a constraint: "These various conditions, which appear first as conditions of self-activity, later as fetters upon it, form in the whole evolution of history a series of forms of intercourse, the coherence of which consists in this: in the place of an earlier form of intercourse, which has become a fetter, a new one is put, corresponding to the more developed productive forces and, hence, to the advanced mode of self-activity of individuals—a form which in turn becomes a fetter and is then replaced by another."[21] It is this proposition that gives a secondary, purely derivative status to the cultural-political processes through which participants revaluate their material-social practices. Marx and Engels conclude that "all collisions in history"—including those they designate as "subsidiary forms, such as all-embracing collisions, collisions of various classes, contradiction of consciousness, battle of ideas, etc., political conflicts, etc."—all these "have their origin, according to our view, in the contradiction between the productive forces and the forms of intercourse."[22]

The controlling model for a development of "productive forces" which breaks the fetters imposed by a prevailing "form of intercourse" is in fact the emergence and formation of the bourgeoisie: "When the estate of the urban burghers...emerged in opposition to the landed nobility, their condition of existence—movable property, craft labor ...—appeared as something positive, which was asserted against feudal landed property."[23] Marx and Engels's analysis isolates two essential characteristics that fitted the rising bourgeoisie for the role of developing society's "productive forces." First, they owned the instruments necessary to their self-activity, in the form of money and the skills and tools of their crafts and, eventually, in the form of capital properly speaking. And second, they acted as separated individuals whose emergent way of life depended upon their ability to advantage themselves,

[21]Ibid.
[22]Ibid., pp. 88–89.
[23]Ibid., p. 84.

as possessive individuals, in market relations. Having identified these specifically bourgeois motivations and conditions of development, Marx and Engels never justify the grounds on which the model of the bourgeoisie provides the general perspective on historical development. Instead, they extrapolate from their account of the bourgeoisie two theses which are by no means self-evident and which remain unsubstantiated in the argument of *The German Ideology*.

First of all, they construe the bourgeoisie's crucial interest in an expanding and autonomous economy as evidence that their participation in the various moral, cultural, and political revolutions of the era was nothing more than an effect of their motivation to develop the "productive forces" of society. When they interpret, for example, the urban burghers' emergence from the bonds of serfdom, they consider the new valuations of freedom and equality not as an innovation in the organization of social relations but rather as the new form of estranged consciousness effected by the transition from one mode of production to another: "Certainly the refugee serfs treated their previous servitude as something accidental to their personality. But here they were only doing what every class that is freeing itself from a fetter does."[24] Similarly, Marx and Engels tend to interpret the bourgeoisie's participation in political revolution as motivated by the economic imperatives definitive of the class and, therefore, as a means of establishing class rule. With the French Revolution in mind, they establish the perspective that led later Marxist historiographers to view that revolution as essentially the conduit to the triumph of capitalist social relations: "The class making a revolution appears from the very start, if only because it is opposed to a *class*, not as a class but as the representative of the whole of society; it appears as the whole mass of society confronting the one ruling class. It can do this because, to start with, its interest really is more connected with the common interest of all other non-ruling classes, because under the pressure of hitherto existing conditions its interest has not yet been able to develop as the particular interest of a particular class."[25] It is this interpretation which has yielded the notion that specifically political values like equality,

[24]Ibid.
[25]Ibid., p. 66. For a critique of the premises and paradoxes of Marxist historians' account of the French Revolution as the event by which the bourgeoisie challenged feudal society and established the conditions of their own class rule, see François Furet, *Interpreting the French Revolution*, trans. Elborg Forster (Cambridge: Cambridge University Press, 1981), esp. pp. 1–10, 81–131.

individual rights and freedoms, and democratic rule are superstructural elements of class ideology.

The second extrapolation Marx and Engels made also became a central tenet of Marxism, namely, that the formation of the proletariat and its historic role are modeled on the bourgeoisie—despite several explicitly drawn distinctions between the two social classes. The bourgeoisie developed their "productive forces" as owners of their own instruments of production, whereas producing classes are proletarianized to the extent that they are dispossessed of the instruments of production; nonetheless, Marx and Engels conclude that the proletariat too is (to be) the class whose interests coincide with the development of society's "productive forces." The developing economy empowered the bourgeoisie as separated individuals, whereas individual proletarians are precisely disempowered by the wage relation and by an industrial system whose motive for productivity remains the capitalists' profit imperative; nonetheless, Marx and Engels conclude that the proletarians too are (to become) an antagonist of the prevailing "form of intercourse" because it stifles *their* productivity. Marx and Engels themselves draw—indeed, as we will see, overdraw—the sharpest distinction between all previous classes and the proletariat by arguing that whereas the former produced or ruled in the context of limited forms of "self-activity," experiencing their own activities as horizon and purpose as well as capacity and means, the proletariat engages in the "negative form of self-activity":

> While in the earlier periods self-activity and the production of material life were separated, in that they devolved on different persons, and while, on account of the narrowness of the individuals themselves, the production of material life was considered as a subordinate mode of self-activity, they now diverge to such an extent that altogether material life appears as the end, and what produces this material life, labour (which is now the only possible but, as we see, negative form of self-activity), as the means.[26]

Having made this virtually absolute contrast between the conditions of proletarian existence and those of every other emergent class in history, particularly the bourgeoisie, while nonetheless retaining the premise that the proletariat, like the bourgeoisie, finds the motive for

[26]Marx and Engels, *The German Ideology*, p. 92.

revolutionary action in their existence as a "productive force," Marx and Engels arrive at the following conclusion:

> Only the proletarians of the present day, who are completely shut off from self-activity, are in a position to achieve a complete and no longer restricted self-activity, which consists in the appropriation of a totality of productive forces and in the thus postulated development of a totality of capacities. All earlier revolutionary appropriations were restricted; individuals, whose self-activity was restricted by a crude instrument of production and a limited intercourse, appropriated this crude instrument of production, and hence achieved a new state of limitation. Their instrument of production became their property, but they themselves remained subordinate to the division of labour and to a single instrument of production; in the appropriation by proletarians, a mass of instruments of production must be made subject to each individual, and property to all. Modern universal intercourse can be controlled by individuals, therefore, only when controlled by all.[27]

Many of the most far-reaching ambiguities of Marx and Engels's thought are at work in this passage. Consider first the question of historical necessity. When Marx and Engels conclude that "modern universal intercourse can be controlled by individuals, therefore, only when controlled by all," they evoke historical necessity in the sense of a condition or requirement of an unprecedented, universal form of intercourse. *If* individuals are to achieve the autonomy and freedom that bourgeois ideology promises them as separated, privately owning individuals, there *must be* a massive reorganization of society, such that all individuals come to control the whole of their interrelations and interactions. This statement expresses the utopian aspect of what Marx and Engels call communist consciousness in *The German Ideology*. The slogan of this consciousness asserts the connection between individuals' freedom and their cooperation: "In a real community the individuals obtain their freedom in and through their association."[28] On the other hand, the passage also advances the notion that the real motive force of socialist revolution is the development of the "productive forces." This line of argument needs to make no reference to the development of communist consciousness, let alone to the values implied by its utopian aspect. Rather, it develops in the direction of another sense of "historical necessity," namely, the notion that capi-

[27]Ibid., pp. 92–93.
[28]Ibid., p. 83.

talism's increasing productive capacity would break, in the form of crises prompted by irreversible economic laws, the relations of production.

These two lines of argument, ambiguously entwined in the same passage of *The German Ideology,* correspond to what Alvin Gouldner has called the two Marxisms: a Critical Marxism that emphasizes the "voluntaristic" dimension of social transformation and the processes of galvanizing revolutionary consciousness, and a Scientific Marxism that emphasizes the objective processes and conditions of historical change. Gouldner summarizes the relation between the two in the following terms:

> Critical Marxism faces two ways: it is a tool of ideological struggle within Marxism itself, at first most especially directed against the determinism and wooden evolutionism of the Second International, as well as a distinct critique of capitalist society. But if Critical Marxism is a later dimension, if it is responding to the prior failures of Scientific Marxism, there is, *also,* in Scientific Marxism itself, an earlier and prior rejection of objective philosophical idealism and of utopian socialism. This is exhibited by the work of Marx and Engels themselves.... Marxism crystallized into a political movement, under the tutelage of Engels and Kautsky, after Marx's death. It was then dominated by a Scientific Marxism opposed polemically to idealism, characterized by an anti-idealistic naturalism alertly focused on the *limits* of voluntarism, and affirming the power of economic structural constraints over human action and reason. Critical Marxism, however, emerges in reaction to *that* reading of Marxism, counteraffirming the role of a voluntaristic consciousness against Scientific Marxism's naturalism, determinism, and its focus on the constraining character of economic structures.[29]

In the passage we are considering from *The German Ideology,* these two Marxisms coexist, undoubtedly because when Marx and Engels are writing in 1845–1846 no discrepancies have opened for them between their emergent theory of the laws of historical change and their expectations about the direction of workers' struggles.

The voices of both Scientific and Critical Marxism can be heard, though pressing toward opposing conclusions, in Marx and Engels's formulation of the relation between the complete deprivation of self-activity and the universal realization of self-activity on the part of the

[29] Alvin W. Gouldner, *The Two Marxisms: Contradictions and Anomalies in the Development of Theory* (New York: Seabury, 1980), p. 165.

proletariat. In the voice of Scientific Marxism, they are declaring that the proletariat, in conformity with an inflexible law of historical movement, is a class whose leadership of society is directly linked to the quantitative increases of the developing economy, like the bourgeoisie before it. The proletariat is, accordingly, a class that has inherited its historic mission from its own antagonist. In this case, the absence of all self-activity literally creates the conditions of complete self-activity. In the voice of Critical Marxism, by contrast, Marx and Engels are not stating an inevitable law of history so much as practicing a political rhetoric charged with irony. This voice confidently and defiantly proclaims that those whose life activity is most degraded by capitalism, subjected to poverty and deprived of freedom and agency, will become the agents of the revolutionary process that will establish their self-activity through the destruction of capitalism.

At their point of greatest divergence, Scientific and Critical Marxism have contrary conceptions of the proletariat. For Scientific Marxism, the proletariat is an entity created by the capitalist "form of intercourse" as its "productive forces" and is destined to act according to the intrinsic law of contradiction between forms and forces of production. For Critical Marxism, the proletariat is the privileged locus of the consciousness that individual realization, well-being, and freedom require a form of community that abolishes private property. It is this divergence which has not yet shown through in *The German Ideology*. Moreover, both voices use the grammar of "dialectics" to designate an impending reversal of the complete deprivation of self-activity into its universal realization.

This dialectical grammar, however, masks the conceptual dualism shared by the two Marxisms. For, how does complete deprivation become total appropriation? How does the class defined as the absence of all agency become the universal historical agent? How does the negative of self-activity become unlimited self-activity? These processes of becoming get short shrift in Marx and Engels. The congealed form of their inaugural paradigm has already removed the terms in which these questions could be addressed, namely, the processes of cultural valuation and political contestation through which workers might repudiate their participation in wage labor because it is impoverishing, coercive, and nonreciprocal. To admit those processes into the theoretical model would also be to acknowledge that the exact forms and contents of such revaluations and contestations is not dictated by economic or historical laws. The congealed paradigm has eliminated culture and politics from its theoretical space and substituted the supposed dialectic of "forms of intercourse" and "productive forces."

As a result, Marx and Engels leave themselves with the dualism between the complete deprivation and the universal realization of self-activity *and* with the unbridged gap between these two concepts, the first a diagnosis of the suffering and disempowerment of industrial workers and the second a utopian resolution imaged as the reversal of disempowerment into empowerment, suffering into self-realization. Since they do not locate the possibility of such a reversal and resolution in the cultural and political practices of workers, they misrepresent their own utopian appeal to a particular idea of community as the intrinsic goal of history (in the Scientific Marxist mode) or as the equally inevitable form of socialist consciousness (in the Critical Marxist mode). But neither the evocation of historical-economic laws nor the triumphant irony of privileged consciousness overcomes the dualism between the deprivation and the realization of self-activity. The problem will, in fact, be continually displaced through the theoretical field of the two Marxisms.

Forms of association

The effort to bridge the conceptual gap between the complete deprivation and the universal achievement of self-activity leads Marx and Engels to postulate an aspect within proletarian practice and experience which prefigures self-activity: namely, the form of association into which workers are pressed by capitalist production and its accompanying industrialization and urbanization of society. According to their assessment, modern workers were in the process of learning a collective and egalitarian form of association through their direct experience of modern techniques of industrial labor. The skills required of workers were being equalized at common levels, and the labor process as a whole was taking the form of a coordination among the activities of many individuals. Workers were, accordingly, becoming a class whose members would experience ever more kinship and identification with one another on the basis of their shared conditions of labor and level of economic well-being. The original dualism, however, ends up being replicated in this conception as well. For the conceptual scheme that postulates the *associated* producers also describes the modern wage laborer as a radically alienated or *isolated* producer. The gap that first appeared as the distance between the deprivation and the achievement of self-activity is now reinscribed within the proletariat itself, as the split between the isolated producer and the associated producers. The former replicates the imperatives of capital within the everyday practices of the worker; the latter prefigures the overcoming of capitalism within those same everyday practices.

By the 1920s Central and Western European Marxists had to acknowledge that there was nothing in the actual development of capitalism which automatically bridged this gap between the isolated producer and the associated producers, that is, between the "proletarian" and the "proletariat." The intermittence of radical and revolutionary orientations on the part of industrial workers, along with the tendency of trade unions to renegotiate the social contract between workers and capitalists—or, more accurately, among unions, corporations, and the state—betrayed the expectation that the momentum of capitalist development led inherently or directly toward social revolution. Moreover, the October Revolution of 1917 had provided a historic example of a socialist revolution pursued without a fully developed, modern working class.

It was in this context that Georg Lukács undertook to reassess the contemporary tendencies of capitalism and the Western workers' movement. To do so, he returned to Marx and reconceptualized the relation between the isolated and the associated producers. Rather than questioning the conceptual scheme which produced this dualism, he reinterpreted it as the historical condition of advanced capitalism. Rather than breaking down the original conception, he rebaptized it. The dualism of the isolated producer and the associated producers became the "dialectic" of *reification* and *class consciousness*. The following passage from *History and Class Consciousness* (1922) reveals the extent to which Lukács reintroduced the very problem he saw in Marx and set out to resolve:

> It could easily appear at this point that the whole process is nothing more than the "inevitable" consequence of concentrating masses of workers in large factories, of mechanising and standardising the processes of work and levelling down the standard of living. It is therefore vital to see the truth concealed behind this deceptively one-sided picture. There is no doubt that the factors mentioned above are *the indispensible precondition* for the emergence of the proletariat as a class. *Without* them the proletariat would never become a class and if they had not been continually intensified—by the natural workings of capitalism—it would never have developed into the decisive factor in human history.
> Despite this it can be claimed without contradiction that we are not

concerned here with an unmediated relation. What is unmediated is the fact that, in the words of the *Communist Manifesto,* "these labourers, who must sell themselves piecemeal, are a commodity, like every other article of commerce." And the fact that this commodity is able to become aware of its existence as a commodity does not suffice to eliminate the problem. For the unmediated consciousness of the commodity is, in conformity with the simple form in which it manifests itself, precisely an awareness of abstract isolation and of the merely abstract relation-ship—external to consciousness—to those factors that create it socially....

On the other hand, the growing class consciousness that has been brought into being through the awareness of a common situation and common interests is by no means confined to the working class. The unique element in the situation is that its surpassing of immediacy rep-resents an *aspiration towards society in its totality* regardless of whether this aspiration remains conscious or whether it remains unconscious for the moment.[30]

Lukács here traces a vicious circle. He is faced with the fact that a basic theoretical axiom of Marxism has not been borne out by the history of the European workers' movement, namely, the notion that workers' association *as* producers motivates them to develop a form of self-organization which prefigures an egalitarian society and com-plete self-activity. Faced with this discrepancy between the theoretical axiom of *associated producers* and historical developments, Lukács takes this very discrepancy to be confirmation of the other pole of Marx's original dualism: the *isolated producer.* The extent to which workers do not become a collective agent of revolution is thus a measure of the effects of *reification,* that is, of their constitutive entrapment as isolated producers within capitalist relations of production. Lukács then reaffirms the first pole of the dualism by reconceiving the *asso-ciated producers* as *class consciousness.* This reconceptualization trans-forms the concrete, prefigurative motivations of workers postulated by Marx into a theoretical cognition presumed necessary for the prole-tariat to be constituted as a revolutionary agent.

That this presumed cognition is theoretical is obvious from Lukács's basic definition: "class consciousness... represents an *aspiration to-wards society in its totality,*" for in Lukács's own understanding the

---

[30]Georg Lukács, *History and Class Consciousness,* trans. Rodney Livingstone (Cam-bridge: MIT Press, 1971), pp. 173–174.

view of society as totality is a theoretical consciousness that does not derive from the lived experience or practices of workers:

> By relating consciousness to the whole of society it becomes possible to infer the thoughts and feelings men [sic] would have in a particular situation if they were *able* to assess both it and the interests arising from it in their impact on immediate action and on the whole structure of society.... Now class consciousness consists in fact of the appropriate and rational reactions "imputed" [zugerechnet] to a particular typical position in the process of production. This consciousness is, therefore, neither the sum nor the average of what is thought or felt by the single individuals who make up the class. And yet the historically significant actions of the class as a whole are determined in the last resort by this consciousness and not by the thought of the individual—and these actions can be understood only by reference to this consciousness.[31]

The vicious circle that Lukács entered with his return to Marx here yields a dangerous tautology. Since class consciousness is the consciousness imputed to a class by Marxist theory, the theory can be tested only by measuring itself against the actions of the class. However, the class's actions are to be judged "historically significant" or, one supposes, historically insignificant only by the already established criteria of the theory, since they alone can identify the situations and interests which give an action its meaning. Not only does this tautology immunize Marxism from the counterevidence of actual developments, but it also fosters the illusion that every nonconforming action undertaken by workers can be explained as further evidence of "reification" and thus a deviation from "class consciousness."

Two important aspects of the potential self-understanding of theory which Marx's own discourse intermittently achieved are definitively abolished in Lukács's. On the one hand, what I earlier identified as the enthymemic strand of Marx's discourse suggests that theory has to argue from values and revaluations and that its mode of address is that of persuasion among participants in a set of practices. The Lukácsian discourse instantiates, instead, the epistemic strand of Marx and its presumed knowledge over and above the practices and experiences of those it "addresses." And, on the other hand, Marx's earliest idea of critical theory was that it serve the "self-clarification of the struggles and wishes of the age." Theory learns from the social struggles and

---

[31]Ibid., p. 51.

aspirations it interprets. Facing the discontinuities of radical action since Marx's era and the changing forms of workers' participation in social struggles, Lukács might have likewise given theory the task of preserving the learning processes achieved, and then disrupted or dispersed, in past social struggles with an eye to their adaptation or revision in light of new social aspirations and struggles. But he imprinted Critical Marxism with virtually the opposite attitude toward its own tasks. Theory becomes a mode of instruction rather than learning, the repository of knowledge "from above" rather than the self-clarification of social movements. This self-understanding has also diminished Marxism's capacity, down through the Frankfurt School, to reevaluate its own most basic conceptions. So long as workers' "failure" to conform to original expectations does not shake the categories of social analysis and historical reflection, the theory can go on refining its account of "reification" and further abstract its conception of "rational interests" without having to face the possibility that it has been disconfirmed.

The Lukácsian dualism reification/class consciousness does not in fact get at either the basis of workers' integration into capitalism or the reasons for their multiform, discontinuous struggles against it. Gouldner argues convincingly that any account of the systemic integration of workers must center not on their allegedly reified consciousness but rather on the disempowerment they undergo in the entire constellation of social, political, and cultural processes which make subordinated social groups dependent. He shows that the sort of dependency and disempowerment which Marx saw in capitalism's "expropriation of peasants and other workers, i.e., their loss of control over the instruments of production, so that they were then constrained to sell their labor power for a wage,"[32] is applicable to a much wider fabric of social relations than just the relations of production. Disempowerment and dependency are key elements in any subordinated group's acquiescence to its rulers. Neither reified consciousness nor even the ideological legitimations of a class structure are sufficient to explain the grip of a "ruling class" on those it rules. At issue, rather, are forms of unequal reciprocity:

> What makes a group a ruling class is that it can satisfy acute and recurrent mass needs, and that *it can prevent others from doing so.* In satisfying

[32]Gouldner, *The Two Marxisms,* p. 334.

a need in this exclusive manner, a new need is generated: a need is generated for the group supplying the need.... Every ruling class, then, does satisfy "its" society's needs, but only on condition that others become its dependents. A ruling class is thus not a military conqueror but is, rather, committed to the maintenance and reproduction of those under it and is involved in reciprocities with them, providing them certain provisions and protections in exchange for hegemony. It is inherent in this hierarchical arrangement, however, that not everyone's needs will be met *equally*; those who control the supplying of needs will be able to advantage themselves; those dependent will not.[33]

Just as reification does not explain workers' integration into the capitalist system, class consciousness cannot explain their struggles against it. The forms of association which are historically relevant to actual workers' struggles do not boil down to their association as "producers"; the relevant forms of association are located, rather, in the web of active social relations and forms of community which empower workers by sustaining or increasing their relative independence from those social groups that seek to monopolize various provisions and protections:

> Scientific Marxism's impulse is to reduce politics to the struggle for power in the state. It thus neglects the importance of protecting and rebuilding the dense infrastructure of communities, institutions, organizations, and groups within which the working class presently lives and through which, even now, some of its own needs could be supplied through self-help and mutual aid, by which its own anxieties can be controlled, and its dependency reduced.... Marx failed to see that, without viable working-class institutions, communities, and groups within capitalism, the dependency and passivity of the working class are heightened, its vulnerability to the regressive politics of fascism and authoritarianism is in modern times intensified, and the working class is unable to cultivate the skills and self-reliance needed to manage its own existence. Without prefigurative working class communities and groups committed to self-help, even "soviets" have little future as a method of political self-management by the working class.[34]

While Gouldner aims this criticism at Scientific Marxism, our discussion of Lukács shows the extent to which Critical Marxism falls prey to the same difficulties in this instance. Lukács renews Marxism's

[33]Ibid., pp. 333–335.
[34]Ibid., p. 346.

blind spot regarding the resources for self-determination and self-organization within the working class. He does not follow the course of economism, for which the categories of self-determination and self-organization are largely superfluous. Nevertheless, his very attempt to assert a Critical Marxism against Scientific Marxism advances conceptions of consciousness and of theory which are heir to Marx's inaugural reduction of culture to consciousness and of social relations to relations of production. On the one hand, Lukács excludes the question of culture in the sense of the material-social practices through which social groups, workers and others, establish their identities and relate themselves to the other social groups with whom they interact in society; he transforms that question into a question of consciousness, indeed, a class consciousness that is itself reduced to the postulated "rational" interests individuals would have if they experienced their place in the relations of production as their only or most relevant social relation. And, on the other hand, Lukács restricts the question of prefigurative forms of association, transposing it from cultural practices and complex social relations over into a field of theoretical knowledge doctrinally occupied by Marxist theory and politically represented by the Party.[35] A Marxism conceived as theory "from above" thus completes the exclusion of culture from social relations; it replaces it with a class consciousness that is indistinguishable from the theoretical operation which distills from social relations as a whole the relations of production and then projects the latter as "totality."

History "from below" has of course been the alternative path taken by twentieth-century Marxists to recover those processes of nineteenth-century class formation and political organization for which Marx wanted his theory to provide the "self-clarification." E. P. Thompson's *Making of the English Working Class* (1963) is the exemplary work in this kind of historical recovery. Its rich detail not only provides an empirically dense description of the forms of resistance and opposition to capitalism in nineteenth-century popular radicalism, but is also meant to retrieve a heritage for twentieth-century Marxism. Juxtaposed

---

[35]Just as "opportunism" becomes the name for those aims of workers which do not conform to the definition of class consciousness, so too the single political instrument of class consciousness is the (Leninist) Party: "In contrast with the right instincts of the proletariat [opportunism] plays the same role as that played hitherto by capitalist theory: it denounces the correct view of the overall economic situation and the correct consciousness of the proletariat together with its organized form, the Communist Party." Lukács, *History and Class Consciousness*, p. 75.

with Lukács's emphases, Thompson's focus on cultural and intellectual traditions has a kind of prima facie justification; his work thoroughly dramatizes the extent to which the culture of subordinated groups has to be counted among their most "historically significant" forms of association and among the experiences most formative of their political organizations and actions.

Nevertheless, Thompson's work has recently been scrutinized and questioned from within the historical and sociological perspective that it has itself established. In *The Question of Class Struggle,* Craig Calhoun has carried out a critical, yet ultimately preserving retheorization of *The Making of the English Working Class.* He challenges the most general conclusion which Thompson drew from the materials he analyzed and which in turn shaped the organization of his narrative, namely, the notion that a *single* working class was in the making during the nineteenth century in England. This organizing theme, Calhoun argues, does not really reflect the social, cultural, and political processes that Thompson uncovers, but rather bends the analysis of them to conform with the Marxian axiom that the development of capitalism brings with it—in the nineteenth century, at least!—an increasing, expanding radicalization of workers. To maintain this axiom, Thompson forces an identification between emergent industrial workers and the culture and politics of popular radicalism.

What Thompson's work shows, as opposed to the story it tells, is a disjunction between a radicalism that arose from one set of "social foundations" and a modern working class that formed out of quite another:

> Thompson's most consistent suggestion of the importance of the ideological legacy of the late eighteenth-century artisans and romantic cultures is that one segment of the working class, and some non-workers, shaped the development of the working class. It is not that the working class made itself. He presents his view, however, as though it were the latter, and as a result tends to obscure the differences among the populations he considers. Relatedly, Thompson sometimes loses track of the change in the social foundations of workers' actions and attitudes over time, both within each different population, and especially as their relative significance changed. None of this suggests that Thompson's argument as to the connection between late eighteenth-century radicalism and workers' movements of the 1830s is false. It does deny that that connection was essentially a continuity of tradition among *a* class.[36]

[36]Craig Calhoun, *The Question of Class Struggle: Social Foundations of Popular*

Thompson discloses the crucial role of culture in the formation of political antagonisms; the most evolved forms of opposition to capitalism had developed in the cultural and ideological traditions of popular radicalism. But he simultaneously holds firm to the Marxian axiom of class formation. To square the evidence with the axiom, he foregrounds culture to the virtual exclusion of social relations and pictures the modern working class as formed primarily by the radical traditions of the preindustrial antagonists of capitalism. Having discovered the roots of radicalism outside the modern working class proper, he has to reverse the emphasis of Marx and Lukács in defining a class formation if he is to preserve the same general thesis that capitalism produces the class that will oppose it. Thompson, Calhoun writes, "maximizes the variable of consciousness, minimizes the variable of social organization. In relation to the latter he virtually ignores the Marxian focus on the social relations established in the workplace by the advent of cooperative labor. Marx makes class an economic category and a social category, in that order. Thompson makes class a cultural category and a political category, in that order."[37]

Calhoun's reinterpretations of English Jacobinism, Luddism, and Chartism show that artisans and industrial workers were enmeshed in very different social relations, as regards both the kinds of bonds connecting the members within these respective social groups and their respective functional roles within the societal structure. The different ways artisans and industrial workers actually conducted their struggles indicate how such struggles are doubly shaped by culture *and* social relations. Or, more precisely, the variable adaptations of available cultural and ideological traditions within specific social relations and in the context of specific forms of empowerment and disempowerment inflected the social movements of the nineteenth century with divergent rather than identical aims:

> Marx was right to place great stress on the analysis of social foundations; he was wrong in holding that the social foundations of mature European capitalism would underpin revolution. This is one of the reasons the present work insists on the importance of the shift from community-based populist radicalism to a great dependence on formal organizations representing larger, less communal populations. This shift marked the

---

Radicalism during the Industrial Revolution (Chicago: University of Chicago Press, 1982), pp. 50–51.
    [37]Ibid., p. 21.

emergence of the typically, and logically, "reformist" modern working class.

This new working class was typically reformist because it could seek a variety of ends within capitalist society. In contrast, the very existence of the older, more traditional communities of artisans and other workers was threatened by capitalism. On a social-psychological level, the most fundamental premises organizing the thought and lives of the older crafts-men were challenged. Their communities, families, and sense of who, exactly, they were all came under attack. The newer working class de-rived this sort of fundamental sense of identity from capitalist society, and struggled over more transient, malleable, and optional goals.[38]

This argument is the heart of Calhoun's conclusions regarding the course of the different social movements. As such, it is insightful and extremely persuasive. It need not, however, lead decisively—or uni-versally—to his theoretical conclusion: "The mutuality of experience in a closely knit community is a much more likely and solid foundation for collective action than is the similarity of experiences among the members of a class defined in external terms."[39] The category of "class," so carefully reexamined by Calhoun in his discussion of Thompson, presents new problems here. Let us consider again the one-sided em-phasis in Marx's and Thompson's respective definitions of the form-ative features of class—the economic and social in Marx, the cultural and political in Thompson. The significance of Calhoun's quarrel with both approaches amounts to more than an argument that the social theorist and the historian should seek a fully balanced account of all four elements. The point, rather, is that concrete collective action results from the particular and contextual interplay of these elements. What counts is the configuration among, to stay with Calhoun's terms, the economic relations in which collectivities function, the forms of social solidarity they have achieved, the adaptability of their available cultural and ideological traditions, and the learning processes they acquire from experiences of political struggle. Such configurations define specific social struggles and their forms of political organization and initiative. But do such configurations also in fact define a "class" or the formation of a "class"? The preponderance of Calhoun's evidence and arguments indicates they do *not*.

As I read Calhoun's reinterpretations and retheorization of Thomp-son, neither those workers whose ideologies were revolutionary and

[38]Ibid., p. 231.
[39]Ibid., p. 226.

whose "concerted action" was radical nor those workers whose ideology and action were "reformist" were acting *as* a class. There is in
fact no reason to suppose that a collectivity in action is a "class," or,
conversely, that "class" ever provides the adequate definition of an
active collectivity. Calhoun seems to hesitate between this view and
the very different view that nineteenth-century workers were potentially
a collective actor as a "class," but did not become one on account of
certain empirical conditions. The latter view retains something of
Marx's distinction between the proletariat as a class "in itself" and as
a class "for itself," and thus interprets the actual developments of the
nineteenth century as evidence that the class "in itself" never became
a class "for itself." Calhoun's hesitation between the two views is
initially indicated by a terminological confusion. On the one hand, he
defines modern industrial workers as a "class" insofar as they have
(externally) definable interests the pursuit of which would require that
they become, as a class, a unified revolutionary agent: "Certain kinds
of goods which workers in the period of the industrial revolution
sought, and especially the resources with which they had to wage their
battles, made collective action a necessity. The common interests of
the workers made them a potentially revolutionary class actor. In this
Marx was right; it was rational for the class to seek those goods, and
there was no other way than as a class."[40] On the other hand, as we
have seen, Calhoun defines the specificity of this same "modern working
class" as being "typically, and logically, 'reformist' . . . because it could
seek a variety of ends within capitalist society." One can't have it both
ways. The alternative view I am proposing avoids this confusion in
terms and concepts by concluding that modern industrial workers are
not *intrinsically* revolutionary or reformist, because "class" does not
define a collectivity's interests, needs, and aspirations and does not
determine its modes of political organization and action. These are
defined and determined by situational configurations of economic, social, cultural, and political relations. Such configurations not only shape
interests and needs, organization and action, but they also at the same
time determine the identity of the collectivity in question.

    This, it seems to me, is the import of the argument Calhoun advances
against Marx but couches as a dispute over empirical conditions:

> Where Marx appears to have been wrong was in arguing that the class
> must supersede all other collectivities for the workers, that those interests

---

[40]Ibid., p. 229.

which they had in common as members of the working class must become their exclusive interests, and that, therefore, it was individually rational for each worker to participate in the collective rational overthrow of capitalist domination by the working class. . . . [T]he empirical conditions do not seem to have been met. Class relations have not, in any advanced capitalist society, been universalized to the point where workers identify primarily with their class, and seek the rational goals of that class. Workers have sought other, less radical ends than the revolutionary transcendence of capitalism; they have aligned themselves on the basis of other, less universal, more mediate collectivities.[41]

To say that workers never identified primarily with the "class" goes far beyond an empirical quarrel with Marx's assessment of the direction and impetus of workers' movements in the nineteenth century. It is tantamount to asserting that "class" never determines what Calhoun, with precision and justification, calls *concerted collective action*. Such an assertion is wholly compatible with his historical interpretations and analyses throughout *The Question of Class Struggle*. This is why the crucial *theoretical* distinction to be drawn in reevaluating the Marxian conception of collective action is not that between community-bound and formally rationalized organizations—that is, *Gemeinschaft* and *Gesellschaft*—however valid those categories may be in distinguishing the link, for artisans and industrial workers respectively, between their "social foundations" and their political organizations. The crucial distinction, rather, is between the categories of *class* and *collectivity*. "Class" is simply not a category of collectivity in action. As Calhoun shows, when (preindustrial) workers undertook concerted collective action against capitalist social relations they did not act as a class; and when (industrial) workers organized "reformist" social movements and political organizations they did so on the basis of "mediate collectivities" other than class. Moreover, "class" does not provide the subordinated groups within advanced capitalist society, whether workers or not, with their *identity* as participants in social relations; since the social relations in which they participate and the "collectivities" to which they belong are multiple and complexly structured, their identity is not fixed solely, or primarily, by their place in the relations of "production." By the same token, then, "class" is not the category that subsumes or gives ultimate coherence to such collec-

[41]Ibid.

tivities or their participants' identity. Neither social action nor social life simplifies to "class."

This conclusion aligns the critique of Marx I have presented with the premises of the pathbreaking work of Ernesto Laclau and Chantal Mouffe. Two lines of critical reflection converge in their *Hegemony and Socialist Strategy,* resulting in a significant rethinking of the relation between socialism and democracy.

(1) On the one hand, Laclau and Mouffe trace the varying, frequently conflicting responses that Marxist politics and political theory have made to the fact that the identity and action of the working class have never coalesced and unified as Marx had anticipated. From these responses they construct what they call a genealogy of the concept of hegemony. "Hegemony" is the concept which took shape with the recurrent recognition that socialist strategy required some process of linking together disparate social forces whose identities, interests, and aspirations were not identical with those of workers or automatically given by their own position in capitalist relations of production. Hegemony acquired the sense of leadership in social and political struggles. There resulted an authoritarian practice of hegemony, exemplified by Leninism. It projects the Party—legitimated as the genuine representative of the real interests of the "proletariat"—to the role of providing "political" direction and leadership over various classes and class fractions which ally in the struggle against a ruling power. In a contrary development, Antonio Gramsci brought Marxist theory to the threshold of a democratic practice of hegemony; it was by means of his shift of the notion of leadership

> from the "political" to the "intellectual and moral" plane, that the decisive transition takes place toward a concept of hegemony beyond "class alliances." For, whereas political leadership can be grounded upon a conjunctural coincidence of interests in which the participating sectors retain their separate identity, moral and intellectual leadership requires that an ensemble of "ideas" and "values" be shared by a number of sectors—or, to use our own terminology, that certain subject positions traverse a number of class sectors. Intellectual and moral leadership constitutes, according to Gramsci, a higher synthesis, a "collective will," which, through ideology, becomes the organic cement unifying a "historical bloc."[42]

[42]Ernesto Laclau and Chantal Mouffe, *Hegemony and Socialist Strategy: Towards a Radical Democratic Politics,* trans. Winston Moore and Paul Cammack (London: Verso, 1985), pp. 66–67.

Gramscian theory remains only on the threshold of a democratic conception of hegemony insofar as it retains the assumption that ultimately
the agent of hegemony in capitalist society is either the working class
or the bourgeoisie, "so that in the end, political struggle is still a zero-
sum game among classes. This is the inner essentialist core which
continues to be present in Gramsci's thought, setting a limit to the
deconstructive logic of hegemony. To assert, however, that hegemony
must always correspond to a fundamental economic class is not merely
to reaffirm determination in the last instance by the economy; it is also
to predicate that, insofar as the economy constitutes an insurmountable
limit to society's potential for hegemonic recomposition, the constitutive logic of the economic space is not itself hegemonic."[43]

   (2) On the other hand, Laclau and Mouffe find in the plurality of
social movements and the ideological polyvalence of popular struggles
in the past two centuries evidence that our historical situation is "char-
acterized by the essential instability of political spaces, in which the
very identity of the forces in struggle is submitted to constant shifts,
and calls for an incessant process of redefinition."[44] The forms of inequality and subordination in modern society are multiple, suggesting
that the potential sites of social antagonism are numerous. While this
is true, the linking together of various demands for equality does not
happen all at once or evenly through the the entire fabric of society.
Such linkages must be actively constructed, and their form depends
upon the cultural, intellectual, and moral configuration which articulates—expresses and joins—the particular plurality of demands. The
inaugural historical moment for this modern, "hegemonic form of politics" was, for Laclau and Mouffe, the French Revolution, which they,
like François Furet, view as a democratic, not a bourgeois revolution.
The "break with the ancien régime, symbolized by the Declaration of
the Rights of Man, would provide the discursive conditions which made
it possible to propose the different forms of inequality as illegitimate
and anti-natural, and thus make them equivalent as forms of oppression. Here lay the profound subversive power of the democratic discourse, which would allow the spread of equality and liberty into
increasingly wider domains and therefore act as a fermenting agent
upon different forms of struggle against subordination."[45] The dem-

---

[43]Ibid., p. 69.
[44]Ibid., p. 151.
[45]Ibid., p. 155.

ocratic discourse could be displaced from the "field of political equality between citizens to the field of equality between the sexes," as in Mary Wollstonecraft; or, as in the emergent socialist discourse, the "critique of political inequality" could be displaced "towards the critique of economic inequality, which leads to the putting in question of other forms of subordination and the demanding of new rights. The socialist demands should therefore," argue Laclau and Mouffe in their most important break with the established political self-understanding of Marxism, "be seen as a moment internal to the democratic revolution, and only intelligible on the basis of the equivalential logic which the latter establishes."[46]

Laclau and Mouffe situate Marx's own theoretical-political project as a particular response both to the possibilities of democratic revolution which were opened in 1789 *and* to the difficulties and uncertainties which characterize the "hegemonic form of politics" after 1848. Marx looked to the model of a sharp polarization of forces which had defined the *political* antagonism of the French Revolution and then transposed that model onto an anticipated *social* antagonism between classes. In this crucial gesture, Marx at once recognized the significance of hegemony and attempted to elude it:

> [Marx's] reflection took place in a moment at which the division of the political space in terms of the dichotomy people/ancien régime seemed to have exhausted its productivity, and was in any case incapable of constructing a vision of the political which could recapture the complexity and the plurality peculiar to the social in industrial society. Marx seeks, then, to think the primary fact of social division on the basis of a new principle: the confrontation between classes. The new principle, however, is undermined from the start by its radical insufficiency, arising from the fact that class opposition is incapable of dividing the totality of the social body into two antagonistic camps, of reproducing itself *automatically* as a line of demarcation in the political sphere. It is for this reason that the affirmation of class struggle as the fundamental principle of political division always had to be accompanied by supplementary hypotheses which relegated its applicability to the future: historical-sociological hypotheses—the simplification of the social structure, which would lead to the coincidence of real political struggles and struggles between classes as agents constituted at the level of relations of production; hypotheses regarding the consciousness of the agents— the transition from the class in itself to the class for itself.[47]

---

[46]Ibid., p. 156.
[47]Ibid., pp. 151–152.

The pertinence of Laclau and Mouffe's criticism is that it pinpoints and historically contextualizes the conceptual strategy which flawed Marx's theory of the social totality. It also clarifies how thoroughly the evasion or elision of the political is part of the inaugural paradigm of Marxian theory.

By way of conclusion I want to stress the connection between this elision of the political and the eclipsing of culture in Marxism. For it is the double effect of these two gestures which has constrained cultural theory and interpretation within this tradition. I have argued that the paradigm of Marxist cultural theory congeals when Marx converts his critical-utopian discourse into a theory based on a conception of social relations and social practices in which cultural valuation and political contestation play only a derivative role. The critical-utopian discourse, however, does not thereby merely disappear. It is readable in what I have called the enthymemic register or strand of the 1844 *Manuscripts,* where Marx argues from values and revaluations to a critical account of social relations in capitalism and an advocacy of political action and social change. It also resonates in the slogans of *The German Ideology* and at various moments in the later writings. What Gouldner calls the pretheoretical "background" of the two Marxisms can be more precisely understood as the strands of this critical-utopian discourse. I have traced how the inaugural paradigm of Marxist cultural theory is formed as this critical-utopian discourse is dislodged and replaced by a series of premises that are shared by both Scientific Marxism and Critical Marxism. Even as Critical Marxism seeks to "correct" its scientistic counterpart, drawing on the "background" discourse to carry out that criticism, it cannot fully recover the critical-utopian impetus. Critical Marxism too remains bound to the reduction of culture to consciousness and of social relations to relations of production. Those reductions, I have argued, eclipse culture and elide politics from Marxism's primary understanding of society and, indeed, from its self-understanding as theory.

Moreover, this double effacement is not only performed *on* the critical-utopian discourse but is prepared for *by* it. Marx's critical-utopian discourse appeals to a vision of classless society which combines an ideal of culture, in the sense of the cultivation of nature and of human capacities, with a radically egalitarian norm of human interaction. Marx projects a conception of community that incorporates the following elements: rational control over the material interchange with nature, rationality being doubly defined as technical knowledge aimed at meeting human needs and reducing the time devoted to work and as decision-making procedures governed by principles of common control and of sufficient provision for all members of society; the multifaceted development of individuals freed from their class identities, that is, from those everyday practices that are structured as a competitive struggle for existence in the context of real or imagined scarcity; and an egalitarian reciprocity through which one's participation in material-social practices that are a means of satisfying others' needs would at the same time be a valued development of one's own satisfactions and needs, activities and capacities. At issue is the fate of this utopian vision in Marxism. Rather than acknowledging that this revaluation of the aims and purposes of social life has to be made persuasive and compelling over against competing visions and ideologies, Marx seeks to secure its validity on other grounds and outside the discursive constructions of politics. In the voice of Scientific Marxism, he turned this critical-utopian idea of community into the intrinsic goal of history; in the voice of Critical Marxism, he turned it into the inevitable form of workers' consciousness. On this level, the elision of the political is part of the self-(mis)understanding of Marxian theory. But the political is also, and already, elided from the utopian vision itself. Marx never imagines that egalitarian reciprocity, or "real community," or universal association, must also be a *political community* which would have continually to renew and transform itself. Because Marx believes that genuine community would eliminate the specifically political processes of deliberation and contestation over values, aims, interests, and so on, he likewise defines the political, this side of utopia, purely as those practices and institutions which ultimately derive from and carry out *class* interests or, alternatively, deviate from class interests and distort them.

4

The Concrete
Utopia of Poetry

From "Beautiful Illusion" to a Poetics of Revolt

Marxist cultural theorists and literary critics have always resisted and attempted to overcome the debilitating effects of the inaugural paradigm of Marxist cultural theory. Just as the historians' attempts to reinsert the formative processes of culture and politics into the analysis of class and collective action are either distorted by the paradigm's limitations or have to break down its most basic premises, so too our efforts at cultural interpretation and literary criticism within the intellectual-political tradition of Marxism encounter such limitations and breaks. I have argued in the previous chapter that the Marxian paradigm began to congeal when Marx abandoned his incipient, largely undeveloped conception of culture as a set of material-social practices, and consequently tended to reduce culture to "consciousness," and to obscure the complex links between culture and politics in favor of a conception that drives both, separately and categorically, from political economy. What then has this meant for the theory and interpretation, specifically, of such cultural practices as art and literature, especially since the supposition of the primacy of political economy has seldom been unquestionably accepted by Marxist critics themselves?

It has meant, first of all, that Marxist criticism does not fully recognize the extent to which the practices of artistic production and aesthetic reception are embedded in moral-political relations and are a site of conflict over the moral-political valuations that inform our participation in social relations more generally. Instead, this problem-

atic tends to be displaced, and obscured, by the supposedly more fundamental question of the relation of the artwork and "society"
conceived as a totality. Since we never have more than a kind of theoretical image of "society," the presupposition that the genuine social
and historical significance of an artwork lies primarily in its relation
to the social totality causes this theoretical image to serve as the implicit
a priori of literary interpretation and analysis. Since the image of "society" is drawn even in Critical Marxism from categories of the economy—from Lukács's image of relations of production and class
consciousness to the Frankfurt School's image of generalized commodification and of "total administration"—, the priority of "society"
over "culture" is at work in the interpretive process even when the
relation of artwork and totality is explicitly construed to deny such a
priority.

This persistence of the base/superstructure model has been amply
shown by Raymond Williams. The artwork/totality relation may be
construed as "reflection" and "typicality" as in Lukács's literary criticism, or as "mediation" and "correspondence" as in Adorno and
Benjamin, or as "homology" as in Lucien Goldmann. Each of these
conceptions separates society and culture categorically; the theoretical
image of the former takes precedence over the interpretive encounter
with the latter, and neither "domain" gets approached as a complex
of interrelated material-social practices. For Williams, the limitation of
these various efforts to relate the artwork to the social totality shows
most tellingly in their inadequacy in approaching contemporary culture, that is, the complex of practices in which we ourselves directly
participate: "None of the dualist theories, expressed as reflection or
mediation, and none of the formalist and structuralist theories, expressed in variants of correspondence or homology, can be fully carried
through to contemporary practice, since in different ways they all depend on a known *history*, a known *structure*, known *products*. Analytic
relations can be handled in this way; practical relations hardly at all."[1]
The same argument, it seems to me, holds true for the analysis of works
from the past, since our "contemporary practice" includes the interpretive reconstruction and political construction of cultural traditions and heritages. As I have already argued with regard to critical
hermeneutics and political-discursive practices, aesthetic reception and

[1]Raymond Williams, *Marxism and Literature* (New York: Oxford University Press,
1977), pp. 106–107.

interpretation are themselves practices through which we participate in context-bound and open-ended conflicts of cultural valuation and in what Laclau and Mouffe call the political articulation of "society." In what follows I will test this perspective against some broad reflections on aesthetics and on poetry that have come from the tradition of Critical Marxism, through a consideration of poems from William Blake's *Songs of Innocence and of Experience*. Blake's contribution to our cultural, and political, heritage lies in the response that his poetry made to the changing relation of art to the evolution of bourgeois society; writing in the volatile decades following 1789, Blake responded both to the possibilities and promises opened by the "democratic revolution" and to the ongoing institutionalization of capitalist social relations. An English Jacobin, he was also a poet who himself reflected constantly on the historical and political possibilities of "imagination." For Blake, poetry is an active imposing of imagination or fantasy against dominant values and institutions. Casting himself in the double role of visionary and voice of condemnation, he attributed both a utopian and a negative power to poetic writing. And it is indeed an interplay of the utopian and the critical, of imagination and negation, that makes his writing resonate with the social and aesthetic preoccupations of such thinkers as Ernst Bloch and Herbert Marcuse, Walter Benjamin and T. W. Adorno. At the same time, Blake's poetry encourages us to consider anew how the politics of revaluation can shape the project of a poet's work and the inner dynamics of poetic language, its processes of figuration, its status as a linguistic act, its forms and techniques, and its effects within reception and interpretation.

From Bloch I have taken the phrase *concrete utopia*. Bloch meant by this that latent utopian possibilities are contained in the experiences of freedom and self-organization which social groups and classes possess, intermittently and fragmentedly, in their everyday existence, political practices, myths, and artistic endeavors.[2] These latent tendencies have as their heritage all the unfinished or abortive efforts in history to extend justice and happiness. The heritage of utopia is thus a discontinuous history, one that must be constructed from cultural traditions and the popular struggles and revolts of the past. The question

---

[2]See Ernst Bloch, "Karl Marx and Humanity: The Material of Hope" and "Upright Carriage, Concrete Utopia," in *On Karl Marx*, trans. John Cumming (New York: Herder and Herder, 1971), pp. 16–45 and 159–173 respectively; and "Indications of Utopia," in *A Philosophy of the Future*, trans. John Cumming (New York: Herder and Herder, 1970), pp. 84–141.

we can draw from Bloch's reflections is this: In what ways is poetry a bearer of utopian hope, of the historical latency that is at once within and beyond society? From Marcuse I will borrow a thesis about art and literature that he advanced in his last published work, *The Aesthetic Dimension:* "The inner logic of the work of art terminates in the emergence of another reason, another sensibility, which defy the rationality and sensibility incorporated in the dominant social institutions."[3] The phrase "terminates in the emergence of" suggests, first, that art is utopian insofar as it anticipates new orders of reason and sensibility that can be secured only through political action and social transformation, and, second, that this utopian anticipation is nonetheless concrete insofar as it stems from what is realized aesthetically in the artwork. Marcuse's thesis leads to a second question about lyric and society: How does the "inner logic" of a poem at the same time manifest a counterlogic against the constraining interactions organized by society?

While Bloch and Marcuse help to frame the questions that a socially critical study of poetry needs to address, their own aesthetic reflections rest on suppositions that cannot be left unchallenged. Bloch maintains that great artworks are part ideology, part authentic utopia. The first task of analysis is to dissolve the ideological shell of the work by exposing the ways its serves particular rather than general interests and legitimates the forms of domination prevalent in its own society; once this ideological shell is dissolved, the utopian kernel of the work is supposed to shine through, a radiant core of meanings and images expressing the strivings and hopes of humanity. Bloch's conception of interpretation shares with the hermeneutics of Heidegger and Gadamer the insight that cultural meanings come forward only from historically situated works and are appropriated only in historically situated contexts. Nevertheless, he tends to view the *valid* meanings of culture as part of a semantic storehouse that preserves itself intact across historical periods and epochs. Hence the questionable notion that interpretation can with assurance separate the valid and true aspect of a work from its ideological and false part. Such a notion goes directly against the grain of Bloch's original insight. *Concrete* utopia precisely does not derive from any pregiven goal of the historical process; the shape of the utopian is a product of the new valuations of justice, freedom,

[3]Herbert Marcuse, *The Aesthetic Dimension: Toward a Critique of Marxist Aesthetics* (Boston: Beacon, 1978), p. 7.

happiness, and so on, which are forged in processes of political struggle and interpretive conflicts. By the same token, the hermeneutical "recovery" of the heritage of utopia has no sure ground of meaning or foothold in truth from which we could then glean the valid significations and discard the ideological shell of a particular work. Bloch's conception of valid meaning and ideological falsehood shares the problems I identified earlier in Habermas's adaptation of Benjamin's idea of "semantic potentials"; both approaches are driven to postulate an essential and separated stratum within communicative practices which are otherwise "functionalized" to ideological purposes of legitimation. At that point, once again the coercive and nonreciprocal aspects of these practices are given a purely external determination. They are derived from social relations presumed to be already constituted independent of the practice in question.

Marcuse's aesthetic reflections accentuate the unity of artistic form. Transcribing Schillerian aesthetics into socially critical terms, he attributes a utopian and critical power to art on the basis of the sharp contrast that individuals experience between the unity and harmony they apprehend in the artwork and the disharmony and conflict that characterize the social relations they encounter in everyday life. This line of argument reverses the main intention of his 1937 essay "The Affirmative Character of Culture"[4] by underscoring the critical rather than the adaptive effects of the experience of art as a compensation for social reality. First in the context of the social and political movements of the 1960s in *Counterrevolution and Revolt* and then in *The Aesthetic Dimension,* Marcuse undertakes to rescue the aesthetic experience of bourgeois culture from the bourgeois idea of culture. Consumer society's relentless assault on art through a commodity culture makes it necessary, according to Marcuse, to restore the uniqueness and autonomy of aesthetic experience.

The shift in polemical purpose from the 1937 essay to the writings of the 1970s is, however, more an extension than a contradiction of the earlier position. The indictment of affirmative culture had already implied that the artwork's separateness and wholeness were, at least potentially, a critique of the social reality from which it separated itself. Marcuse counters the directions taken by the idea of cultural revolution

[4]Herbert Marcuse, "The Affirmative Character of Culture," *Negations,* trans. Jeremy J. Shapiro (Boston: Beacon, 1968), pp. 88–133. For my discussion of Marcuse's concept of "affirmative culture," see above, pp. 5–9.

in the 1960s with a renewed insistence on the two-sidedness of the aesthetic:

> At stake is the "affirmative character" of bourgeois culture, by virtue of which art serves to beautify and justify the established order. The aesthetic form responds to the misery of the isolated bourgeois individual by celebrating universal humanity, to physical deprivation by exalting the beauty of the soul, to external servitude by elevating the value of inner freedom.
> But this affirmation has its own dialectic. There is no work of art which does not break its affirmative stance by the "power of the negative," which does not, in its very structure, evoke the words, the images, the music of another reality, of another order repelled by the existing one and yet alive in memory and anticipation, alive in what happens to men and women, and in their rebellion against it.[5]

The Aesthetic Dimension extends this defense of the separated art of bourgeois society. According to Marcuse's thesis, art rejects the divided order of society by adhering to the specifically aesthetic aim of achieving a Beautiful Illusion (*schöne Schein*). Art constitutes the affective and utopian support of a critical consciousness of society. This is not to say that it is a form of critical consciousness. To the contrary, Marcuse's later aesthetics insists that art has an affective rather than cognitive power and that its value lies in the aesthetic sublimation of reality rather than in any critical reflection on reality. In this way, Marcuse alters Marxism's conception of art as a mode of illusory consciousness without questioning the categorical framework within which that conception arose. For Marcuse, art is indeed an illusion or appearance for consciousness. But its mode of separation and difference from social reality—that is, the socially organized real material activity which Marx also sharply differentiated from art—is so complete as to turn art into a contradiction of existing society. The postulated contrast between the wholeness of aesthetic form and the dividedness of social reality thus becomes something like the affective analogue of the critical theorist's cognitive condemnation of that same reality. The classical Marxian divide between "society" and "culture" reasserts itself in the modified form of the divide between theoretical understanding and aesthetic experience. While this modification may seem significantly to alter the valuation of "art," it does so by so thoroughly privileging the

[5]Herbert Marcuse, *Counterrevolution and Revolt* (Boston: Beacon, 1972), p. 92.

affective and "aesthetic" dimension of reception over the interpretive or hermeneutical dimension as to virtually eliminate the concreteness of aesthetic understanding and valuation. The specificity of actual artworks and the discriminating, concretizing work of interpretation are subordinated to the wholly generalized social interpretation of aesthetic experience per se.

Against Marcuse I will advance the alternative thesis that the social dialectic of art does not arise from the conflict between a divided reality and a unified work, but rather takes the form of conflicts *within* the work, including the conflict between its unity and its division. I am guided in part by Adorno's notion, expressed in his essay "Lyric Poetry and Society," that the criticism of poetry needs to attend "to ways in which various levels of society's inner contradictory relationships manifest themselves in the poet's speaking."[6] We will also, however, have to examine critically Adorno's view of the relationship of modern lyric and society, for he tends to view the unifying movement of a text as the shape taken by its constitutively antagonistic relation to "society" as a totality. The demand for "something purely individual" from lyric poetry is, he argues, "in itself social in nature. It implies a protest against a social condition which every individual experiences as hostile, distant, cold, and oppressive; and this social condition impresses itself on the poetic form in a negative way: the more heavily social conditions weigh, the more unrelentingly the poem resists, refusing to give into any heteronomy, and constituting itself purely according to its own laws."[7] By contrast, I do not think that we can presuppose that the unifying dimension of the work is—necessarily and categorically—the manifestation of a resistance to oppressive social conditions, any more than we can presuppose the opposite, namely, that its unifying dimension is the mark of its subjugation to "ideological closure." Such judgments have to be made contextually and through specific interpretations.

My thesis that the social counterlogic of a poem arises from its internal contradictoriness as a *text*, not from its wholeness as a "beautiful appearance," is based on a very different premise, namely, that literature is a practice that acts upon language and therefore enters into a complex relation to those language practices—or discourses—that shape the social relations of the context in which it is produced and

[6]T. W. Adorno, "Lyric Poetry and Society," *Telos* 20 (Summer 1974), 65.
[7]Ibid., p. 58.

of the context in which it is received. The utopian power of poetry can only lie in its concrete connections, as a language practice, with its relevant social contexts rather than in its capacity either to separate itself from those contexts or to set itself above them.

Aesthetic receptivity is not an affective experience galvanized by either the unity of form as conceived by Marcuse or the autonomous principle of artistic construction in Adorno's sense. Poetic language solicits, incites, calls for a reading that at once lets the effects of poetic condensation erupt across the poem and ties those effects to the situation or act of writing itself. Reading always entails this double movement—receptivity to a language that is multivalent and overdetermined and moments of decision in which the multivalence and overdetermination are reconnected to the place or situation from which the poem has arisen. And this site of the poem's genesis is social. An analogy might be made between the reading of poetry and psychoanalytic interpretation. The analyst listens with what Freud called a suspended or floating attention in order to hear what reverberates within the subject's discourse and its silences. On the other side of the dialogue, the subject is pressed toward what Lacan called the "moment to conclude," where he or she feels the pressure of the unconscious and integrates it into his or her actual discourse with the analyst, allowing the unconscious to interrupt the false continuities and coherence which up to then have resisted it. The two sides of reading poetry are an interplay of this kind between floating attention and the moment-to-conclude. The reader, however, is more like the patient than the analyst, in that interpretations, usually in the name of their own coherence, tend to resist the effects of the poetic text. Such decisions always take place, even when they are masked, as in the rhetoric of deconstructive criticism. Every interpretive moment-to-conclude links the interpretation and the text as the two historically—and socially—situated poles of aesthetic experience. The transaction between writing and reading is thus at the same time an encounter between the social situation of literary production and the social situation of literary reception. Just as the cultural heritage is not given but is constructed through this transaction and this encounter, so too aesthetic experience is not given but is *formed* in the interplay of writing and reading.

Blake understood the relation between writing and reading as a form of struggle. "Opposition is true Friendship"—this proverb concludes one of the "memorable fancies" in *The Marriage of Heaven and Hell*. Blake invents an encounter between himself and an Angel whom Blake challenges "to shew me my eternal lot," after the Angel has bid him to "consider the hot burning dungeon thou art preparing for thyself to all eternity." The Angel takes him beneath the earth to look upon the void in which appears the orthodox vision of the Inferno, filled with "black & white spiders," "a black tempest," "a cataract of blood mixed with fire," "the scaly fold of a monstrous serpent," and even "the head of Leviathan . . . advancing toward us with all the fury of a spiritual existence." When the Angel leaves Blake behind, this vision of eternal doom disappears:

> My friend the Angel climb'd up from his station into the mill; I remain'd alone, & then this appearance was no more, but I found myself sitting on a pleasant bank beside a river by moon light hearing a harper who sung to the harp, & his theme was, The man who never alters his opinion is like standing water, & breeds reptiles of the mind.
> But I arose, and sought for the mill, & there I found my Angel, who surprised asked me, how I escaped?
> I answered. All that we saw was owing to your metaphysics: for when you ran away, I found myself on a bank by moonlight hearing a harper. But now we have seen my eternal lot, shall I shew you yours? he laughed at my proposal; but I by force caught him in my arms, & flew westerly thro' the night. . . .[8]

Blake's parable is of the struggle between the angelic imagination of hell and the infernal imagination of heaven. When Blake forces the Angel to see heaven in the mode of the diabolical imagination, a place where monkeys and baboons chained together engage in an eternal orgy of cannibalism and self-cannibalism, the Angel recoils:

> So the Angel said: thy phantasy has imposed upon me & thou oughtest to be ashamed.

This ends their brief friendship, because Blake will not tolerate the Angel's inability to see that he too has created a vision through the imagination, the degraded imagination of orthodox religion and philosophy:

> I answered: we impose upon one another, & it is but lost time to converse with you whose works are only Analytics.

---

[8] *The Complete Poetry and Prose of William Blake*, rev. ed., ed. David V. Erdman (Garden City, N.Y.: Anchor, 1982), pp. 41–42.

Blake practiced the writing of poetry not in order to unveil objects of contemplation or to preserve the kernel of unvarying truth or to produce the harmonies of the beautiful illusion, but rather as the active imposition of "imagination" or "fantasy" as a form of discursive struggle against the dominant values organizing the social experiences and practices in which he participated.

A Poetics of Moral Revaluation: "A Poison Tree"

Having questioned the theoretical frameworks within which Bloch and Marcuse elaborated the relation of utopia and poetry, let us now address the questions that we owe to their initiatives within Marxist cultural theory.

In what ways is poetry a bearer of utopian hope, of the historical latency that is at once within and beyond society?

How does the "inner logic" of a poem at the same time manifest a counterlogic against the constraining interactions organized by society?

I will attempt to address these questions by means of an interpretation of Blake's poem "A Poison Tree":

> I was angry with my friend;
> I told my wrath, my wrath did end.
> I was angry with my foe:
> I told it not, my wrath did grow.
>
> And I waterd it in fears
> Night & morning with my tears:
> And I sunned it with smiles,
> And with soft deceitful wiles.
>
> And it grew both day and night.
> Till it bore an apple bright.
> And my foe beheld it shine.
> And he knew that it was mine.
>
> And into my garden stole,
> When the night had veild the pole;
> In the morning glad I see;
> My foe outstretched beneath the tree.[9]

Much depends on the relation of the first stanza to the rest of the poem as it unfolds what happened to the wrath that was not told to the foe.

[9]Ibid., p. 28.

Every time one reads the poem, I believe, the first stanza has the force of a moral statement. The past tense establishes the twin perspective of Blake's action *then* and his judgment *now*. The danger or unhappiness of a wrath that grows, as against a wrath that ends, establishes a set of values or preferences that virtually goes without saying. And all of this is then confirmed in the account of the ensuing anguish that he experienced and the harm he brought on his foe. The poem reads as a kind of confessional utterance in which Blake the speaker shares with the reader a reflective judgment on the actions of Blake in the past, anchored in the view that telling one's wrath is healthy and not telling it is harmful and even self-destructive.

Another extreme, however, emerges against this reading and contradicts its every detail. The last two lines of the poem, breaking the consistent past tense of the rest, can be taken at face value:

> In the morning glad I see;
> My foe outstretched beneath the tree.

A transcendent joy! He has gotten his satisfaction, and his wrath has finally been expressed, yielding the sheer delight of seeing an enemy destroyed. One might try to avert this reading by arguing that the phrase "glad I see" is not really in the present tense, but rather is an elliptical construction for something like "glad I was to see." But the amoral reading can draw on other aspects of the poem's total structure. First of all, there are two oppositions in the first stanza, not only telling as against not telling one's wrath, but also the difference between friend and foe, suggesting that there is no undestructive means of expressing wrath toward a foe but that it must be enacted. Second, the poem's words and syntax are not particularly charged with affective connotations; the tone is flat, and this second reading leaves it so by construing the first stanza not as a moral statement but as a statement of fact: wrath can be expressed and immediately dissipated with a friend, but not with a foe. Indeed, one can take this reading to its logical conclusion and say that the poem as a whole, far from being a confessional utterance, is more like a set of instructions on how to do in an enemy and feel relief, even joy.

Either of these readings can account for itself, bringing the various details of the poem into line. In this sense, the poem generates both. Neither reading, on the other hand, can account for the possibility of the other, except to declare that it is the product of misreading; they can only accuse each other of naive moralism and amorality respectively. It is inadequate, however, to leave off with these results and declare that the poem is formally or logically undecidable, a pure oscillation between two mutually exclusive meanings. For this undecidability also represents two contrary experiential situations, remorse and remorselessness, condemnation and coldness, constituting an ethical impasse that the reading of the poem need not yet accept, that is, decide to affirm.

The very flatness of the poem's tone allows each reading to invest the poem with the affects appropriate to it. In the first reading, the poem bespeaks the solemn awe of one witnessing an action that the speaker himself can hardly believe he committed. The second reading, on the other hand, takes the speaker's final joy at face value and, in turn, invests the atonal surface of the poem with the connotation of coldness. But the conjoining of coldness and joy calls into question the joy itself. The tone becomes the symptom of a joy that is derived from an altogether different emotion, namely, the wrath that has had to wend its way through elaborate detours in order to manifest itself in the fatal deception of the foe. The conceit which gives the poem its title is the image of this circuitous transformation of wrath into fear, duplicity, and finally deception:

> And I waterd it in fears,
> Night & morning with my tears:
> And I sunned it with smiles,
> And with soft deceitful wiles.
>
> And it grew both day and night.
> Till it bore an apple bright.

Without making reference to any moral judgment against duplicity and deception, we discover in the image of the watering and sunning of the wrath (tree) that there opened within the subject a split between the inner feeling (fear) and the outward show of fraternity (smiles, soft deceitful wiles), which from that moment on precludes any direct connection between emotion and action. This distortion of experience is not subject to a moral condemnation in the sense of a judgment against the speaker himself, for he has made no choice which could be judged. He has suffered the effects of an anger that cannot immediately express and resolve itself.

The conceit of the poison tree, its simplicity and completeness extending over the last three stanzas as a whole, nonetheless has at its center an indeterminate element—the "apple bright." All the other single elements of the image equating untold wrath with a tree easily find their appropriate equivalents. Within the logic of the conceit, the image of the apple is only vaguely motivated, as by the idea that it is the "fruit" of his wrath. The meaning of "apple bright" is otherwise unspecifiable from the standpoint of the conceit itself.[10] It could be anything—an object, a situation, a person—so long as it fulfilled one general condition: that it be, in the eyes of the foe, an *enviable possession* of the speaker's. Here indeterminacy is an extreme instance of metaphorical condensation. A thousand and one narratives could be told that revolved around an episode in which a character's enemy, thinking he is about to deprive the protagonist of a valued possession, falls to his own ruin:

> And my foe beheld it shine.
> And he knew that it was mine.
>
> And into my garden stole,
> When the night had veild the pole;

These lines resist the poem's moral reading more than any other passage, for they show that this foe could be counted on to try to rob the subject of his possession. Blake had calculated exactly what his foe's reactions and actions would be, having imputed to the other the same destructive antagonism that he had discovered within himself. This equality between protagonist and antagonist likewise causes the amoral reading to lose its force. The apparent difference between protagonist and antagonist has been dissolved into their essential identity with each other.

At this point, the indeterminacy of the apple and the prototypical nature of the narrative yield a significance that exceeds the grasp of either the moral or the amoral reading. The prototype narrative and the image of the "apple bright" are like a vortex that pulls everything into itself. Anything could be the enviable possession around which the deadly struggle between Blake and the foe revolves. Possessiveness is not merely an element of their antagonism but its cause; it pre-forms their relation to each other as a relation of equality and envy, their

---

[10]If one were immediately to draw the meaning of the image from its biblical source in order to supply what is missing in the conceit, the poem could be construed as a satire on the Eden myth. The speaker would then be God, who ensnares his foe—humankind—with the temptation of something enviable.

mirroring of each other being so complete that the protagonist need only calculatively impute his own aims and motives to the other in order to make his scheme a success. Possessiveness pre-forms their relation *socially*. The conditions of the central image-narrative are in fact met only in a social relation in which the practices of exchange make *any* object or situation or person susceptible to an (economic) designation that at once makes its value *the same for all individuals* and turns it into *something to be possessed*. Only under these conditions does the equality of individuals necessarily take the form of antagonism between individuals. Envy, a term borrowed from the ethics of pre-capitalist societies, here names the market-mediated intersubjectivity that capitalist social relations tend to extend to all manner of relationships.

The unusual power of this simple poem derives from the play of the image of the "apple bright." It is at once the poem's most abstractly indeterminate and its most concretely, socially determined image. The figurative movement of the image has three distinct moments. First, as an element in the conceit, the "apple bright" stands for the *effect of unexpressed wrath,* a result arrived at in the course of the narrated events. Second, and to the contrary, as a metaphor of the social process of abstraction that forms the very interrelation and interactions of individuals, the "apple bright" stands for the *cause of the antagonism* from which the story originated. The conceit substitutes effect for cause. The "apple bright" is thus, at the third moment of its figuration, the trope called a metalepsis. The metalepsis here takes the form of a contradiction between *what is narrated* and *the narrative* itself, for we have discovered the social cause of the poem's narrative in the image that initially stood for the psychological effect of what was narrated, namely, the speaker's unexpressed wrath. In order to have followed this figurative swerve in the poem's language, we have made a break with the two readings, the moral and the amoral, that the text has engendered.

In "A Poison Tree," the critique of bourgeois society is expressed not thematically but in the very articulation of the text and in the dynamic that it provokes. Linguistic theory has distinguished between a text's *énoncé* ("statement") and its *énonciation* ("utterance"), that is, between what is said and the saying of it. In our context, Roman Jakobson's original terminology suffices, distinguishing the *narrated event* and the *speech event*. At the level of the narrated event in "A Poison Tree," an unexpressed wrath results in the destruction of an antagonist by ensnaring him with an enviable possession. The speech event of the poem, I am urging, should be grasped in social and indeed political terms. The text has generated two conflicting and irreconci-liable readings; each apprehends the poem's status as speech event in a particular way, as a confession or moral judgment in the one case, and as a cold statement of fact or scenario for destructive action in the other. Neither of these readings can be a true understanding of the text, because neither can explain or cancel the other. Our interpretation has been forced beyond the moral and the amoral reading. The poem must rather be interpreted in terms of its generation of these two partial, blind readings. It generates these readings because they correspond to the two poles of ethical consciousness through which individuals actually live the social relations of capitalist society. The moral reading corresponds to a false morality of goodwill and honesty—which would have been, by the way, the simple object of a satire had Blake kept the poem's notebook title: "Christian Forebearance." The amoral reading, on the other hand, corresponds to that form of individualism in which individuals, having been made interchangeable by the market-mediated relation in which they meet, are deprived of the very individuality in the name of which they act.

The dialectic of the text consists in imposing the moral and the amoral readings, which represent these two poles of ethical experience, and then forcing these two readings back to the figure of the "apple bright" in order to make the poem understandable. Both readings are doomed to fail, since they take the "apple bright" as the effect of wrath rather than as the social cause of the antagonism between individuals. The metalepsis, in breaking our interpretation from the two readings, gives form—or figure—to the difference between this act of poetic speech and the lived morality of capitalist social relations.

Let me explain this formulation of poetic form by contrasting the results of the analysis with the position that Marcuse held. For Marcuse, aesthetic experience marks the difference between the real and the possible by presenting an image or appearance whose completeness separates it from the existing conditions and prevalent experiences of social life. Art is sublimation in the sense that it transforms the real into the beautiful appearance; accompanying this aesthetic sublimation, Marcuse argues, is a process of desublimation that occurs in aesthetic perception: "The transcendence of immediate reality shatters the reified objectivity of established social relations and opens a new dimension of experience: the rebirth of rebellious subjectivity. Thus, on the basis of aesthetic sublimation, a *desublimation* takes place in the percep-tions of individuals—in their feelings, judgments, thoughts; an inval-idation of dominant norms, needs, and values."[11] Now, Blake's "A Poison Tree" does indeed invalidate dominant forms of experience and of ethical consciousness, those which are embedded in the socially organized practices and interactions of bourgeois society. But the poem accomplishes this not by means of the beautiful appearance of aesthetic wholeness but rather in the contradiction within the text between the· readings it generates and its genesis of the readings. The "dominant norms, needs, and values" the poem negates are as integral to the inner workings of the text as they are inherent in actual social life. What is felt, thought, judged within the historical forms of ethical consciousness that the possessive individual must inhabit are themselves a part of the poem's aesthetic dimension, here as the dynamic of the readings which corresponds to the polarity in that ethical consciousness. It is not the unity but the active division of the text that invalidates these social-ethical forms.

So, too, the utopian power of the poem lies not in its protection of an aesthetic appearance of wholeness but in its concrete act of speaking. The concreteness of utopia does not, however, as Bloch would have it, reside in the semantic storehouse of images of happiness and free-dom. The utopian is more closely tied to the negative. The poem an-nounces a morality that cannot yet be lived in society or represented in poetry. The poem voices its revaluation of values in a fracture be-tween the *énoncé* and *énonciation*. The utopian dimension of the poem is enacted in a poetic speaking which manifests the struggle between the social conditions of the poet's speech and the latent possibilities of speech. The movement of figuration, through the three moments of the trope of the "apple bright," invalidates the two readings capable of giving the narrated event (*énoncé*) and the conceit (tree = wrath) consistency and in this way negates those forms of ethical experience that can be lived in the social context of the poem. What the poem says is negated in the saying of it. What I have called poetic form or figure is here just this difference between *énoncé* and *énonciation*, an enactment of the divergence between the real and the possible, the lived and the utopian. "A Poison Tree" points toward a future in which its own story and its mode of telling would no longer be necessary.

I want to conclude these remarks on "A Poison Tree" with reference

[11]Marcuse, *The Aesthetic Dimension*, pp. 7–8.

to Adorno, since he, in contrast to Marcuse, suggests precisely that it is the negative imprint of society on the form of the artwork, not the artwork's transcending formal unity, which is crucial to our understanding of the relation of modern lyric and society. And it seems to me that Adorno gives significant direction to the socially critical theory of art when, for example, he sets a critical task like the one I have tried to take up here, namely, to assess the "ways in which various levels of society's inner contradictory relationships manifest themselves in the poet's speaking." Or when, as in his *Aesthetic Theory*, he points to the intimate connection between the social and the aesthetic problems that a writer or artist has to solve in the very construction of text or artwork: "The unresolved antagonisms of society reappear in art in the guise of immanent problems of artistic form."[12]

The interpretive and analytical problematic that Adorno initiates tends to give way to a categorical and epochal opposition between "art" and "society." Modern art becomes primarily an antagonist— and, then, the primary antagonist—of modern society:

> [Art] is social primarily because it stands opposed to society. Now this opposition art can mount only when it has become autonomous. By congealing into an entity unto itself—rather than obeying existing social norms and thus proving itself to be "socially useful"—art criticizes society just by being there. Pure and immanently elaborated art is a tacit critique of the debasement of man [sic] by a condition that is moving towards a total-exchange society where everything is for-other. This social deviance of art is the determinate negation of a determinate society.[13]

Or again:

> It is by virtue of its separation from empirical reality that the work of art can become a being of a higher order, fashioning the relation between the whole and its parts in accordance with its own needs.[14]

Such an opposition between "art" and "society" marks the basic impasse of Critical Marxism's renewal of cultural theory. The conceptualization of "art" depends upon the a priori established by Adorno's

---

[12]T. W. Adorno, *Aesthetic Theory*, trans. C. Lenhardt (London: Routledge & Kegan Paul, 1984), p. 8.
[13]Ibid., p. 321.
[14]Ibid., p. 6.

theoretical image of "society." According to that image, "society" is a totally administered, economically rationalized world in which all social relationships are saturated by the law or logic of commodity exchange. The theoretical image in turn justifies—and generalizes to a virtually absolute degree—the one protest against bureaucracy and capitalism which animates Adorno's socially critical stance, namely, the claim that individuals, subjected to the reifying effects of commodity relations and instrumental rationality, suffer an intolerable and unchanging isolation and loss of community and solidarity.

"Art" is then called upon to incarnate the countermovement to this reification. On my reading of *Aesthetic Theory* and the critical essays that preceded it, Adorno's theoretical image of "society" generates three essential propositions about art which establish its antagonistic— and, for Adorno, socially critical—role. First, art is a practice governed by the laws immanent in its traditions, its materials, and its formal aims, and therefore stands as the counterpoint in modern society to the generalized laws of commodity exchange which govern all other practices. Second, and relatedly, the pursuit of artistic aims and the making of artistic objects which spurn marketability and utility, even at the cost of their communicativeness, makes art the counterpoint of instrumental rationality: "A free society would situate itself beyond the irrationality of its false costs and the means-end rationality of utility. This ideal is encoded in art and is responsible for art's social explosiveness."[15] For these reasons art is, third, the practice in which the modern individual, whether as artist or critic, preserves an arena of activity and experience in which those aspects of subjectivity and individuation that resist the organizational power of "society" find concrete and externalizable expression.

This threefold determination of "art" by the theoretical image of "society" is already at work in the essay on lyric poetry and society. And there it gives rise to an account of modern lyric which attempts to mediate the polarity "society" and "art" with the category of language. Adorno thus conceives language as simultaneously the element in which the socially estranged voice of the poet realizes its individuality *and* the sedimented presence of the "society" from which the poem recoils:

---

[15]Ibid., p. 323.

through the individual and his [*sic*] spontaneity, objective historical forces rouse themselves within the poem, forces which are propelling a restricted and restricting social condition beyond itself to a more humane one. These forces, therefore, must belong to an all-embracing configuration and in no sense to merely naked individuality, blindly opposing itself to society.... The specific paradox belonging to the lyric poem— this subjective, personal element transforming itself into an objective one—is bound to that specific importance which poetry gives to linguistic *form*, an importance from which the primacy of language in all literature (prose forms as well) derives. For language itself has a double aspect. Through its configurations it submits to all possible stirrings of emotion, failing so little that one might almost think that it is language which first produces feeling. On the other hand, language remains the medium of concepts and ideas; and establishes our indispensable relation to generalities and hence to social reality. The most sublime lyric works, therefore, are those in which the subject, without a trace of his material being, intones in language until the voice of language itself is heard. The *subject's* forgetting himself, his abandoning himself to language as if devoting himself completely to an object—this and the direct intimacy and spontaneity of his *expression* are the same. Thus language begets and joins both poetry and society in their innermost natures.[16]

Adorno thus looks to the social character of language in search of the link between "art" and "society," which have otherwise been polarized into radical antagonists or opposites. But in fact he merely transfers his own dualism of "art" and "society" into his conception of language. To conceive the two-sidedness of language as its emotive-expressive capacity and its conceptual-generalizing capacity does not so much link the individual expressiveness of poetry to the social relations in which the poet participates as it links poetry to theory—for it is the theorist's image of "society" which ultimately, and a priori, establishes "our indispensable relation to generalities and *hence* to social reality."

What I have, by contrast, attempted to show through the interpretation of "A Poison Tree" is that the link established by language between lyric and society has to do with the interplay between one discursive practice (poetry) and another (in this instance, the moral interactions of possessive individuals). The latter is a material-social practice that organizes actual social relations. Not only does the poem not recoil from the socially constraining discourse; it in fact takes such discourse up as an organizing principle of its narrative and its metaphors. This element of "existing reality" is a condition of expressibility

---

[16]Adorno, "Lyric Poetry and Society," pp. 61–62.

for the poem itself, not something it strives to escape. The critical-utopian power of Blake's poem comes from its capacity to innovate a communicative interaction which exceeds the rules of communicative interaction that govern the social relations in which it is, and remains, situated. That innovation, which in this case was performed through the process of figuration that broke through what I called the "moral" and "amoral" readings of the poem, provokes an *alternative* interaction in the form of a reading that goes beyond the values embedded in the prevailing interactions governed by market-mediated intersubjectivity.

Poetry and Politics: "London"

I now will consider one of Blake's most overtly political poems, "London," in the context of Harold Bloom's effort, in *Poetry and Repression*, to discredit the notion that it is a political poem at all. Bloom advances this contention by means of a systematic reading of the poem which places it within the problematic of "influence" and "misreading" by which he has undertaken to reconstruct the literary tradition as endless rhetorical-psychological outbreaks of anxiety on the part of poets seeking to overcome or avert the strength of their poetic Fathers: culture as the drama of the Oedipus complex, without mothers and without daughters. While my criticism of Bloom's reading of Blake does not imply that he exemplifies Marcuse's position, it does illustrate how indissociable the "aesthetic experience" is from interpretation as a form of ideological struggle in which the political significance of art, in itself, and for us, is constantly contested.

I begin with Bloom's conclusions on "London," because they only apparently result directly from his labors of interpretation:

> Blake's poem is not a protest, not a prophetic outcry, not a vision of judgment. It is a revisionist's self-condemnation, a Jonah's desperation at knowing he is not an Ezekiel. We misread Blake's poem when we regard it as prophecy, and see it as primarily sympathy with the wretched of London, because we have canonized the poem, and because we cannot bear to read a canonical poem as being truly so altogether negative and self-destructive a text.[17]

Bloom's rhetoric here masks the fact that he is quite at peace with the disappearance of any political meaning in "London." Bloom does not

[17]Harold Bloom, *Poetry and Repression* (New Haven: Yale University Press, 1976), p. 44.

read the apocalyptic visions of Blake as the call for Paradise on Earth, secular redemption, but reads them religiously as Revelations. Thus, in an earlier, brief commentary on "London" in *The Visionary Company*, he has its images of death and blood slide quickly from the vision of possible revolt into signs of ultimate destruction and transcendent salvation, signs of a final redemption from nature and society, rather than as the hope for the transformation of society and the redemption of nature:

> The Chimney Sweeper's cry (" 'weep! 'weep!'") in notes of woe appalls the forever blackening church in the literal sense of "appall"; it makes the church pale and so exposes the church as a whited sepulcher. The hapless Soldier's sigh runs down palace walls in the blood of the victims he is compelled to slaughter. But this blood presages the king's blood, as David Erdman observes, and indeed the blood of all men when the apocalypse tears down nature as well as society.[18]

This reading already turns regicide and the possibilities of social liberation into weak forecasts of the Last Judgment, the spilling of the king's blood being but a brief diversion on the way toward the spilling of everyone's blood. The political character of the poem has, in the earlier reading, become subordinate, the mere vehicle of a metaphor whose tenor has nothing to do with human history except as theological images.

Bloom is undoubtedly right to say that "London" fits comfortably within the canon because it has been taken as expressing Blake's "sympathy with the wretched of London." Indeed, Blake does not show himself to be sympathetic in this poem. The reason, though, is that he considered Pity, Mercy, and Humility mere abstractions lived as virtues and hiding the human misery that concretely makes them possible. The political power of "London" lies elsewhere, in the very fact that it touches on the resources of revolution rather than contemplating the lot of the unfortunate. The wretched of Blake's London suffer, and what Blake hears in that suffering is the hope that the wretched themselves will become the agents of their own, very secular redemption.

> I wander thro' each charter'd street,
> Near where the charter'd Thames does flow.

---

[18]Harold Bloom, *The Visionary Company* (1961; Ithaca: Cornell University Press, 1971), pp. 46–47.

And mark in every face I meet
Marks of weakness, marks of woe.

In every cry of every Man,
In every Infants cry of fear,
In every voice: in every ban,
The mind-forg'd manacles I hear

How the Chimney-sweepers cry
Every blackning Church appalls,
And the hapless Soldiers sigh,
Runs in blood down Palace walls

But most thro' midnight streets I hear
How the youthful Harlots curse
Blasts the new-born Infants tear
And blights with plagues the Marriage hearse[19]

Structurally and semantically, the entire poem turns on the phrase "The mind-forg'd manacles I hear." It does so syntactically as well, since this is not only the main clause of the second stanza, but also serves the same function for the third, unless one takes the two subordinate clauses in the third stanza as connected to the reiterated "I hear" of the first line in stanza four. (As always in the illuminated poems, Blake's punctuation does not settle the question.) In any case, the phrase "mind-forg'd manacles," because of its position and its powerful if enigmatic meaning, has to be read in light of what comes before and after.

The common inclination to read "mind-forg'd" to mean "self-imposed" intuitively justifies itself when the phrase is looked at independent of its context. In context, the notion that all those whom Blake hears, every Man and every Infant, suffer through some fault of their own is not easily acceptable. Bloom, emphasizing that *forge* means to fabricate in the double sense of to make and to counterfeit, here by means of the *mind,* and that *manacles* means hand-cuffs and is related to *manus,* reads in the phrase the dualism of mind and body: " 'Mind-forg'd manacles' is a phrase deliberately evoking the Western metaphysical problem of dualism, since 'manacles' for 'hand-cuffs' involves *manus* or hand, and hence bodily act, which is at once made and yet feigned or counterfeited by the opposing principle of mind."[20] I will come back to the place of this in Bloom's interpretation of the poem as a whole, but it is difficult to see Blake affirming the dualism of mind and body; in the language of *The Marriage of Heaven and Hell,* "Man

[19]*The Complete Poetry and Prose,* pp. 26–27.
[20]Bloom, *Poetry and Repression,* p. 40.

has no Body distinct from his Soul for that calld body is a portion of Soul discerned by the five Senses, the chief inlets of Soul in this age."[21] I suggest staying closer, for the moment, to the essentially *auditory* aspect of the image. In every cry, voice, and ban Blake hears something more, something else, the clanging of shackles. Even before the phrase's meaning is settled, this auditory experience of hearing "mind-forg'd manacles" has pushed Blake beyond a mere perceptual receptivity to what is going on around him. In fact, the meaning of this experience will only gradually specify itself in the next two stanzas. The jarring phrase ending the second stanza exceeds and even unsettles its immediate context.

On the other hand, the subject has from the first lines of the poem described himself as moving counter to the city: "I *wander* thro' each *charter'd* street, Near where the *charter'd* Thames does flow." To wander in city streets that are mapped, officially sanctioned and named, and so on, is more than a paradox. It is a gesture of opposition, which as yet has no content beyond a kind of identification with the natural against the processes of commercialization and civic organization; Blake thus identifies his own movement with that of the river, which *flows* despite being *charter'd* in the sense of divided up for purposes of commerce and industry. He continues:

> And mark in every face I meet
> Marks of weakness, marks of woe.

The reiteration of the word *mark* nuances each instance in a distinct way. "Marks of weakness" suggests signs or symptoms that betray weakness, whereas the "marks of woe," an image of the very crevices and lines in the people's faces, suggests that the pain of existence has been inflicted, indeed gouged on the victims. There is, then, in these two uses of 'marks' an ambivalence between viewing the people's passivity as submissiveness or as victimization.

That Blake himself *marks* in every face these marks of weakness, marks of woe, has the sense of noticing or, more strongly, taking note of. This first perception is itself not merely passive, though it is not quite active either. More important, though, the distinctive nuance of this first "mark" differentiates Blake from those he sees; their sheer passivity, whether from lack of courage or excess of pain, contrasts

---

[21]*The Complete Poetry and Prose*, p. 34.

with Blake's own reflective perception. This slight differentiation of the wandering poet from the suffering populace then shifts in the second stanza to what is apparently a radical distinction between the people and Blake, whose imaginative hearing now discerns self-imposed chains in every cry of child'or adult. It is as though Blake has been suddenly and dramatically estranged from the entire population of London. But it is precisely the excess of meaning in the phrase "mind-forg'd manacles" which keeps this moment of estrangement from becoming permanent, let alone a celebration of the poet's superior insight.

My description of the first two stanzas gives them a narrative quality, as though each line marks a shift or development in the poet's relation to the city. I think this is the case in "London," which distinguishes it from most of Blake's shorter lyrics. Various elements indicate such a narrative structure: the fact that Blake is wandering through the city, that the first two stanzas involve the generalization of everyone and everything, while the last two specify the chimney-sweeper, the soldier, and the harlot, and finally that the last stanza emphatically places itself at midnight whereas the events of the earlier stanzas are daytime occurrences. The poem does not, in other words, articulate a single situation or a fixed relation between Blake and the city's populace; rather, the poem moves, with drastic transformations, through a series of such relations. At each moment in this development, Blake hears something more and something different.

The last two stanzas give the pivotal "mind-forg'd manacles" an altogether new meaning—a meaning that at the same time reverses Blake's relation to the voices of suffering that he hears. There appear three pairings of a dispossessed individual and a social institution: the chimney-sweeper and the church, the soldier and the state, the prostitute and marriage. Human beings suffer from self-imposed chains in the sense that the constraining institutions of church, state, and marriage are all human constructs, the products of the collective actions of human beings. But these human constructs, having attained their separate existence as objective forces in social life, confront every individual, every separated human being, as something already there, a reality greater and more powerful than oneself and the agent of one's suffering. This reversal whereby human activity becomes passivity—the subject turned into an object—while the products of activity themselves become agents—the object turned into a subject—Marx a few decades later would call alienation. Blake here calls it "the mind-forg'd manacles," and it is what he means elsewhere by *abstraction*.

In the final two stanzas Blake again hears—the cry, the sigh, and the curse—, but now with a sense that these manifestations of suffering have the active power to condemn and protest:

> I hear
>
> How the Chimney-sweepers cry
> Every blackning Church appalls,
> And the hapless Soldiers sigh,
> Runs in blood down Palace walls
>
> But most thro' midnight streets I hear
> How the youthful Harlots curse
> Blasts the new-born Infants tear
> And blights with plagues the Marriage hearse

David Erdman, whose *Blake: Prophet against Empire* stands as the most significant reading of Blake within the political culture and ideological tendencies of the late eighteenth century, has insisted on the politically charged nature of the chimney-sweeper's cry, the soldier's sigh, and the harlot's curse. Lord Stanhope, protesting the presence of Prussian soldiers in England to ensure the repressive measures ("every ban") of Pitt and the king, had

> urged citizens to arm and to fraternize with their fellow countrymen, the British common soldiers. The latter are Blake's "hapless Soldiers" whose "sigh Runs in blood down Palace walls"—and whose frequently exhibited inclination in 1792–1793 to turn from grumbling to mutiny is not taken into account by those who interpret the blood as the soldier's own and who overlook the potentially forceful meaning of "sigh" in eighteenth century diction. In the structure of the poem the soldier's utterance that puts blood on palace walls is parallel to the harlot's curse that blasts and blights. And Blake would have known the curses that were often chalked or painted on the royal walls. . . . A number of cognate passages in which Blake mentions blood on palace walls indicate that the blood is an apocalyptic omen of mutiny and regicide.[22]

The dialectic of poetry and politics is a dialectic of speaking and hearing. At first, the suffering voices were all one, the undifferentiated chorus of every Man's and every Infant's cry, so that Blake's poetic speaking emerges as a virtual condemnation of suffering humanity, as

---

[22]David V. Erdman, *Blake: Prophet against Empire*, 3d rev. ed. (Princeton: Princeton University Press, 1977), pp. 278–279.

though it lacks the imagination and energy that set the poet himself against the existing society. This moment in the process is at once concluded and exceeded in the hearing of "mind-forg'd manacles." Blake, in other words, discovers the possibility of poetic speaking in his estrangement from passive suffering. In the final stanzas, however, this estrangement of the poet finds a new relation to the suffering voices because they can now be heard as raised against the people's own alienation, against the institutional forms which are the inhuman creations of humanity.

Poetic imagination is not thereby identical with popular political consciousness. Their interaction is left open in this poem, as it historically must be. "London," like "A Poison Tree" in a different way, points toward a future that would radically alter its own relation to reality. The poetic imagination, for Blake, is prophetic in the sense that its action, its praxis, anticipates the possibility of the political explosion of the imagination as a material, popular force. That possibility emerges within the inner logic of the poem itself; the incipient voices of suffering and revolt have, in the course of the poem's development, altered the meaning of its most volatile image: the "mind-forg'd manacles" are finally heard clanging in rebellion.

One of the Proverbs of Hell thematically expresses the dynamic of the last stanza of "London": *Prisons are built with stones of Law, Brothels with bricks of Religion.* Blake's concept of *contraries* is often ambiguous for the reason that it intertwines what I will call historical and eternal contraries. Critics like Bloom consistently endeavor to transform Blake's historical contraries into eternal contraries. My reading of "London" sees the particularizing reference to chimney-sweeper, soldier, and harlot as a process of concretization which searches for the dynamic of institutions in the social existence of the oppressed— the child laborer, the lower-class man pressed into the military service of the state, and a woman constrained to sell her sexuality as a commodity. Bloom goes in the opposite direction. Just as he reduces the possibility of the bloody rebellion of the common soldier to a mere symbolic forecast of ultimate Revelation, so too he does not consider the harlot as a harlot, for she must be Nature: "I want to reaffirm my own earlier interpretation [that is, in *The Visionary Company*] of the Harlot here as Blake's perpetually youthful Harlot, Nature, *not* the human female, but the natural element of the human, male or female."[23] Bloom likewise spurns the sense of the harlot's curse as her speaking

[23]Bloom, *Poetry and Repression*, p. 43.

and, explicitly rejecting the usual but not very interesting reading of "curse" as venereal disease, proposes that it must mean menstruation: "The harlot's curse is not, as various interpreters have said, venereal disease, but is indeed what 'curse' came to mean in the vernacular after Blake and still means now: menstruation, the natural cycle in the human female."[24] Now, if the harlot is not a woman but Nature or the natural element of human beings and if her curse is menstruation or a sheer natural fact, then the poem's final stanza has nothing to do with the historical experience of the family, morality, and prostitution but expresses how "every natural fact equals every other natural fact," since the curse merely "blasts or scatters another natural fact, the tearlessness of the new-born infant."[25] In other words, Blake ends the poem saying menstruation equals birth equals marriage, since in Bloom's view Blake considers marriage to be essentially the institutionalization of a natural fact. In this interpretation, the poem abjectly renounces the natural element of human existence as such. There is then no institutional struggle, no woman's suffering and protest, no historical contraries; there are only eternal contraries.

Blake's proverb—"Prisons are built with stones of Law, Brothels with bricks of Religion"—helps keep us to the political-poetic dialectic of the final stanza:

> But most thro' midnight streets I hear
> How the youthful Harlots curse
> Blasts the new-born Infants tear
> And blights with plagues the Marriage hearse

Marriage and prostitution are locked together as contraries in the sense that without marriage, there would be no prostitution. Being a harlot is thus not a natural state of being, but a social condition of being created by the repressive force of its opposite, the institution of marriage. In turn, the harlot's suffering—which I take to be specified here as her bastard child, though Blake scholars, including Bloom, seem generally to believe that the infant is the child of the harlot's customer and his wife, as if Blake might have assumed that youthful prostitutes transmit diseases but don't have babies—then gives itself voice as the denunciation of that which created it: the Marriage hearse. Otherwise one is left with the very unBlakean *contresens* that prostitution is evil

[24]Ibid., pp. 39–40.
[25]Ibid., p. 43.

because it destroys marriage, whereas the whole power of the poem rests on the recognition that marriage creates prostitution. Out of the dynamic of the harlot's voice Blake hears that marriage, in its morality and its restraint on desire, is a hearse—the conveyor of dead bodies. Blake's association with the early development of feminism around Mary Wollstonecraft's *Vindication of the Rights of Woman* shows in the poem's ending, where a woman's voice becomes rebellious, articulate, cursing. The poem comes to anticipate—in this interaction of suffering and imagination, passivity and revolt, being marked and speaking—the destruction of church, state, and marriage by those whom these "mind-forg'd manacles" create as victims, workers and women. The contraries of the last two stanzas are precisely not eternal, but are the historical contraries of specific institutions and human beings. The very articulation of the poem involves the discovery that these contraries have been historically constructed; it also foretells a process in which the dehumanized objects of the institutions will become the human subjects who destroy those institutions.

The interpretation I have proposed contrasts with Bloom's in construing "London" to be a thoroughly political poem, one which repudiates paternalistic sympathy and seeks the resources of political solidarity and rebellion, and which manifests, through its structure and syntax, a changing, still unsettled relation between poet and populace, poetic imagination and political consciousness. My interpretation also, therefore, contrasts with E. P. Thompson's exactingly historicist reading of the poem. By "historicist" I mean an interpretation developed from the assumption that the poem's meaning is ultimately determined, and delimited, by the historical context in which Blake wrote. Thompson's historicism both illuminates and obscures "London."

Thompson first of all takes the political and intellectual culture in which Blake actively participated as the informing context of the poem. That orientation yields a rich and clarifying approach to several of the poem's words, images, and allusions. Thompson argues, for example, that the negative connotations that Blake gives the word "charter'd" place the poem within the political debate between Edmund Burke and Thomas Paine. For Burke, the chartered rights of the English were part of an "entitled inheritance" granted by the king and maintained through traditions and customs. Paine challenged Burke's traditionalism on the grounds that rights which someone had the power to grant or withhold by means of charter were not rights at all, but privileges from which some were excluded even as others were included. Drawing on various of Paine's phrases to gloss Blake's vocabulary, Thompson quite persuasively argues that Blake, who "shared much of Paine's political outlook . . . , thus chose 'charter'd' out of the biggest political argument that was agitating Britain in 1791–3, and he chose it with that irony which inverted the rhetoric of Burke and asserted the definitions of 'exclusion,' the annulling of rights, 'negative operation' and 'giving, selling, and buying freedom.' "[26]

Thompson then extends his historicist premise. He embraces the notion that the poem's meaning is ultimately limited to just those significations that fall within the horizon of expectations of Blake's contemporaries and, more specifically, of his fellow participants in radical Dissent in the 1790s. The acceptable range of meaning becomes that which the poem ostensibly would have communicated to those whose intellectual, cultural, and political formation most closely resembled Blake's own. Thompson, for example, dismisses the claim made by Bloom and others that "London" alludes to a story in Ezekiel and associates the poem, instead, with certain passages in Revelation on the grounds that those associations would have more likely occurred to Blake's "contemporaries":

> There is, further, the question of what response the word "mark" is most likely to have called up among Blake's contemporaries. I assert that the allusions called first to mind will have been either to the "mark of Cain" (Genesis iv.5) or to the "mark of the beast" in Revelation [xiii.16–17]. And the more radical the audience, the more preoccupied it will have been with the second. For generations radical Dissent had sermonized and pamphleteered against the beast (Antichrist) who had his servitors "which worshipped his image" (Revelation xvi.2): social radicalism equated these with usurers, with the rich, with those successful in buying and selling.[27]

In Thompson's specific argument the reference to buying and selling in Revelation 13 is crucial:

> And he causeth all, both small and great, rich and poor, free and bond, to receive the mark in their right hand, or in their foreheads:
> And that no man might buy or sell, save he that had the mark, or the name of the beast, or the number of his name.

[26]E. P. Thompson, " 'London,' " in Michael Phillips, ed., *Interpreting Blake* (Cambridge: Cambridge University Press, 1979), p. 10.
[27]Ibid., pp. 12–13.

The potential relevance of this passage to the poem is not in dispute. And it seems plausible enough to say that Blake's fellow radicals may have associated the first stanza's uses of "mark" with the biblical "mark of the beast" and, further, sensed a critical attitude toward commerce in the allusion. However, the specific role that this line of interpretation plays for Thompson is questionable. For it is used to exclude other lines of interpretation, specifically those which evoke the passage from Ezekiel (which I will discuss on their own terms in a moment). The axiom implicit in Thompson's method requires that proposed meanings be rejected if they do not fulfill two conditions: on the one hand, they would have to resonate with the suppositions and expectations of the work's original audience, and, on the other, they would have to contribute to the semantic unity of the work.

With the appeal to semantic unity Thompson completes his historicist assumptions. He supposes that the poem will have an underlying semantic unity—a "symbolic organization" commensurate with the meanings that the poem's contemporaries would have found decipherable and acceptable. It is within this methodological framework that Thompson summarizes his interpretation of "London," emphasizing only those associations and resonances which contribute to the theme of buying and selling:

> Blake's "London" . . . is seen, or suffered, from within, by a Londoner. And what is unusual about *this* image of the-human-condition-as-hell is that it offers the city as a unitary experience and not as a theatre of discrete episodes. For this to be so, there must be an ulterior symbolic organization behind the literal organization of this street-cry following upon that. . . . The tone of compassion falls upon those who are in hell, the sufferers; but the tone of indignation falls upon the institutions of repression—mind-forg'd manacles, blackning Church, Palace, Marriage hearse. And the symbolic organization is within the clearly conceived and developing logic of market relations. Blake does not only list symptoms: within the developing imagery which unites the poem he also discloses their cause. From the first introduction of "charter'd" he never loses hold of the image of buying and selling although these words themselves are never used. "Charter'd" both grants from on high and licenses and it limits and excludes; if we recall Paine it is a "selling and buying" of freedom. What are bought and sold in "London" are not only goods and services but human values, affections, and vitalities. From freedom we move (with "mark") to a race marked by buying and selling, the worshippers of the beast and his image. Then we move through these values in ascendant scale: goods are bought and sold (street-cries), child-

hood (the chimney-sweep), human life (the soldier), and, in the final verse, youth, beauty, and love, the source of life, is bought and sold in the figure of the diseased harlot who, herself, is only the other side of the "Marriage hearse." In a series of literal, unified images of great power Blake compresses an indictment of the acquisitive ethic, endorsed by the institutions of the State, which divides man from man [*sic*], brings him into mental bondage, destroys the sources of joy, and brings, as its consequence blindness and death. And it is now evident why the final verse is no afterthought but appeared to Blake as the necessary conclusion to the poem. . . . [T]he harlot not only provides a culminating symbol of the reification of values, she is also a point of conjunction with the parallel imagery of religious mystification and oppression: for if this is Babylon, then the harlot is Babylon's whore who brought about the city's fall "because she made all nations drink of the wine of the wrath of her fornication." For English radical Dissent in the eighteenth century, the whore of Babylon was not only the "scarlet woman" of Rome, but also *all* Erastianism, all compromise between things spiritual and the temporal powers of the State, and hence, very specifically, that extraordinary "Erastian" formation, the Church of England. . . . Hence the harlot is able to unite in a single nexus the imagery of market relations and the imagery of ideological domination by the agency of a State Church, prostituted to the occasions of temporal power.[28]

How then do this interpretation and the one I have advanced actually differ, especially in light of several shared emphases? Thompson treats "London" as a sequence of images all of which can be deciphered with reference to a common element; the images are symbolically associated—some very directly, others more or less obliquely—with the single theme of buying and selling. The poem thus becomes a unified statement about social conditions in London. Rather than a statement about social conditions, the poem in my reading is about the political relation between poet and populace, and it does not in fact make a statement so much as it narrates ongoing and unfinished changes in that relation. Second, the poem's informing trope is not buying and selling but rather "mind-forg'd manacles." In contrast to a sequence of semantically equivalent images, I discern within the informing trope an interaction among incommensurate meanings. The first two stanzas give "mind-forg'd manacles" the meaning of the self-imposed chains of a populace that passively and slavishly accepts restrictions and prohibitions,

---

[28]Ibid., pp. 21–23. For an extension of Thompson's approach to "London," and a thorough critical comparison of Thompson and Bloom, see Michael Ferber, " 'London' and Its Politics," *ELH* 48 (1981), 310–338.

whereas the last two stanzas recast "mind-forg'd manacles" into a trope of the alienating force of oppressive social institutions: at the level of imagery, Blake first hears "mind-forg'd manacles" as sounds of enslavement and submission, then as sounds of rebellion and uprising. The difference between the two readings comes down to opposing constructions not only of the poem's "message" but, more important, of the kind of utterance it actually is: a semantically unified statement versus a semantically shifting, syntactically fractured narrative; in short, a well-wrought poem versus a "text."

And, indeed, Thompson's rejection of the textuality of "London" fits with his restricted sense of its intertextuality. The controversy over the pertinence of Revelation and of Ezekiel is, for Thompson, settled by the fact that the buying and selling motif associated with the "mark of the beast" would have more readily come to mind among contemporary radicals and also places the allusion within the poem's symbolic grid. The Ezekiel reference Thompson tendentiously dismisses as mere verbal similarity. Both the argument for Revelation and that against Ezekiel stem from the tacit assumption that a biblical allusion will be evoked only if it is consonant with Blake's own meanings. Such an expectation is at the very least at odds with Blake's notion of "corrosive" writing and "diabolical" readings which suggests an actively negative or antagonistic relation to the Bible. Bloom identifies just such an intertextual antagonism between "London" and the ninth chapter of Ezekiel. By reexamining his argument, we can get beyond the restrictive, one-dimensional transmission of meanings from text to text and at the same time make good our challenge to Bloom's construction of intertextuality as cultural belatedness and agonized misreading.

Ezekiel tells of his vision of God calling forth six men of the city of Jerusalem and commanding them to slay the inhabitants without mercy for their wickedness. A seventh man, "with a writer's inkhorn by his side," accompanies them. The connection with "London" is reinforced, as Bloom points out, by the occurrence in the biblical passage of the rhyme *sigh* and *cry* as in the poem's third stanza:

> And the glory of God of Israel was gone up from the cherub, whereupon he was, to the threshold of the house. And he called to the man clothed with linen, which had the writer's inkhorn by his side:
> And the Lord said unto him, "Go through the midst of the city, through the midst of Jerusalem, and set a mark upon the foreheads of the men that sigh and that cry for all the abominations that be done in the midst thereof."

> And to the others [the six men, each with "a slaughter weapon in his
> hand"] he said in mine hearing, "Go ye after him through the city, and
> smite: let not your eye spare, neither have ye pity:
> Slay utterly old and young, both maids, and little children, and women:
> but come not near any man upon whom is the mark; and begin at my
> sanctuary." Then they began at the ancient men which were before the
> house.

That "London" is complexly related to this passage from the Old
Testament is beyond doubt. The question is how Blake's writing enters
into an intertextual or dialogical relation to the precursor text. Bloom
begins with an assumption which, by the time he writes *Poetry and
Repression,* has become axiomatic in his criticism: the precursor-text
will be stronger than its rewriting and will induce a virtually unmas-
terable anxiety on the part of the later or "belated" poet, who has
missed all opportunity of being an original voice. Thus, Bloom immediately decides that the Blake of "London" wishes he could be
Ezekiel. Of the wandering "I" of the poem, he asks:

> Is it an Ezekiel-like prophet, or someone whose role and function are
> altogether different? To "wander" is to have no destination and no
> purpose. A biblical prophet may wander when he is cast out into the
> desert, when his voice becomes a voice in the wilderness, but he does
> not wander when he goes through the midst of the city, through the
> midst of Jerusalem the City of God. There, his inspired voice always has
> purpose, and his inspired feet always have a destination. Blake knew all
> this, and knew it with a knowing beyond our knowing. When he begins
> by saying that he *wanders* in London, his Jerusalem, his City of God,
> then he begins also by saying "I am not Ezekiel, I am not a prophet, I
> am too fearful to be the prophet I ought to be, *I am hid.*"[29]

In Bloom's conception of cultural and literary history, the past always
dominates the present because every poet supposedly wants his present,
the moment of his creativity, to be without precedent and radically
free from the past. Since this wish is purely imaginary, the Father will
always weigh heavily upon the Son. Thus, if "London" is written out
of a reading of Ezekiel, it must mean that Blake wants to be Ezekiel,
and that since he cannot he will be doomed to struggle unsuccessfully
for his own identity against this influence.

An opposing sense of intertextuality allows us to see in the dialogue

---

[29]Bloom, *Poetry and Repression,* p. 37.

between texts written in different historical and social conditions a genuine measuring of just those historical and social differences. "London" is a dialogical rewriting of Ezekiel and actively differentiates itself from a prophetic mode that listens to the voice of God, even as God himself is willfully deaf, as in the eighth chapter from which Bloom quotes: "Therefore will I," God warns, "also deal in fury; Mine eyes shall not spare, neither will I have pity; and though they cry in Mine ears with a loud voice, yet I will not hear them." Blake does hear, and it is through this hearing of the voices of suffering that his poetic voice develops through the course of the poem and acquires its prophetic power—which is necessarily unlike that of Ezekiel. Prophecy becomes agitation, vision participates in the dialectic of social struggles, and the imagination discovers itself to be an actual and potential element of political consciousness.

It is interesting that Bloom summarily dismisses any analogy between Blake and the man with the inkhorn: "There are six angels of destruction, with only Gabriel (according to the Talmud) armed with the inkhorn that will spare the righteous. Unlike Gabriel, Blake does not necessarily set a mark, since his 'mark in every face I meet,' primarily is intransitive, meaning 'remark' or 'observe.' "[30] The reasons for connecting the two figures, beside the fact that both are writers, can be seen in *The Marriage of Heaven and Hell*. In a passage in which Blake is attempting to articulate his own historical role by identifying with, yet differentiating himself from, Isaiah and Ezekiel, he announces that the modern apocalypse will take the form of an expansion of human possibilities and the human senses, and that his own place in this process is through the practice of a demonic writing:

> The ancient tradition that the world will be consumed in fire at the end of six thousand years is true. as I have heard from Hell. . . .
> This will come to pass by an improvement of sensual enjoyment.
> But first the notion that man has a body distinct from his soul, is to be expunged; this I shall do, by printing in the infernal method, by corrosives, which in Hell are salutary and medicinal, melting apparent surfaces away, and displaying the infinite which was hid.[31]

"London" shows the poet himself coming to see, or hear, what is hidden beneath the still fixed contraries of victimizing institutions and victim-

<hr>

[30]Ibid., p. 41.
[31]*The Complete Poetry and Prose*, p. 39.

ized human beings. He differs from the man with the inkhorn in that he goes through the city not in order to separate out the righteous but to find the resources of his own infernal writing in the concrete experience of London's population itself. Bloom can conjure away the connection between poetry and society, imagination and secular redemption, because he places the poem within a cultural framework that arbitrarily obliterates the difference between Ezekiel's Jerusalem and Blake's London; the latter's inhabitants are not even worthy of slaughter or salvation: "In the opening dialectic of presence and absence, precisely what is absent is prophetic direction and prophetic purpose"—Bloom's reading denies that these could be discovered in the course of the poem's own interaction with reality—; "what is present are chartering and marks. So voice is absent, and only demonic writing is present. Blake's defensive reaction-formation to the call he cannot answer is to be a wanderer, and to mark passively rather than mark actively with the *taws* [marks] of righteousness and wickedness, life and death. But righteousness and wickedness are alike absent; present only are weakness and woe, neither of which merits a *taw*, whether of ink or blood."[32] In Bloom's reading, then, which is not just a reading of the poem but of history, Blake's tribe is a weak parody of Ezekiel's, and so Blake can speak only a dejected self-condemnation.

Integrated into the very mode of Bloom's hermeneutical practice is a thoroughgoing obliteration of the interaction of poetry and society, which is displaced by an interaction between the poem and its cultural precursor. The sheer antecedence of the precursor twists the belated poem into a tortured rejection of itself and its world. It is this vision of history and culture that allows Bloom's various interpretations of "London" to transform its symbols of revolt into weak signs of the Last Judgment, its harlot into repudiated Nature, and its political-prophetic voice into self-abuse. In the process, our own cultural experience is suspended between the original texts of the tradition and a Last Judgment which, for Bloom, is more fictive or poetic than religious anyway. Bloom effaces the historical specificity of Ezekiel's prophetic mode as well as Blake's, and he denies modern prophecy a future. The prophetic imagination becomes significant only insofar as it is, on the one hand, a belated version of its precursor, and, on the other, looks forward to a purely illusory Redemption. The only history

[32]Bloom, *Poetry and Repression*, p. 41.

is the history of poetry severed from its tribal and social reality and disengaged from its own complex temporality.

Blake's poetry in fact engages the cultural past as part of its concrete struggle against the present for the future. I have argued that in "A Poison Tree" and "London" the utopian dimension of poetry is enacted in poetic speaking as the concrete struggle between the conditions of the poet's speech and the possibilities of speech. Each of these poems enacts the hope for conditions of existence and experience which would make its own speaking unnecessary. "A Poison Tree" points to a future in which its own story and its mode of telling would no longer be possible. And "London," through its internal development, opens onto new possibilities in the relation between the poetic imagination and popular consciousness. The inner logic of Blake's writing negates the fetishization of the poem as a monument, as an expression separated from time and change.

By the same token, simply "placing" Blake "in his own time" would forget that the future is an indispensable dimension of his poetic dialogue with time and history. When Marx contrasted what he considered the bourgeois revolutions of the eighteenth century with what he hoped from proletarian revolution in the nineteenth, he saw in each a specific disharmony of form and content:

> The social revolution of the nineteenth century cannot draw its poetry from the past, but only from the future. It cannot begin with itself before it has stripped off all superstition in regard to the past. Earlier revolutions required recollections of past world history in order to drug themselves concerning their own content. In order to arrive at its own content, the revolution of the nineteenth century must let the dead bury their dead. There the phrase goes beyond the content; here the content goes beyond the phrase.[33]

Blake has to be "placed" *between* the opening of the democratic revolution in 1789 and the actual development of capitalist society since. Historically he is a poet of the American and French Revolutions, but what defines his imagination is that, unlike the revolutions that stirred it, it did not stop, rigidifying the forms of freedom and destroying the content of freedom. Blake was *not* of his time; his poetry demands a future that capitalist society inhibits and resists. I conclude with this

[33]Karl Marx, *The Eighteenth Brumaire of Louis Bonaparte* (New York: International Publishers, 1963), p. 18.

juxtaposition of Blake and Marx not in order to place Blake within Marx's frame of reference but to resituate Marx within a *political* and *cultural* process that includes, as a productive and prophetic moment, the poetry of Blake. This becomes all the more necessary in our own historical moment in the twentieth century. What for Blake was a future that could free him from his present has disappeared within the fabric of our own political and cultural inheritance. We look back at Blake across a wide gap. We live the reality that exists because the revolutions Blake and Marx anticipated did not occur. We are more the heirs of Blake's restraining reality than of his imagined future. To put it another way, his poetry still speaks to us because we have not been freed to hear it.

Part Three

CULTURE AND PSYCHOANALYSIS

5

The Social Constitution
of Subjectivity

"Culture" and "Civilization" in Psychoanalysis

With uncharacteristic vehemence, Freud declared, "I scorn to distinguish between culture and civilization." Writing in 1927, he may well
have been aiming his polemical tone at the stirrings of fascist ideology
with its opposition between the Germanic soul and emotion (*Kultur*)
and mere manners, codes, and rationality (*Zivilisation*). Or he may
have been aiming at a whole tradition, reaching back to Schiller and
Kant, in which culture was opposed to civilization as inwardness to
behavior.[1] In either case, Freud's attitude signals the degree to which
he considered culture to involve the whole of human experience and
activity, a continuum along which psychoanalysis does not hesitate to
link the everyday and the monumental. Indeed, what often appears to
literary scholars, for example, as Freud's reductive understanding of
art and literature derives from this tendency to view the entire range
of symbolic interactions and affective connections as elements in a
continuum of culturally significant, socially situated processes. On the
other hand, the complete context of Freud's remark discloses the need
for carrying out a critique of the psychoanalytic theory of subjectivity,
even as we place it at the center of the critical theory of culture:

---

[1]On the significance of the opposition between "culture" and "civilization" in modern
German intellectual life, see Norbert Elias, *The History of Manners: The Civilizing
Process,* vol. 1, trans. Edmund Jephcott (New York: Pantheon, 1982), pp. 1–34.

Human civilization, by which I mean all those respects in which human life has raised itself above animal status and differs from the life of beasts—and I scorn to distinguish between culture and civilization—, presents, as we know, two aspects to the observer. It includes on the one hand all the knowledge and capacity that men [sic] have acquired in order to control the forces of nature and extract its wealth for the satisfaction of human needs, and, on the other hand, all the regulations necessary in order to adjust the relations of men to one another and especially the distribution of the available wealth. The two trends of civilization are not independent of each other: firstly, because the mutual relations of men are profoundly influenced by the amount of instinctual satisfaction which the existing wealth makes possible; secondly, because an individual man can himself come to function as wealth in relation to another one, in so far as the other person makes use of his capacity for work, or chooses him as a sexual object; and thirdly, moreover, because every individual is virtually an enemy of civilization, though civilization is supposed to be an object of universal human interest. It is remarkable that, little as men are able to live in isolation, they should nevertheless feel as a heavy burden the sacrifices which civilization expects of them to make a communal life possible.[2]

Marxist commentaries on Freud, from Marcuse's *Eros and Civilization* to Michael Schneider's *Neurosis and Civilization*,[3] have at once admired the subtlety of this description of the social and cultural totality and been dismayed by its lack of any historical specification, its inability to see that each set of relations identified, from the domination of nature to the domination of human beings by other human beings, has distinctive forms in the different eras of history, and its disregard for the particular way in which the capitalist mode of production isolates individuals and creates special conflicts between the "individual" and "society."

Concerned with the same set of uncritical underpinnings in psychoanalysis, I will approach a critique of Freud from a different direction. The importance of Jacques Lacan's "return to Freud" lies in its transformation of the psychoanalytic problematic into a theory of subjectivity as it is constituted by and through language. It is this discovery

---

[2]Sigmund Freud, *The Future of an Illusion*, in *The Standard Edition of the Complete Psychological Works*, ed. and trans. James Strachey et al. (London: Hogarth, 1953–1974), XXI, 5–6.

[3]Herbert Marcuse, *Eros and Civilization: A Philosophical Inquiry into Freud* (New York: Vintage, 1962); and Michael Schneider, *Neurosis and Civilization: A Marxist/Freudian Synthesis*, trans. Michael Roloff (New York: Seabury, 1975).

of the place of speaking and of the social character of communication in general that renews the possibility for psychoanalysis to contribute to a cultural theory that can in fact be integral to the critical theory of society. Lacan too scorns to distinguish culture and civilization, but in the sense that he defines culture as the social bond, as that which ties the subject to the community, though not in the manner of an organism's integration into an environment. "I designate [the social bond] with the term discourse, because there is no other way to designate it once one sees that the social bond is established only in anchoring itself in the manner that language is situated and imprinted... on .the speaking being."[4] The question of culture must be grasped as the relation of the speaking being to the discourses that constitute the social bond. At the same time, the immanent critique of psychoanalysis will require the recognition that neither the constitution of the subject nor the institutions of discourse are separate from forms of domination which have evolved historically.

Speech as Play

The need for a theory of the processes whereby the subject is constituted by language and becomes self-constituting through language has attained an urgency in the contemporary world. This issue intervenes in a vast array of philosophical, social, and political contexts. The search for a universal grammer or a universal pragmatics of human communication has gone hand in hand with the widespread strain, in the cybernetic society, on the connections between social experience and communication, collective action and language. It is precisely because psychoanalysis has engaged the modern individual in his or her most abject states of isolation and helplessness that it can, when read against the grain of many of its most basic concepts, yield a vision of the conditions of self-activity.

I propose, then, to pursue an immanent critique of psychoanalysis in order to draw from it the bases of a socially grounded theory of subjectivity. I begin with an example of Freud's interpretation of the most elementary level of the issue: namely, childhood and children's play, a domain that remains a privileged field of psychoanalytic investigation. Without accepting the whole framework of Huizinga's notion of the "play element in culture," I believe that it is pertinent to make

[4]Jacques Lacan, *Le séminaire, Livre XX: Encore* (Paris: Seuil, 1975), p. 51.

play, which is inseparable from the human being's earliest experiences of speech, a reference point in this inquiry into the social and subjective conditions of cultural creation.

Freud's famous discussion in *Beyond the Pleasure Principle* of the game played by his grandson as he first acquired a basic phonemic and semantic opposition of his language, *fort! da!*, "gone," "there," broaches a kind of experiential knot in which language, play, desire, and—as I will argue—institutions are intertwined. Freud's text, whose conclusions I will dispute, exemplifies a quality that Lacan, in another context, compared to the procedures of a good archaeologist: "he leaves the work of the excavation in place—such that, even if the dig is not completed, we can know what the unearthed objects mean."[5]

The grandson's game is described as follows:

This good little boy, however, had an occasional disturbing habit of taking any small objects he could get hold of and throwing them away from him into a corner, under the bed, and so on, so that hunting for his toys and picking them up was often quite a business. As he did this he gave vent to a loud, long-drawn out "o-o-o-o," accompanied by an expression of interest and satisfaction. His mother and the writer of the present account were agreed in thinking that this was not a mere interjection but represented the German word *"fort"* ["gone"]. I eventually realized that it was a game and that the only use he made of any of his toys was to play "gone" with them. One day I made an observation which confirmed my view. The child had a wooden reel with a piece of string tied round it. It never occurred to him to pull it along the floor behind him, for instance, and play at its being a carriage. What he did was to hold the reel by the string and very skilfully throw it over the edge of his curtained cot, so that it disappeared into it, at the same time uttering his expressive "o-o-o-o." He then pulled the reel out of the cot again by the string and hailed its reappearance with a joyful *"da"* ["there"]. This then was the complete game—disappearance and return.[6]

Freud easily relates the form of the game to the child's disciplined acceptance of his mother's regular departures from the house. The game "was related to the child's great cultural achievement—the instinctual renunciation (that is, the renunciation of instinctual satisfaction) which he made in allowing his mother to go away without protesting" (p. 15). The theoretical import of this relation between libidinal renun-

[5]Jacques Lacan, *Les quatre concepts fondamentaux de la psychanalyse: Le séminaire, Livre XI* (Paris: Seuil, 1973), p. 166.
[6]Freud, *Beyond the Pleasure Principle, S.E.* XVIII, 14–15. Hereafter cited in the text.

ciation and play Freud poses as a question: "How then does his repetition of this distressing experience [the mother's leaving] as a game
fit in with the pleasure principle?" (p. 15).

Freud first considers the possibility that, since the game ends by
reenacting the mother's return, it is a straightforward manifestation of
the pleasure principle. This he immediately rejects because "the first
act, that of departure, was staged as a game in itself and far more
frequently than the episode in its entirety, with its pleasurable ending"
(p. 16).

Two interpretations are then proposed which Freud retains, though
he carefully subordinates the first of these to the second. At a first level,
the game provides the subject with "mastery" over an unpleasant situation. He is transformed from the passive recipient of another's action,
which he finds painful, into the active agent of a fantasy which repeats
this situation. At a second level, the game expresses the child's wish
for revenge. Here another reversal occurs. The child dominates rather
than being dominated, gives pain rather than receiving pain: "Throwing
away the object so that it was 'gone' might satisfy an impulse of the
child's, which was suppressed in his actual life, to revenge himself on
his mother for going away from him. In that case it would have a
defiant meaning: 'All right, then go away! I don't need you. I'm sending
you away myself' " (p. 16). At two moments in his short commentary,
Freud insists on the primacy of revenge in relation to mastery. This
argument, part of the polemic of *Beyond the Pleasure Principle* as a
whole, disputes the claim that there exists an independent instinct of
mastery. Freud believes that the presence of the wish for revenge is
what gives active mastery through repetition its libidinal support. For
this very reason, however, the interpretation of the game leads to a
recognition of the dominance of the pleasure principle. Consequently,
this carefully worked out example remains indecisive for the book's
overall argument. It has not clearly involved something *beyond* the
pleasure principle.

What Freud considers a reversal from passivity to activity in the
child's relation to the mother in fact encompasses two completely different forms of intersubjectivity. At first the child is wholly dependent
on the mother's love for the satisfaction of his vital needs. He not only
attains from her all satisfactions but also suffers the withholding or
neglect of such satisfactions. He has, Freud tells us, been a "good boy"
who has responded to parental discipline, "and above all, he never
cried when his mother left him for a few hours" (p. 14).

Freud's grandson's assumption of speech in his game is not simple "mastery." The game has two quite distinct aspects. The child's articulation of the phonematic opposition, "o-o-o-o"/"da," marks his entry into speech, his emergence, as a subject who speaks, into the symbolic field around him. "The child," writes Lacan in one of his commentaries on this episode, "begins to involve himself in the system of the concrete discourse of his surroundings by reproducing, more or less approximally, in his *Fort!* and his *Da!*, the vocables he receives from it."[7] There is, however, a moment anterior to this one: namely, the emergence of the spool, which is not so much a symbol of the mother as the symbolization that absents her. As Lacan argues in many different contexts a child's dependence on its mother is a dependence on her love; she is "all-powerful" to the extent that her special role in the care of the child gives her the power to select and articulate the child's desire. In Lacanian terms, it is from the Other that the subject receives the signifiers of his or her desire. The often fruitful ambiguity in Lacan's notion of "the Other" must be resolved here. The Other can refer to the child's mother to the extent that she is virtually the exclusive provider. By the same token, in this capacity she is but the *representative* of Otherness in the more radical sense that Lacan gives to this term. What is radically Other is precisely "the concrete discourse of [the subject's] surroundings"; language, in Marx's phrase, is "the *Dasein* of the community." The mother, in her role as exclusive provider, represents, or is made to represent, the community. Her exclusive hold on discourse defines her "omnipotence."

Let us, then, reconnect the two aspects of the game. The initial symbolization, the emergence of the spool as symbol, negates the mother's hold on discourse, her presumption to represent the Other. The child is not the agent of this negation, nor does the negation itself imply any violence against the mother. It is merely the precondition for the child's involvement in "the concrete discourse of his surroundings" as the Otherness that is beyond his immediate relation to the mother. This primordial symbolization causes the child to pass from his status as a being who is "spoken to" and "spoken for" into the subjectivity of speech. He becomes a speaking being. This first symbolization, then, is at once negating and creative. Its negativity is impersonal and silent; in this, it indeed resembles the "death drive" which Freud eventually

[7] Jacques Lacan, "Fonction et champ de la parole et du langage en psychanalyse," *Ecrits* (Paris: Seuil, 1966), p. 319.

describes as a purely impersonal, silent force. The force of this negativity is also what springs the subject into language, breaking the other's hold on discourse. The other aspect of the game, the playful alternation of "o-o-o-o" and "da," marks an altogether new relation of the subject to his mother and his surroundings in general. It is his first experience of participation in the concrete discourse of the community.

This interpretation of the *fort-da* games does not follow those Lacan developed first in the so-called Rome Discourse and then in Seminar XI, but it does take up two central problems he broaches. On the one hand, all Lacan's remarks and commentaries on this episode revolve around the thesis that "the moment in which desire becomes human is also the moment the child is born into language."[8] And, on the other hand, Lacan's later commentary insists that the game's status as a *repetition* of a situation that was traumatic (the mother's leaving) entails something radically *new,* in that the repetition cannot be the same as that which it repeats. My interpretation is specifying this "something new" as a change in the subject's relation to others and to language.

In the game, an *interpersonal reality* (the subject's relation to his mother) is reenacted as an *intrapersonal fantasy* played with spool, string, and toys. At the same time, however, this transposition from the interpersonal to the intrapersonal, from reality to fantasy, springs the subject into language, so that his playing of the game, his speaking, unfolds a new horizon of *intersubjectivity.*

From his experience of the concrete discourse around him, the child has recognized that meaning, in coming from the Other, is not the exclusive province of the mother. The negativity that disrupts the mother's hold on discourse pushes the child into language and speech as the praxis of his relations with others. Indeed, no particular relationship among human beings, even a mother-child relation as intense and exclusive as this one, exhausts or fully embodies the interactions which language inaugurates, which, that is, the subject's relation to the Other makes possible. The *fort-da* game, then, opens a field of playing and speaking which can develop various permutations and transformations. There is no reason to assume that the game, however much it takes its significance from repetition, does not *also* contain the possibility of new uses, elaborations, applications. The very genesis and dynamic of the game include the capacity to create interactions with others, whether children or adults. It is not hard to imagine that Grandfather

[8]Ibid.

Freud himself was perhaps invited to play, to join in the game rather than merely observe it.

What Freud observed were the actual, rather than possible, applications of the game. And it was from these that he constructed the second level of his interpretation, where the game receives its libidinal determination from the wish for revenge it supposedly represents. It will be necessary to slow down the pace of Freud's interpretation, which so quickly marshals the evidence it needs—evidence that is, on the one hand, gathered not from the episode itself but from the boy's behavior a year later (when he was two-and-a-half) and even three years after that, or, on the other hand, is adduced axiomatically from other observations. The wish for revenge is stated as a translation of the game which makes it addressed only to the absent mother: " 'All right, then, go away! I don't need you. I'm sending you away myself.' " To support this translation, Freud reports that a year later, when the little boy's father was "at the front," he "would take a toy, if he was angry with it, and throw it to the floor, exclaiming: 'Go to the fwont' " (p. 16).

Rather than immediately connecting the game the child played at age one-and-a-half to this later action, Freud could have asked, What might have happened? What possibilities are opened by this accession to language? The child, called by language to speak, enters speaking as a practice whose possibilities point beyond any specific language interaction he in fact encounters. By the same token, the actual interactions around him limit the interactions in which he can participate— which is why he plays, and why this play appeals to possibilities beyond the situational context of his immediate experience. The situations of the child's experience are organized by specific institutions that orient the actions and interactions of the participants and are, to that very extent, constraining.

The context of Freud's grandson's experience is the restricted or "nuclear" family. The effects of this institutional constraint on discourse and interaction are everywhere apparent in Freud's description. Without cynicism, we can characterize what the child is told by the very organization of the household and the relationships taking place within it: mommy will meet all your needs—mommy cannot, and does not want to meet your every need—you must want what mommy wants. The result is the child's self-control, the conflict in which propels him toward play as self-activity: "He did not disturb his parents at night, he conscientiously obeyed orders not to touch certain things or go into certain rooms, and above all he never cried when his mother left him for a few hours" (p. 14). The exclusiveness of the child's relation to the mother, the intensity of his dependence and love, are organized by a social practice peculiar to the restricted family: "At the same time, he was greatly attached to the mother, who had not only fed him herself but also looked after him without any outside help" (p. 14). This familial context presents the child with two contrary but interwoven demands: he must find his satisfactions and enjoyments in the one person devoted to him, and, on the other hand, he must adapt to the pattern of restrictions and renunciations imposed on him.

To safeguard this restricted field of experience he must not only develop the self-control which makes his mother's wishes his own; he also develops the intense rivalry toward father and sibling which Freud put at the heart of the Oedipus complex: "He had heard at that time"—when he was two-and-a-half—"that his father was 'at the front,' and was quite far from regretting his absence; on the contrary he made it quite clear that he had no desire to be disturbed in his sole possession of his mother" (p. 16). This possession was then a short while later permanently disturbed: "a second child had been born and had aroused him to violent jealousy" (p. 16n). It is clear from Freud's account of this child's early experiences that the sheer exclusiveness of the maternal care he received led him not only to wish for the absence or destruction of his father and sibling, but actually brought him to the point where the mourning of his mother's death could find no expression, no speech, to be exchanged with others: "When this child was five and three-quarters, his mother died. Now that she was really 'gone' ('o-o-o'), the little boy showed no signs of grief. It is true that in the interval a second child had been born.... "

Although it is necessary to guard against a reductively sociological explanation of this child's symptoms and suffering, two conclusions are unavoidable: first, that the organization of everyday life by the social institution of the restricted family left a clear imprint on the course of his childhood experience, and, second, that Freud's decision to interpret the libidinal content of the *fort-da* game as the child played it at age one-and-a-half clearly derives from the observations made between the time the child was three-and-a-half and nearly six.

Against this, let us propose an interpretation that reconceptualizes the game as an entry into language and speech. The wish for revenge is not the exclusive or even the primary meaning of the game; insofar as this particular interpretation is valid, it applies only to the socially restricted meaning the game took on within the limited set of interactions and relationships that continued to shape the child's experience. As play, as speaking-playing, on the other hand, the game is an appeal to, an opening onto, a leap toward interactions which the situational context of the child's experience does not immediately provide. The game is dialectical in its development: it is the site of a struggle between the *self-activity of speaking-playing* and *the institutionally constrained discourses and interactions* in the situation itself. The libidinal contents of the game, the wishes it expresses, are multiple in their determination, in the sense that the game, as negation and creation, can draw on a diversity of repressed wishes. Such indeterminacy is in keeping with Freud's own view that fantasies are generally multivalent and not tied to particular mental structures, as opposed to his interpretation of the *fort-da* game as revenge, which mechanically derives the fantasy from a single libidinal source.

Play is activity, and as such it negates the constraints imposed on human interaction and creates new possibilities of interaction, even as it is stamped with restrictions and the wishes formed by repression. The *fort-da* game illustrates that language is a two-sided process in which the subject is constituted by the speech of others and becomes self-constituting through speech; this dialectic, however, is not only that of cultural creation but also involves the social and institutional forms that determine experience itself. Whereas Freud saw his grandson's "cultural achievement" in the instinctual renunciation of his wish for his mother's satisfactions, I have attempted to locate the moment of cultural creativity in the very entry into speech and play, which becomes possible only with the negation, however limited or fragmentary, of the constraints on speaking as interaction.

The theoretical import of this discussion will serve to introduce a more systematic critique of psychoanalysis. Let me reiterate a guiding thesis. The critical theory of society and culture requires a theory of subjectivity and lived experience, and in turning to psychoanalysis to develop that, it discovers another task as well: to disclose those points in psychoanalytic theory where historical forms of domination—principally the social division of labor and the social organization of sexual difference—have to become integral and primary elements of that theory itself.

The procedures, as opposed to the contents, of Freud's own reflections generally lead away from this possibility. The psychical apparatus takes on an ahistorical character, such that the social conditions of human experience appear secondary to the predominantly natural or biological or mechanical functioning of the psyche. The importance of Lacanian theory lies precisely in the fact that it restates the psychoanalytic problematic in social and cultural terms, while at the same time maintaining the integrity of the psychoanalytic experience. Lacan's reformulations of Freud make possible, I will argue, a genuinely dialectical, as opposed to dualistic, theory of subjectivity. Put another way, Lacan inaugurates the immanent critique of psychoanalysis.

All the major categories of Freud's descriptions of the "psychical apparatus"—pleasure-ego and reality-ego, pleasure principle and reality principle, ego-instincts and sexual instincts, life instincts and death instincts—are fraught with ambiguities. In this instability of concepts can be detected Freud's unreflected response to the forms of domination prevalent in modern society. The shifts and reversals that these categories undergo indicate the points where it is possible and necessary to see that the contradictions of society interlace with the constitution of human subjectivity.

The intellectual procedures informing Freud's metapsychological writings exhibit two tendencies:

(1) The construction of a model of psychological processes invariably begins with a description of the most simplified or "primitive" form of the "psychical apparatus" and proceeds, in the manner of building blocks, toward an ever more complex model designed to account for human experience and interaction. However much Freud qualifies the primitive psychical apparatus as a hypothesis or fiction, a merely logical beginning point, the building-block approach to the investigation has an indelible effect on the results. It casts the problematic as essentially the relation between a "living organism" and its "environment," so that the specifically historical, cultural, and social dimensions of the problematic do not explicitly enter into the theoretical model until the basic premises and dynamic of that model are already well established.

(2) As Freud uncovers the elements of contradiction in the theory, he maps these across a linear exposition, leaving one of two impressions: either that he has dropped particular formulations as they have come to appear inadequate, or that he has established a developmental sequence in human life which corresponds to the building-block format of the theoretical explanations. In other words, the linearization of contradictions yields a sequence of concepts or, alternatively, of stages of growth in which each step forward apparently supplants what pre-

ceded it. This method accords with Freud's propensity to dualistic rather than dialectical formulations, in that it preserves the identity of each basic category or concept.

These two general tendencies are, however, counteracted by another, leaving Freudian theory open to the possibility of continual renewal and radical reformulation. The "evidence" or "facts" that provoke and support Freud's theoretical models do not derive from the observations of an organism and its environment but rather from the experience of the psychoanalytic situation itself—that is, from an experience taking place within language in the form of the psychoanalytic dialogue. The cause posited behind the dialogue, and the theory, is the unconscious, which is not known by means of the observation of its positive existence but is recognized by its effect in a process of interpretation.

Lacan's project has been the attempt to give language and intersubjectivity primacy within the theory as well as the practice of psychoanalysis. He recognizes that the *Umwelt*, the environment or outer world, of even the newborn is preeminently social. From birth, the human being is affected by actions, gestures, wishes, and intentions that are already imbued with the symbolic and that occur within the constraints of specific, historically determined institutions. In Lacan's terms, the subject is, from the outset, radically dependent on the field of the Other—for the objects of one's satisfactions, for the benchmarks of one's identity, and for the language that will make one's interaction with others possible.

To read Freud's theoretical writings from this standpoint is no easy task, given the two tendencies delineated above. Indeed, in the appropriation of such works as "Formulations on the Two Principles of Mental Functioning," the *Papers on Metapsychology,* and *Beyond the Pleasure Principle,* Lacan jettisons, though in a polemically subdued manner, two propositions that are fundamental in Freud: first, that "in the beginning" the psychic apparatus is all ego, in the sense that everything it perceives is counted as a part of itself, and, second, that the original form of the sexual drives is autoerotic in the sense that the organism has no need of an object outside itself.

Pleasure and Reality

Freud's 1911 essay "Formulations on the Two Principles of Mental Functioning" establishes the opposition between the pleasure-ego and the reality-ego as the fundamental dualism of the psyche. The model gives a priority to the pleasure principle archaeologically and to the reality principle teleologically. The original pleasure-ego avoids stimuli and seeks pleasure in the form of a reduction of stimuli. Freud posits a time when the psychical apparatus merely hallucinated whatever it required to extinguish the "demands of internal needs" and sustain its sleeplike state. "It was only the non-occurrence of the expected satisfaction, the disappointment experienced, which led to the abandonment of this attempt at satisfaction by means of hallucination. Instead of it, the psychical apparatus had to decide to form a conception of the real circumstances of the external world and to endeavour to make a real alteration in them."[9] This second moment, then, marks the ascendency of the reality-ego.

Whereas the pleasure-ego leads to hallucinatory satisfactions, the reality-ego is the vehicle for actions. Its capacity to make "the appropriate alteration of reality" comes with the development of the senses, consciousness, attention, and memory, all of which comprise the psyche's reality-testing ability. Action not only stands in opposition to hallucination but also provides a form of "motor discharge" wholly distinct from that produced "under the dominance of the pleasure principle," such as "expressive movements and the play of features" and "manifestations of affect."[10]

In developing this construct, which associates hallucination as well as affective gestures and vocalizations with the pleasure-ego, external perception and action with the reality-ego, Freud brackets the problem of intersubjectivity at the very point where he alludes to its peculiar role in the development of the *human* psyche. The following passage appears in an extended footnote intended to clarify the dualism of pleasure-ego and reality-ego:

It will be rightly objected that an organization which was a slave to the pleasure principle and neglected the reality of the external world could not maintain itself alive for the shortest time, so that it could not have come into existence at all. The employment of a fiction like this is, however, justified when one considers that the infant—provided that one includes with it the care it receives from its mother—does almost realize a psychical system of this kind. It probably hallucinates the fulfillment of its internal needs; it betrays its unpleasure, when there is an increase

[9]Freud, "Formulations on the Two Principles of Mental Functioning," *S. E.* XII, 219.
[10]Ibid., p. 221.

of stimulus and an absence of satisfaction, by the motor discharge of screaming and beating with its arms and legs, and it then experiences the satisfaction it has hallucinated [that is, we can assume, because the mother has been prompted to provide a real satisfaction]. Later, as an older child, it learns to employ these manifestations of discharge as methods of expressing its feelings.[11]

Freud thus defends his *fictional model* of the psychical apparatus with the claim that the life of the human infant is an *empirical approximation* of it. The situation of the infant's complete dependence on others for its very existence and sustenance "almost realize[s]" the model's assumption of an original pleasure-ego, in that the baby receives its gratifications without taking any actions to alter reality. It is not enough, however, for the relation between child and mother to approximate the theoretical account of the "psychical apparatus"; this relation should rather be the very basis and object of the theory from the outset.

There can be no simple transition from manifestations of affect (pleasure principle) to action (reality principle), for the very reason that neither takes place except through the mediations of intersubjectivity. Even the infant's earliest involuntary gestures and vocalizations occur within the context of an unbalanced, nonreciprocal intersubjectivity. The agitation and motor discharge of an infant who is incapable of directly achieving the needed object enter a symbolic register; they are treated, by the Other, as a request or demand. Independent of any intentionality on the part of the child, his or her simplest cry is received and responded to as what Lacan calls a "request for love." Crying is an utterance which is proffered by the child but intentionalized by the Other. A nonreciprocal intersubjectivity is instituted. The child's signifying act, in running ahead of his or her intention, finds its meaning only as it comes back to the child from the Other. Neither the pleasure nor the reality principle has dominance here. For even the simplest "manifestation of affect," which Freud associates with the pure pleasure-ego, is *between* pleasure and reality. The push toward pleasure and the orientation toward outside reality are both mediated by the relation to others and to the symbolic. This relation is constitutive of subjectivity itself.

The dialectic of the request unfolds an interhuman reality anterior to any possible reality-ego which could attain predominance in the

[11]Ibid., p. 220 n.

"psychical apparatus." Because of the slow maturation of the human being's sensory-motor capacities, there are no reality-altering actions that are not already situated in and affected by the social network of a human community. The hypothetical reality-ego which Freud describes physicalistically as a motor discharge that alters a neutral, external field of objects is a pure fiction, just as much as the supposed "original pleasure-ego."

The prematurity of birth in human beings, their extended dependence on others for the most basic vital needs, is the reference point for another central category of Lacanian theory—namely, the concept of the *mirror phase*. Drawing on ethological studies and the researches of Charlotte Bühler and Elsa Köhler, as well as his own early work on paranoia, Lacan began in the mid-1930s to construct a theory of the fundamental structure and processes of the ego, in the more restricted sense given this term by Freud in *The Ego and the Id* and by Anna Freud in *The Ego and the Mechanisms of Defense*. Lacan interprets a series of psychological phenomena connected with the capacity of very young children (six to eighteen months of age) to recognize their image in the mirror and to distinguish even earlier, from about the tenth day after birth, the human face. Following Bühler, he examined the importance of "transitivism," where children will, for example, cry when a playmate has fallen down or "claim to have received the punch that they themselves have thrown, without this being a lie."[12]

Lacan sees in these phenomena the close connection between identification with another and identification with the image of one's own body, such that the aggression that the sheer presence of another like myself can provoke suggests that my most primitive identifications with the image of my own body were fraught with ambivalence. The infant's recognition of the human form and then of its own form in the mirror indicates a level of visual and mental development that outstrips the development of the nervous system as a whole. In the experiences of the mirror phase, "the child anticipates, on the mental plane, the conquering of the functional unity of its own body, which has not been accomplished on the plane of voluntary motor activity."[13] The subject's identification with the visual *Gestalt* of his or her body—"I am that one," said Narcissus—establishes the ego as an "ideal unity, a beneficent *imago*" which "is valorized with all the distress primordially

---

[12]Lacan, "Propos sur la causalité psychique," *Ecrits*, p. 180.
[13]Lacan, "L'agressivité en psychanalyse," *Ecrits*, p. 112.

connected with the infant's intraorganic and relational discordance."[14] The subject, in other words, first grasps the self-sufficiency of his or her body not in its real activity but as an image, that is, as a reality estranged from the body's actual capacity for independent action. Self-identity is thereby caught in the conflict between the experience of an uncoordinated body invested with needs, affects, and unmastered movements, and an imaginary body that forms the core of the subject's ego. At the same time, this experience marks the original split in the subject's relation to the body; the erotogenic body is divided from the body image.

Ambivalence, oscillating between playful jubilation and aggression, thereby becomes constitutive of the subject's earliest experience of self and others and makes possible the widest range of interpersonal re-actions—from jealousy, unprovoked violence, and the false attribution of agency to imitation, sympathy, and love. Human beings' capacity to project their own feelings into the image of the other or to discover their own feelings through the image of the other demarcates, for Lacan, the overlap in human experience between madness and being human as such. This theme, prominent in his writings in the 1930s and 1940s, anticipates the problematic of Michel Foucault's *Madness and Civilization*. Lacan at once repudiates the Enlightenment conception of "man" as a quintessentially rational being and pleads against the forms of brutality, incrimination, and confinement that Enlightenment inflicts upon the insane. In a characteristic rhetorical gesture, Lacan carries this polemic into his own basic concepts and calls the fundamental structure of the ego *paranoiac*.

Against the Freudian conception of a reality-ego that confronts external objects as a neutral field, Lacan's theory of the ego pivots on two alternative premises: (1) that the subject's ego is at first itself estranged and external, an *imago* which has reality in being external but, as an image, is imaginary and ideal, and (2) that consequently human desire and the relation to reality are always mediated by the subject's relation to others. Lacan summarizes these premises with reference to the Hegelian conception that self-consciousness constitutes itself in relation to another self-consciousness:

The first effect of the *imago* on the human being is an effect of the *alienation* of the subject. It is in the other that the subject identifies with

[14]Ibid.

himself [*sic*] and even first experiences himself. A phenomenon that will seem less surprising if one recalls the fundamental, social conditions of the human *Umwelt*—and if one evokes the intuition that dominates all of Hegel's speculation.

Human desire is constituted, he tells us, under the sign of mediation; it is a desire to have one's desire recognized. It has as its object a desire, that of others, in the sense that man has no object constituted for his desire without some mediation, as can be seen in his most primitive needs in the fact that even his feeding must be prepared and provided.[15]

From the earliest stages of development, the external world is imprinted with the human image. Moreover, this external reality is a field of objects which, being points of mediation among human beings, never correspond immediately to organic tendencies. Rather, this field is always already comprised of objects "with the double possibility of instrumental and symbolic uses."[16] The earliest human experiences are of an *Umwelt* that is social, a world of tools, symbols, and the desires of others.

Neither Freud nor Lacan adequately integrates a conception of human autonomy into the theory of psychological development. Freud limits himself to references to the reality-adjusted ego without ever taking into account the social and historical nature of reality. Lacan, while acutely aware of this falsification in Freud, leaves his development of an alternative conception allusive and fragmentary. He is constrained, on the one hand, by the way he pursues the strategy of making psychoanalysis pass through phenomenology in order to free it from its mechanistic and biological tendencies; ever after he must also continually denounce the construct of the autonomous ego which guided the entire Husserlian project. On the other hand, Lacan's fascination with structuralism never completely escapes the effects of the structuralist tendency to reduce or exclude the question of the subject.

Clearly psychoanalysis precludes any conception of the subject's autonomy as a given, or a priori, condition. Nor is autonomy simply acquired developmentally and then securely maintained. As Lacan's frequent recourse to the Hegelian dialectic of master and slave indicates, freedom and autonomy are achieved in processes of struggle, a labor in which the subject works through relations of domination and dependence.

[15]Lacan, "Propos sur la causalité psychique," p. 181.
[16]Lacan, "L'agressivité," p. 111.

Any definition of human autonomy has to focus on, I will argue, the interactions, discourses, and activities through which any subject lives his or her existence *with others*.

The mirror-identifications and the dialectic of the request institute a complex temporality in the developmental processes of human beings. The movement toward self-activity, in its double aspect of verbal and bodily activity, follows a distinctively social dialectic that is neither linear nor natural. The mirror phase, along with the series of identifications it governs, influences both bodily activity and the acquisition of language, but with different, even contrary effects. On the one side, the mirror phase projects the subject beyond his or her existing level of motor integration and autonomy; it thus institutes the anticipatory orientation in time which is required for development and maturation. In this, it inaugurates the affective oscillation between jubilation and depression. On the other hand, the fact that mirror-identification precedes the child's entry into language as a speaking subject—that is, his or her birth as a subject—has another, discordant set of effects. For the subject, the not-yet-a-subject, first grasps his or her autonomy in the imaginary register by means of the *Gestalt* that fixes one's own body as a complete and self-sufficient form. This imaginary autonomy is not only in conflict with the real dependence on others and the inner chaos of the body, but it will also come into conflict with the real autonomy which is discovered in the acquisition of language—an autonomy which depends upon the symbolic register and which manifests itself not as self-sufficiency and completeness but as participation and interaction. In this sense, the imaginary coordinates of identity at once condition and retard the access to language. The mirror phase, then, projects the subject toward the self-activity of the body, but at the same time fixes the subject in those archaic identifications against which the self-activity of speech will manifest its negativity.

The dialectic of the request is the Lacanian formulation which addresses the fact that human beings are not born with language but are born into a world saturated with language. The theoretical import of the formulation is that it does not succumb to either behaviorist or rationalist conceptions of language learning. Language is neither acquired behavioristically nor innately present in the subject as a "deep structure." Because of the mediating role of the request, the subject is constituted by the effects of others' immersion in language before he or she becomes a speaking subject. Vital needs prompt the helpless infant to cry. Crying is invested by the Other as a request for love; this investment is reinforced in the infant's experience by his or her total dependence, such that the request generalizes the particular need ("Do something for me!" "Come here!" we might translate). What the child's provider does in response, however, is itself particular—a feeding that stimulates the mouth, a caress on the back of the neck, a pat on the belly, a soothing murmur, a caring look. In Freud's vocabulary it is the "memory-traces" of these gratifications which comprise the primal layers of the unconscious. Lacan in turn calls them *signifiers*. According to the psychoanalytic interpretation of dreams and symptoms, the associative and substitutive interplay of these elements of the unconscious is "structured like language." These memory-traces are not signs or indicators of the vital needs or tendencies. They are the residue or remainder left behind by the unbalanced and nonreciprocal dialogue between the subject and the Other. Just as crying is an utterance that is proffered by the infant but intentionalized by the Other, so the free-floating signifiers that the subject receives back in the Other's response are not immediately intentionalizable: the particular gratification cannot be *asked for* but only desired.

The primally repressed—that is, unintentionalizable—signifiers which are desire thus constitute the subject and connect his or her body to a matrix of social interactions. Language already mediates, indeed, constitutively mediates, the relation between the body and others before the subject enters this domain of intersubjectivity as one who speaks. This split in the subject's relation to the signifier, as the unintentionalized constituent of desire and as an element to be deployed in a signifying act, defines the "division of the subject." The acquisition of language, which Lacan justifiably calls the "second entry into language," brings into the child's experience a concrete and lived autonomy. When Freud's grandson discovers his capacity to intentionalize a set of signifiers, *fort-da,* he liberates himself, even if only momentarily, from a relation in which his request is tied to the dominance of another. By the same token, however, the leap into the autonomy and self-activity of speaking outstrips the actual organization of the child's daily life and continuing dependence on others. Speech itself fosters an anticipation which is utterly distinct from that of the mirror phase; speaking, as self-activity, installs within experience a utopian expectation of self-developing interactions in which the individual's autonomy lies in participation, not in imaginary self-sufficiency. The mirror-identifications institute the coordinates of an identity prior to language, that is, before the emergence of a genuine subjectivity in language. This divergence between identity and subjectivity makes it impossible for the dialectic of development to take a predetermined sequential course, whether this is conceived in biological, sexual, linguistic, or moral terms. Self-activity in language requires working beyond the imaginary forms of one's own identity as much as working beyond the domination of another.

While the mirror-identifications antedate and condition the access to language, speaking launches the countermovement that mobilizes, negativizes, and points beyond any imaginary crystallization of identity. This dialectic between verbal self-activity and imaginary identity has a corollary in the body's activity. The autonomy figured in the identification with the image of one's own body anticipates the subject's actual control over the body, but these two forms of autonomy are not the same. The self-activity of the body is the capacity for moving, gesturing, playing, and making. It is the erotogenic body in motion, just as speech has its impetus in the erotogenic body freed from its dependence on another's will. Human autonomy has nothing to do with self-sufficiency; indeed, it is the active overcoming of imaginary self-sufficiency. Autonomy, as the self-activity of the body and speech, of doing and speaking, *praxis* and *logos,* enters human experience as a concrete and lived possibility that overshoots and struggles against whatever is given as reality.

An understanding of which constraints on this possibility of self-activity are necessary and which are unnecessary does not immediately enter human consciousness, whether in its ordinary cognitions or its scientific knowledge. This is a question psychoanalytic theory generally refuses to entertain. Such a refusal deftly leaves aside the ambiguities of the utopian, which precisely mixes the possible and the impossible, but it also therefore evades the other side of this question—namely, the necessity for a theory of subjectivity to develop as a critical theory of society. Here is the deeper significance of Freud's failure to provide an elaborated concept of autonomy and, with it, a theory of cognition.

A general theory of cognition is ultimately indissociable from theory's understanding of its own epistemology. Human knowledge cannot, especially when it pretends to be a scientific knowledge of the forms of everyday cognition, detach itself from the lived experiences out of which genuine subjectivity emerges. It will either foster the utopian core of those experiences or defend against them; it will either seek to destroy and transform the constraints imposed on self-activity or attempt to justify them. The concrete utopia that sustains human development cannot be understood except through a knowledge of society. Neither a scientific psychology nor a social science can justifiably repudiate the double necessity of utopian and critical consciousness.

This problematic, in which science is inseparable from politics in the development of an understanding of human social, psychological, and cultural life, never becomes visible in Freud and never completely breaks into the clear in Lacan. I have, following Lacan, criticized the Freudian dualism of pleasure principle and reality principle on the grounds that human experience and subjectivity, because they are from the beginning social, are neither governed originally by the pleasure principle nor finally by the reality principle. Although Freud insists on the hypothetical, even fictional, status of the two principles, he never formulates the dialectic which actually grounds them: that between *constrained interaction* and *self-developing interaction,* the dialectic I have been extrapolating from the Lacanian concepts of the mirror-identifications and the request by confronting these concepts with the self-activity of the body and of speech.

Now, it is precisely in the context of an assumed dualism between the reality principle and the pleasure principle that Freud reflects on science in the essay "Formulations on the Two Principles of Mental Functioning." "It is *science,*" he writes, "which comes nearest to succeeding in [a conquest of the pleasure principle]; science, too, however, offers intellectual pleasure during its work and promises practical gain at the end." The qualification that Freud adds here does not really counter the main point, which is made in the context of a distinction between science and religion. Religion does the work of the reality-ego in demanding the renunciation of pleasure, but, according to Freud, religion must in turn offer the promise of a reward in the afterlife. He reduces this promise to "a mythical projection" of the "revolution in the mind" whereby it gives up "a momentary pleasure" for "an assured pleasure at a later time." On the other hand, religions "have not by this means achieved a conquest of the pleasure principle" because this mythical projection itself represents the resurgence of fantasy and the pleasure principle.[17]

The superiority of science over religion is, then, for Freud, twofold. Science excludes fantasy, and it has the ability to alter reality in the form of bringing about "practical gain in the end." Art enters into these schematizations as "a reconciliation between the two principles

[17]Freud, "Formulations on the Two Principles," pp. 223–224.

in a peculiar way." The artist is someone dissatisfied with reality "who allows his erotic and ambitious wishes full play in the life of phantasy. He finds his way back to reality, however, from the world of phantasy by making use of special gifts to mould his phantasies into truths of a new kind, which are valued by men as precious reflections of reality."[18]

This entire account develops from a false correlation made earlier in the essay: "a closer connection arises, on the one hand, between the sexual instincts and phantasy and, on the other hand, between the ego-instincts and the activities of consciousness."[19] However common-sensical the association of fantasy with sexuality and thought with self-preservation may appear, it cannot so easily be projected onto the production of collectively effective discourses like science, religion, and art.

Freud lacks any workable framework within which to grasp the interrelation of religion, scientific knowledge, and art in historical terms—starting with the recognition that this very problematic and the sharp distinctions among these forms of discourse emerge only with the rise of modernity and of capitalism. As a result, he tenaciously holds onto the dualistic distinction of pleasure principle and reality principle. To displace the Freudian problematic into this field of historical and social questions requires pressing the immanent critique of psychoanalysis to its limits. Let us once more, therefore, locate the problem within Freud's interpretation of children's play, for it is here that we can see the consequences of his recourse to the dualism of pleasure and reality:

> With the introduction of the reality principle one species of thought-activity was split off; it was kept free from reality-testing and remained subordinated to the pleasure principle alone. This activity is *phantasying,* which begins already in children's play, and later, continued as *day-dreaming,* abandons dependence on real objects.[20]

Freud here interprets play as a stage in psychological development which is abandoned in the course of maturation, as though an advance has taken place when fantasy "abandons dependence on real objects." As the reinterpretation of the *fort-da* game has shown, play has an open, outward-seeking orientation that comes up against the con-

[18]Ibid., p. 224.
[19]Ibid., p. 222.
[20]Ibid.

straints imposed on interaction by a reality which is socially organized. Surely fantasy does become interior in the course of the "developmental process." But why? Certainly not simply because "reality" makes the fantasy "useless," a distraction from the demands of sheer self-preservation, but rather because the organized and instituted forms of interaction which comprise the *social* reality of the child's world do not tolerate the development of the fantasy as free interaction. The interiorization of fantasy, its transformation from play to day-dreaming, cannot, therefore, be straightforwardly valued as maturation. Interiorization marks rather the obstruction of the possibility of an expanded realm of intersubjectivity. The constraining elements of Freud's grandson's experience clearly derived from the institution of the nuclear family as it organizes the social world of childhood. What we call the maturation of the individual in our era is at the same time the retardation of self-constituting activity. As fantasy is forced to be interiorized, it loses its connection with real objects in the sense that it is inhibited from realizing itself as speaking-doing, that is, as play.

The social dialectic, then, that determines the operation of the pleasure principle and the reality principle lies in the conflict between the institutionally constrained discourses and interactions of social reality and self-constituting interaction through language and activity. The dynamics of this conflict fall outside the parameters of psychoanalysis only because of the way in which psychoanalysis has tended to draw its own boundaries and define itself as a science of psychology. We can already, in anticipation of the problematic that will have to be developed, suggest the consequences of examining the interrelation of science, religion, and art in light of a social dialectic of discursive and expressive forms. Hence, the following hypotheses: (1) A science of society has to be able to *imagine* another social order if it is to *know* this one, and the rich sources of this utopian imagination lie, though not ready at hand, in the diverse expressive forms that traditional, bourgeois science has continually repudiated in order to found its own concept of scientific knowledge. (2) The form of religious experience that serves as Freud's model is the Protestant ethic, which, as the predominant "spirit of capitalism," reconstituted the symbolic forms of religious life precisely by interiorizing them and so creating what Freud himself recognized as the kernel connection between "modern neurosis" and "civilized morality." (3) However much traditional aesthetics promotes a conception of art as the *reconciliation* of pleasure and reality, it is the task of interpretation to augment the critical theory of society by disclosing how artistic practices enact the historical *contradictions* that obtain between the constraints of social reality and the concrete utopia of human speaking.

Processes of interiorization transform play into day-dreaming in psychological development, have historically caused the symbolic field of religion to retract from its collective forms to private spirituality, and have increasingly segregated art from social experience as a whole.

All these cultural transformations are closely connected to the predominant effect of capitalism on the social constitution of subjectivity, be it that of the master or of the slave, namely, the constitution of the subject as a *separated individual*. Lacan took up this theme, though he cast it more narrowly as a critique of social Darwinism, in the concluding section of the 1948 essay on "Aggressiveness in Psychoanalysis." I quote the passage at length in order to emphasize the importance of a problematic that does not in fact remain in focus in the development of Lacanian theory:

> The satisfaction of human desire is not possible except as mediated by the desire and the labor of the other. If, in the conflict of Master and Slave, it is the recognition of man by man [sic] that is at stake, it is also the case that this recognition is promoted by the radical negation of natural values, whether it is expressed in the sterile tyranny of the master or the fecund tyranny of the slave.
>
> We know the reinforcement that this profound doctrine has given to the constructive sparticism of the slave recreated by the barbarism of the Darwinian century.
>
> The relativizing of our sociology by the scientific collection of the cultural forms that we are destroying in the world, as well as the analyses, exhibiting truly psychoanalytic characteristics, in which the wisdom of Plato shows us the dialectic common to the passions of the soul and of the city, can instruct us as to the reason for this barbarism. It is—to use the jargon which responds to our approaches to the subjective needs of man—the increasing absence of all those saturations of the *superego* and the *ego ideal* which are realized in all sorts of organic forms in traditional societies, ranging from the rites of everyday intimacy to the periodic festivals in which the community manifests itself. We no longer know them except in the most thoroughly degraded forms. Moreover, in abolishing the cosmic polarity of the male and female principles, our society knows all the psychological incidences proper to the modern phenomenon of the so-called *battle of the sexes*. An immense community, on the boundary between the "democratic" anarchy of the passions and their desperate leveling by the great winged hornet of narcissistic tyr-

anny—, it is clear that the promotion of the *ego* in our existence ends up, in accordance with the utilitarian conception of man which supports it, realizing ever more completely man as an individual—that is, in an isolation of the soul ever closer to his original helplessness.[21]

Lacan here tries to specify the historical process that produces the sufferings which brought psychoanalysis into being: namely, the erosion and destruction of the symbolic practices that tie a subject's desires, identity, and actions to the social bond as a whole. Lacan does not, however, get beyond a style of social criticism that is fraught with uncritical nostalgia. Nor does he bring the critical force of this analysis to bear on his reconstruction of Freudian theory; there he is prone to neglect that side of the psychoanalytic conception of dialogue which involves the springing of the subject into speech.

In the account of the *fort-da* game in the Rome Discourse, for example, he sees in the child's playing before the mirror a drama of isolation, imaginary identification, and domination: *"Fort! Da!* It is indeed already in his solitude that the desire of the child has become the desire of the other, of an *alter ego* that dominates him and the object of whose desire is henceforth his own affliction."[22] Just as Freud projects onto his grandson's play the experiences that befall him later in his life within the restricted family, Lacan here imputes to the mirror game the tragic dimensions of solitude and domination which the game actively seeks to transcend. It is essential not to collapse the distinctive moments of the dialectic of desire and interaction; the child's mirror play is already marked with the liberating negativity of speech. In making himself disappear before the mirror, the child is experimenting with the desire of the Other. He assumes his mother's desire in order to know where, as an object, he stands in relation to it. He enacts a question: Isn't it true that, in leaving, she wants me to disappear? However, he does not then succumb to overwhelming emptiness. To the contrary, having taken up the subjective position of the other and having survived his own disappearance, he discovers his subjectivity, his power to speak, and his orientation beyond dependence on the will of this other. The playful assumption of the desire of the other has freed him from his domination by that desire and breaks the closed circle of ego and alter ego.

"Language," Jean Baudrillard has written, "because it cannot as such

[21]Lacan, "L'agressivité," pp. 121–122.
[22]Lacan, "Fonction et champ de la parole," p. 319.

be consumed or possessed by those who speak it, always preserves the possibility of the 'essential' and of a syntax of exchanging (a structuring of communication)."[23] The history of Freud's grandson is the struggle between the eruption of that possibility and its obstruction. The solitude of his play in his mother's absence is but a moment which is required for his entry into language. It is the empty space between dependence and participation, bondage and mutuality, subordination and inter-dependence. Wherever this push toward participation, mutuality, and interdependence is blocked, there we find the conditions for a solitude that is lived as isolation, as the subject's withdrawal from the syntax of exchanging and communication. Between domination and creative interaction there lie, then, these two forms of solitude, the one a new form of being dominated and the other the precondition of freedom and creativity.

Reification: The Self-Preservative "Instinct" in Bourgeois Society

The dualism of pleasure principle and reality principle does not retain its prominent position in Freudian theory. It is replaced, or resituated, by the dualism of the life instincts and the death instinct. *Beyond the Pleasure Principle* clearly discloses the uncertain or ambiguous character of the principles of pleasure and reality. Even so, Freud still fails to reflect on the contradictory foundations of his metapsychological theory. The theory is guided, on the one hand, by the dialectic and phenomenology of psychoanalytic interpretation, that is, the therapeutic practice of psychoanalysis, and, on the other hand, by the intent to develop a scientific psychology whose idea of science is derived from biology, neurology, and the physical sciences. Nowhere is the incompatibility of these two tendencies clearer than in *Beyond the Pleasure Principle*. Freud's effort to combine a theory of human subjectivity with a biological investigation into the nature of life and death yields an improbable text whose dialectical brilliance is overshadowed by a scientific speculation that verges on pure fiction. An entire strand of the Lacanian revision of Freud is a relentless effort to rescue the dialectical core of this particular text and bring it back to its origins in the psychoanalytic experience. Once again the task here will be to carry

---

[23]Jean Baudrillard, *Le système des objets: La consommation des signes* (Paris: Gallimard, 1968), p. 223.

Lacan's immanent critique of psychoanalysis over into a critical theory of society.

Freud introduces his investigation by acknowledging that the pleasure *principle* is *divided;* its force breaks up as it breaks across the human psyche:

> In the course of things it happens again and again that individual instincts or parts of instincts turn out to be incompatible in their aims or demands with the remaining ones, which are able to combine into the inclusive unity of the ego. The former are then split off from their unity by the process of repression, held back at lower levels of development and cut off, to begin with, from the possibility of satisfaction. If they succeed subsequently, as can so easily happen with repressed sexual instincts, in struggling through, by roundabout paths, to a direct or substitutive satisfaction, that event, which would in other cases have been an opportunity for pleasure, is felt as unpleasure. ... The details of the process by which repression turns a possibility of pleasure into a source of unpleasure are not yet clearly understood or cannot be clearly represented; but there is no doubt that all neurotic unpleasure is of that kind—pleasure that cannot be felt as such.*
>   *(*Footnote* added in 1925:) No doubt the essential point is that pleasure and unpleasure, being conscious feelings, are attached to the ego.[24]

Lacan's concept of the division of the subject or Freud's of primal repression implies that this splitting up of the pleasure principle is a primary, not a secondary characteristic of human psychological life. It is important therefore not to consider Freud's description as applying to "neurotic" as opposed to "normal" experiences, unless we grant, as Freud often did, that neurosis is a virtually normal state in modern societies. Indeed, the problem that must be made clear here concerns the ways in which the conflictual division between the unconscious and "the inclusive unity of the ego" owes its specific forms to the social constitution of the ego. Freud's neglect of this question leads him to ignore two implications in his discussion of the pleasure principle.

First, the fundamental complication of the pleasure principle involves temporality. Repression marks the split between what *is* pleasurable and what *would have been* pleasurable. The inhibitions, symptoms, and anxieties of experience in the present block the subject's access to his or her own history, and it is this unlived and as yet untold history that will repeat itself in those phenomena that Freud discusses through-

[24]Freud, *Beyond the Pleasure Principle,* S.E. XVIII, 11.

out the book as instances of the repetition compulsion. The temporality of the human subject, as it is constituted in the dialectic of his or her history, lived and unlived, told and untold, defines the processes of psychoanalytic interpretation as such, but remains obscured in Freud's search for a "scientific" description of the pleasure principle.

As a consequence, a second problem is never adequately posed. If the reality the ego faces is recognized as an essentially human and social reality, then the conflict between what is and what would have been pleasurable opens onto the question of what *might become* pleasurable under changed circumstance. This question is not merely hypothetical, nor does it fall within the exclusive province of the scientific investigator. The orientation toward the future and toward another reality must be counted among the cognitive capacities of the human being caught in the conflict between pleasure and unpleasure, between desire and reality. Moreover, a cognition that is critical of reality also implies the possibility of renouncing what is now pleasurable, not in the mode of repression, which hampers the possibilities of the present under the impact of an unlived and untold past, but in the mode of a liberation which, comprehending the past and demanding a new future, condemns the present, including its pleasures, since what is pleasurable is itself conditioned by the social organization of reality.

Readers of Freud, apologists and critics alike, have long recognized that his conception of the reality-ego's ability to alter reality in fact involves nothing more than its ability to adjust to reality, that is, to alter its relation to the external world. Freud thus associates human cognition with self-preservation, which stands throughout his writings as the exemplary *ego-instinct*. In *Beyond the Pleasure Principle* this central manifestation of the reality principle has to be related to the new hypothesis of a death instinct, that is, of an overriding tendency within the living organism to return to a state of the total absence of stimuli. Freud's uncertainty as to where to place the self-preservative instinct, with the life instincts or the death instinct, is only apparently resolved when he ultimately concludes he must revise the longstanding psychoanalytic tenet that the sexual instincts and the ego-instincts are opposites and redesignate both as parts of eros, against which is posed the death drive. Before arriving at that solution Freud attempts to categorize self-preservation as a death instinct; I will argue that this extraordinary paradox has a historical truth which Freud tacitly recognizes but finally abandons. It is the following argument, with its singularly unscientific logic, which the new dualism of eros and death drive will serve to eradicate:

> The hypothesis of self-preservative instincts, such as we attribute to all living beings, stands in marked opposition to the idea that instinctual life as a whole serves to bring about death. Seen in this light, the theoretical importance of the instincts of self-preservation, of self-assertion and of mastery greatly diminishes. They are component instincts whose function it is to assure that the organism will follow its own path to death, and to ward off any possible ways of returning to inorganic existence other than those which are immanent in the organism itself. ... What we are left with is the fact that the organism wishes to die only in its own fashion.[25]

Freud's allegiance to a dualistic conceptualization, in which opposing terms have an unambiguous identity of their own, prevents him from letting this formulation stand. Its biologistic assumptions are typical of those throughout the book. The reason that he entertains this formulation at all is twofold—first because the psychoanalytic experience has constantly disclosed a conflict between the sexual impulses and the aims of self-preservation, and second, because it is in fact necessary, as we shall see, to link self-preservation and death.

Freud founders here because he continues to assume that the problem can be posed as the unmediated relation between the individual and a natural (or pseudonatural) environment. The biologistic speculations in which Freud's reflection is cast are the symptoms, not the cause, of this basic assumption. Another starting point is required. For it is not possible to describe the supposed "instincts serving the self-preservation of the individual" without recognizing the historical specificity of the social conditions under which self-preservation becomes the individual's private responsibility. Any purely psychological concept of self-preservation fails to recognize the historical development of the modes of the production and reproduction of material life—that is, of the social formations which determine how individuals find provision for their vital needs and organic preservation.

To the extent that the capitalist mode of production reconstitutes human praxis as a relation between things, reification enters into the constitution of subjectivity. The capitalist organization of the produc-

[25] Ibid., p. 39.

tion and reproduction of material life causes other human beings and nature to appear to the subject as so many objects that are either means or obstacles to the acquisition of exchange value. The Freudian problematic must shift, because between the living human organism and its environment is the mediation of society. The body, the subject, and the outside world are differentiated and related to each other according to historical forms of social organization. In contrast to the mirror-identifications and the dialectic of the request, reification does not confront the human being from birth; it lurks in the future, for the subject's full assumption of the role of reified social agent is integrally a part of what defines his or her maturity. The ego is destined to be reduced to its capacity for calculation, the ability to assess actions, objects, forces, the motives of others, and so on, in terms of their potential for furthering or hindering the private appropriation of exchange value, whether in the form of the wage or of capital. The subject-object relation assumes a form that obeys the laws of mathematical calculation. The calculating ego faces the outer world as a field of measurable objects. Needs and desires become secondary as the ego passes through the detour that makes the acquisition of value its primary aim. While outer reality is reduced to a set of measureable objects to be exploited and from which the ego is privately to appropriate value, inner reality becomes an object to be controlled as an instrument productive of value.

For the separated individual, self-preservation is the mere "manipulation and procuring" (Kosík) of objects. The subject, in order to find sustenance in a world organized by capitalist social relations, is in effect expelled from the community, in that the bourgeois mode of self-preservation sets the individual against others. The total life of society cannot appear to the subject as the interconnected whole of human activities but instead appears as the calculable relations between things. The thief or the rogue, Lazarillo de Tormes, for example, was thus among the first literary prototypes of the respectable burgher. They are both antisocial.

The reified ego must dominate, discipline, and control the body to keep it from interfering with the aim of acquiring exchange values. What the body wants is reencoded as mere need, that is, as a measurable quantity. Capitalist calculation, carried out in the ledger of the private enterprise, computes this need as "necessary labor." This code imposes itself on the worker as the connection between needs and wage; insofar as the worker measures his or her needs by the wage, the need-code establishes slave morality in its bourgeois form. Providing for one's own existence is thus subjected to the principle of homogeneity that governs the processes of calculation, instrumentalization, and the rationality of economic ends. Self-preservation is organized as a destructive assault on the body, on others, and on nature. And it positions the homogeneous subject, whether entrepreneur or producer, as the agent of this destruction. The production of value is bound up with an abstractly regulated violence against human and natural life. All of this yields a thesis that brings us back to Freud: *self-preservation, in its capitalist form, manifests the death drive.*

Freud cannot avoid registering, in his practice and in his theory, the effects of this conjunction of preserving and destroying, for it is the social condition of human experience in the bourgeois era. Freud's attempt to come to grips with this dialectic can be discerned in his hesitation over where to place the self-preservative instinct, with eros or with the death drive. Similarly, when Freud saw in sadism a phenomenon that apparently combined destructiveness and love, he developed a concept, "instinctual fusion," which is suggestive in the context of our discussion. "But how can the sadistic instinct, whose aim it is to injure the object, be derived from Eros, the preserver of life?" he asks. "Is it not plausible to suppose that this sadism is in fact a death instinct which, under the influence of narcissistic libido, has been forced away from the ego and has consequently only emerged in relation to the object? It now enters the service of the sexual function."[26] Even entertaining the supposition of a death drive, Freud's formulation can nonetheless be restated: the death drive cannot appear, cannot become a part of the subject's wishes or behavior, unless it is "fused" with eros. Freud himself gives expression to this notion in *The Ego and the Id,* forthrightly admitting that the death drive is at once a necessary postulate but nowhere observable: "we are driven to conclude that the death instincts are by their nature mute and that the clamour of life proceeds for the most part from Eros."[27] There are now two questions to be pursued: (1) If the so-called death drive is silent and does not take hold of the subject except when "fused" with eros to become a destructiveness or aggressiveness directed at others, is it nonetheless possible to clarify the concept of a pure, unmixed death drive? And (2) what are the consequences of recognizing that the fun-

---

[26]Ibid., p. 54.
[27]Freud, *The Ego and the Id,* S.E. XIX, 46.

damental "fusion" of eros and the death drive in our own social experience is reification, insofar as it integrates aggression and destruction
into the means of self-preservation?

Lacan never integrates the concept of reification into the psychoanalytic problematic, which remains, therefore, without this critical historical dimension. What he does do, however, is tirelessly address the
first of the questions I have just posed by displacing the concept of the
death drive over into the question of the subject's relation to death.
His reference points are philosophical rather than biological. In the
Rome Discourse and other writings in the 1950s, Lacan appropriates
the Heideggerian notion of being-toward-death and adapts it to Hegel's
dialectic of master and slave. The *relation* to death is a human and
cultural experience; language introduces human beings to the symbol's
double capacity to make something disappear and to memorialize it,
imprinting being with history and with death:

> The first symbol in which we recognize humanity in its vestigial traces
> is the tomb, and the intermediary of death is recognizable in every re-
> lation where man [*sic*] comes to the life of his history.
> Which is the only life that lasts and is true, since it is transmitted
> without being lost in the perpetual tradition from one subject to the
> next. How can one not see how completely this life surpasses the life
> inherited by an animal, in which the individual fades into the species
> since no memorial distinguishes its ephemeral appearance from that
> which will reproduce it again in the invariability of the type.[28]

Human beings discover their identity, and their humanity, in relation
to a community and recognize that this community precedes their individual existences and will survive their deaths. Evoking the themes
of Hegel's *Phenomenology of Spirit*, Lacan links the most extreme
forms of the "death drive" to the fact that the relation to death emerges
only in the subject's relation to the consciousness of another: "Man's
[*sic*] freedom is wholly inscribed within the constituting triangle of:
the renunciation that he imposes on the desire of the other through
the threat of death for the enjoyment of the fruits of that other's
bondage—the voluntary sacrifice of his life for the reasons that give
human life its measure—and the suicidal renunciation of the vanquished, which deprives the master of his victory and abandons him
to his inhuman solitude."[29] It is the last "of these figures of death" that

[28]Lacan, "Fonction et champ de la parole," p. 319.
[29]Ibid., p. 320.

compels Lacan's attention, for suicide is a reality from which the psychoanalyst cannot turn away. Viewed as the last recourse that the subject has when subjected to the domination of another's will, suicide becomes at the same time a figure of freedom. Life and death, Eros and Thanatos, are here enfolded together: "[Suicide] is not in fact the perversion of an instinct, but rather that desperate affirmation of life which is the purest form in which we recognize the death drive."[30] This is more than a paradox. It suggests that at the limit of a person's relation to the community is an absolute solitude which, in becoming self-destruction, renounces and negates that which has already negated the subject and so affirms the life in community which has been denied. Lacan therefore views the therapeutic task of psychoanalysis as the labor of making the alternative concretely possible: "the question of the termination of analysis is that of the moment at which the satisfaction of the subject discovers how to realize itself in the satisfaction of everyone, that is, of all those with whom this satisfaction associates itself in a human undertaking."[31]

This conception places the dialectic of subject and community between the two extremes of a suicidal affirmation of life against domination and the subject's discovery of his or her own satisfaction in the satisfaction of the community. I consider such an interpretation culturalist, to the extent that Lacan construes the dialectic of intersubjectivity purely from the effects of language as such. The historical resonances of the master-slave relation fade into the question of culture disconnected from that of society. The problematic that presses against Lacan's whole reflection without ever breaking into the clear is this: that the community itself is divided, and that this division, comprised of the social division of labor and the social organization of sexual difference, assumes historically specific forms that inflect the subject's experience of him- or herself and of the community. So, too, these modes of social domination determine the specific forms of isolation and of participation that any subject confronts.

Psychoanalysis as Social Allegory

If domination is recognized in its social bases, we can all the more radically discover the possibility of freedom in the most fundamental

---

[30]Ibid.
[31]Ibid., p. 321.

dimension of culture—language and the self-constituting power of the speaking subject. Children's play has already suggested the terms of the problem. Any actual interaction, preformed and dictated by a specific social institution, the family, in this instance, limits the possibilities of interaction which emerge in the experience of speech as the activity that at once ties the subject to others and points beyond institutionally constrained relations to others. The negativity of the springing of the subject into language makes possible creative, undominated self-activity *with others*. Because the community itself is divided, the dialectic of subject and community does not take place between the poles of solitude and integration.

The experience of the subject, who is constituted by and constituting through language, is lived within the struggle between the unrealized community and those social institutions which, deriving from the divisions of the community, shape the situations, interactions, and arrangements of everyday life. Thus whenever the subject discovers, in a collective undertaking, the interlocking of his or her own satisfactions with the satisfaction of others, that undertaking itself unfolds within the effects and the struggles of the social community's divisions.

Reification is the pervasive effect of the capitalist division of labor. The struggle between domination and self-activity takes shape, in the modern individual's life, in the polarity of work and play. The adult's labor and the child's play mark the presence of the death drive in what Freud conceived as its two forms, the bound and the unbound. For the subject of alienated labor, self-preservation is the fusion of destruction and production. For the child, speaking-playing is a creative praxis that negates the domination of another. In labor, the death drive combines with eros; in play, the unbound, pure death drive frees eros.

Although the Lacanian reflection on the relation to death does not yield this formulation, it does approach it. The relation to death defines the subject's tie to the community as the ambiguity of the subject's radical dependence on the field of the Other and the possibility of his or her freedom with others. This relation to death is not a violence turned against the self or others; it is a movement, or force, or "drive," which comes from the very fact that the subject is not from birth integrated into the world of others. Indeed, this unabsorbed remainder that always subsists between the subject and the Other, between being and meaning, is how Lacan understands the unconscious.

Once it is acknowledged, on the other hand, that any problematic of the subject and the community has to be worked out in terms of the social dialectic of institutions, then the two forms of the death drive, bound and unbound, have to be read across the political dynamic of institutions and groups. Gilles Deleuze and Félix Guattari, in their *Anti-Oedipus*, attempt to do this by reconstructing the psychoanalytic categories in terms of a radical distinction between individual fantasy and group fantasy; this distinction corresponds to the one that I have made between fantasy as speaking-playing and the interiorized fantasy of the "day-dream":

> we see that the individual fantasy is itself plugged into the existing social field, but apprehends it in the form of imaginary qualities that confer on it a kind of transcendence or immortality under the shelter of which the individual, the ego, plays out its pseudodestiny: what does it matter if I die, says the general, since the Army is immortal? The imaginary dimension of the individual fantasy has a decisive importance over the death instinct, insofar as the immortality conferred on the existing social order carried into the ego all the investments of repression, the phenomena of identification, of "superegoization" and castration, all the resignation-desires (becoming a general; acquiring low, middle, or high rank), including the resignation to dying in the service of this order, whereas the drive itself is projected onto the outside and turned against the others (death to the foreigner, to those who are not of our own ranks!). The revolutionary pole of group fantasy becomes visible, on the contrary, in the power to experience institutions themselves as mortal, to destroy them or change them according to the articulations of desire and the social field, by making the death instinct into a veritable institutional creativity.[32]

Within the social order of capitalism, it is reification, the transformation of the exchanging of human activity into a set of calculable relations between things, that reconstitutes the subject as a separated individual, that converts play into the interiorized fantasies of the ego, that binds the death drive to eros and makes self-preservation an act of aggression.

When Freud incorporates the postulate of a death drive into his reflections on the nature of human society and history, he describes the struggle between the libidinal binding of humanity by eros, which he equates with "civilization" (*Kultur*), and the human aggressiveness that pits individuals against one another:

[32]Gilles Deleuze and Félix Guattari, *Anti-Oedipus: Capitalism and Schizophrenia*, trans. Robert Hurley, Mark Seem, and Helen R. Lane (Minneapolis: University of Minnesota Press, 1983), pp. 62–63.

I may now add that civilization is a process in the service of Eros, whose purpose is to combine single human individuals, and after that families, then races, peoples and nations, into one great unity, the unity of mankind [sic]. Why this has to happen, we do not know; the work of Eros is precisely this. These collections of men are libidinally bound to one another. Necessity alone, the advantages of work in common, will not hold them together. But man's natural aggressive instinct, the hostility of each against all and of all against each, opposes this programme of civilization. The aggressive instinct is the derivative and main representative of the death instinct which we have found alongside of Eros and which shares world-dominion with it.[33]

At the core of this vision of society and history there reappears the assumption that I have resisted and criticized in its various manifestations—namely, the notion that a psychology or a sociology can be founded on the naked relation of the individual and society, as though each is a simple entity. It leads Freud to reduce the aggressiveness of individuals toward one another and toward social grouping as such to "man's natural aggressive instinct." However, here, as in the analysis of the *fort! da!* game, the preciseness of Freud's account leaves open another line of reflection. For this antisocial aggressiveness is not in fact a primary category in psychoanalytic theory; rather, it is "the derivative and main representation of the death instinct." In other words, the aggressiveness that counters the libidinal binding of human beings is not the death drive as such but is rather, to employ another of Freud's metaphorics, the mixing of the death drive with eros. A few pages earlier in the sixth chapter of *Civilization and Its Discontents*, Freud pinpoints the theoretical importance of this distinction:

It was not easy, however, to demonstrate the activities of this supposed death instinct. The manifestations of Eros were conspicuous and noisy enough. It might be assumed that the death instinct operated silently within the organism towards its dissolution, but that, of course, was no proof. A more fruitful idea was that a portion of the instinct is diverted towards the external world and comes to light as an instinct of aggressiveness and destructiveness. In this way the instinct could be pressed into the service of Eros, in that the organism was destroying some other thing, whether animate or inanimate, instead of destroying its own self.[34]

[33]Freud, *Civilization and Its Discontents*, S.E., XXI, 122.
[34]Ibid., p. 119.

If the rivalrous and destructive relation between human beings marks a "confluence," "admixture," or "fusion" (these being Freud's other metaphors) of the death drive with the libidinal, binding power of eros, we might therefore ask: How can the social bond include both a binding and unbinding, a creative and destructive, tendency, and how can the subject's life instinct become destructive? I have suggested that such a contradiction, at work in the social bond and in the structure of subjectivity, has a precise *historical* meaning connected to the fundamental tendencies of capitalist society.

Capital, altering the social organization of production, institutes, for the first time in history, homogeneity as a purely economic mechanism which asserts its dominance over all other aspects of human existence and experience. Capital drives a wedge into social life, splitting the economic from the symbolic and splintering the symbolic into fragmentary experiences and interactions. The social bond in capitalist society is contradictory. The economy, in becoming the mechanism that binds all members of society together in an abstract universality, at the same time absolutely separates them. It causes human beings to face one another as objects, instruments, and rivals. Moreover, as the economy asserts its autonomy and primacy as the determining element of the social bond, it opposes itself to the symbolic—that is, to the very practices in which all libidinal and affective ties among human beings develop. The social bond is torn by a centrifugal and a centripetal force. The economy moving for itself exerts a centripetal force that pulls all human activity and interaction into the orbit of the production and exchange of economic values; at the same time, its centrifugal force expels the symbolic domain of expressions and interactions which human beings experience as the possibility of activity *for itself.*

To pose a simple antagonism between the individual and society is a falsification. It is necessary to recognize that the contradiction afflicting the social bond in capitalist society also passes into subjectivity itself. The split between the economy and the symbolic produces a division in the subject, namely, the conflict of the reified ego with the body and its drives, with fantasy and interaction. As the production and acquisition of exchange values are imposed on the subject as the mode of securing material existence, the death drive is fused with that aspect of the life instincts we call self-preservation. Just as the autonomous economy binds individuals by separating them, so the individual must carry out the very production and maintenance of life by means of actions destructive of others, of nature, of the self. The integration of the death drive into the ego's means of self-preservation is a special achievement of capitalism, an effect of commodification. The "aggressive instinct" is not so natural after all, however pervasive in our social and psychological life.

Here we must stretch Freud's terms to their limit. Struggling against this fusion of the instincts of life and death, of self-preservation and destruction, is the symbolic, where human beings, their subjectivity constituted in the possibility of self-constitution through interaction, glimpse and are driven toward free, developing interaction, and it is here that we must point to the death drive—the death drive in its silent, nonderivative, nonrepresentable force. The death drive clears away all that inhibits and restrains free human interaction. It founds the symbolic. It is the force in the emergence of the spool, the precondition of *fort! da!* as speaking-playing. All of Freud's conceptualizations keep suggesting that mastery, domination, and rivalry are not the death drive but its fusion with eros; they represent the bound form of the death drive. It is necessary, then, on the other side, to affirm the instituting and creative power of the death drive in its pure and silent force. The death drive frees eros. Human liberation requires not some ultimate liberation *from* the death drive, but the constant liberation *of* it, "making [it] into a veritable institutional creativity."

Freud's failure to grasp the specific way in which the capitalist mode of production constructs the "self-preservative instinct" has consequences on several levels. It causes him constantly to shift ground in his formulations regarding the sexual instincts and the ego-instincts; it stamps his various reflections on society and history with the kind of anachronistic projections that preclude any truly social and historical problematic. Finally, the failure to recognize that self-preservation is not an instinct at all, but rather a socially determined, practical relation of human beings to reality, causes Freud to take refuge in biological concepts whenever the purely psychological description of subjectivity founders, rather than seeing in the ambivalences and impasses of psychological theory the need for a social theory adequate to the discoveries of psychoanalysis itself.

The dialogue that Horkheimer and Adorno carried on with Freud in their *Dialectic of Enlightenment* inaugurated a critical reassessment of Freud starting from the historical specificity of the ego, rational thought, and reality as Freud understood them. They forged their concept of the "dialectic of enlightenment" in order to show that the optimal forms of bourgeois thought, culture, ethics, and politics tend

toward self-destruction; the universality and freedom which enlightenment originally promised are increasingly obliterated by the real
cause of bourgeois consciousness itself: commodification, the process
that strives to transform all objects, activities, and interactions into
abstract values subject to economic calculation.

I will follow the initial steps of Horkheimer and Adorno's critique,
but will continue to develop it in a direction that goes against the grain
of the whole Frankfurt School reading of Freud. For Horkheimer and
Adorno, as for Marcuse, psychoanalysis was important essentially as
a theory of instinct, whereas I believe that the critical theory of society
must draw on psychoanalysis as an interpretive practice capable of
generating a theory of intersubjectivity. *Dialectic of Enlightenment*
itself moves toward a conception of cultural history in which the reign
of instrumental reason, on the one hand, and unbridled instinct, on
the other, acquires an implacable necessity that is but the nightmarish
inversion of the logic of history which orthodox Marxism distilled from
Marx's analysis of capital.

Like Max Weber, Horkheimer and Adorno note the strange com-
plicity between Protestantism and the development of capitalism. Eth-
ically the body becomes an alien force to be controlled; at the level of
the labor process the body becomes, for the producer, an instrument.
The subject's mature relation to the body is a relation to its productive
capacity, its labor power, a measurable quantity that is sold in the
marketplace like any other commodity. The Protestant ethos had a
special role in the historical reconstitution of this relation to the body.
"Christianity," Horkheimer and Adorno write, "extolled the virtues
of work but declared the flesh to be the root of all evil."[35] In bourgeois
society, reason and the ego face social reality as a world of things from
which abstract value is to be extracted, whether in the form of capital
or of the wage. The bourgeois claim of universality—the universality
of "Man," of freedom, and of culture—is the ideological mask of the
social domination inherent in the relation between labor and capital.
The truth in this claim lies on another level from its ideological expression; the separation of the reality-oriented ego from the body, which
founded the ethical organization of bourgeois experience, is extended
to the producing classes insofar as the institution of wage labor separates the laboring subject from the laboring body. Bourgeois univer-

---

[35] Max Horkheimer and Theodor W. Adorno, *Dialectic of Enlightenment*, trans. John
Cumming (New York: Seabury, 1972), p. 231.

sality is not the given, inalienable "rights of man," but rather the tendency of bourgeois alienation to impose itself on the producers as the condition of their own existence. The truly universal drive in the bourgeois era is the hegemonic aim of reconstituting subjectivity through the reorganization of material production and the labor process.

Enlightenment, according to Horkheimer and Adorno, is the intellectual side of this hegemonic process. Enlightenment rationality develops a "form of knowledge which copes most proficiently with the facts and supports the individual most effectively in the mastery of nature. Its principles are the principles of self-preservation."[36] Just as it reconstitutes the producer's body as an instrument, capitalism forms, for the wage laborer and for the entrepreneur, the calculative ego as the psychological agency through which the subject relates to a reified reality. The critique of Freud's historical speculations insists on the historical specificity of the relation between ego and reality established by bourgeois thought and science:

> Like science, magic pursues aims, but seeks to achieve them by mimesis—not by progressively distancing itself from the object. It is not grounded in the "sovereignty of ideas," which the primitive, like the neurotic, is said to ascribe to himself; there can be no "over-evaluation of mental processes as against reality" where there is no radical distinction between thoughts and reality. The "unshakable confidence in the possibility of world domination," which Freud anachronistically ascribes to magic, corresponds to realistic world domination only in terms of a more skilled science. The replacement of the milieu-bound practices of the medicine man by all-inclusive industrial technology required first of all the autonomy of ideas in regard to objects that was achieved in the reality-adjusted ego.[37]

This argument sheds light on Lacan's frequent suggestion that the historical parameters of psychoanalysis are defined by the emergence of the subject of modern science. On the other hand, Horkheimer and Adorno's uncritical affirmation of the self-regulative and autonomous subject of liberal bourgeois society can be corrected by reiterating Lacan's notion that modern neurosis must be seen in relation to the erosion of those symbolic practices which, in connecting the body and desire to a communal context, prevented the "superego" and the "ego

---

[36]Ibid., p. 83.
[37]Ibid., p. 11.

ideal" from becoming the intrapsychic processes of the isolated individual.

Another hypothesis can be derived from Freud's efforts to link neurosis to mythic thinking, superstition, and religious ideas. The forms of rational calculation that capitalism created, in separating out the production of economic value as an autonomous force in social life, could not truly abolish religion and myth. Rather, these symbolic-affective domains tend in the development of capitalism to disintegrate as collectively articulated discourses and to be relocated within the privatized subject of the bourgeois order: they become unconscious in the Freudian sense.

A systematic reformulation of fundamental Freudian concepts follows from this. The reified ego, with its rational, self-preserving orientation toward outer reality, is that moment in the structure of subjectivity which is governed by the laws of commodity production, exchange, and consumption. It is less a "psychological mechanism" than a field of perceptions, actions, and relations marked by the dominance of exchange value; reification is the historical result and continuous effect of those processes that transform the interhuman activities of producing, exchanging, and consuming into value production, exchange, and consumption. Capitalism tears material production from the affective and symbolic matrix in which it existed for artisans and peasants, and even for slaves in the ancient mode of production, and reconstitutes it as the economy, that is, as the homogeneous domain of rational calculation and of the abstract sign of value.

Freud's theory of narcissism centered on the notion that the reality-ego is built up as the relation to outer reality is desexualized. This "desexualization" is not a psychological process; it is the effect of the social process that in the history of modern society, and in the history of the individual's so-called maturation, dissolves or displaces the subject's affective and symbolic relations with others and institutes the calculable relation to *things,* that is, to persons, objects, and activities as bearers of the monetary sign. Reification is thus precisely a process, not an achieved condition, of capitalist society; it is the relentless transformation, in the history of society and of the individual, of the affective into the calculable, of the symbolic into the sign or value.

The reified ego's relation to the body is complex and contradictory. With respect to the labor process, the body is an instrument, a tool that one "owns" and sells in the marketplace; it is a rationally calculable means for securing exchange value (the wage). Lacan has placed the body as image within the earliest human experiences; as we have seen, the mirror-identifications have the conflicting effects of provoking the subject's anticipation of bodily activity, conditioning yet retarding the access to language, and creating the most basic emotional ambivalences through the subject's identification with others. As the subject becomes an agent within the social relations of capitalism, this primordial relation to the body as image is reinvoked within an altogether different dialectic. On the one hand, the fragility of the isolated individual, producer or entrepreneur, facing the social world as an inert reality, is ideologically encoded as the individual's self-sufficiency; this central element of bourgeois ideology thus finds its subjective coordinates in the reversion to the mirror phase. On the other hand, the real basis of this reversion—the commodification of labor—destroys the free activity of the body which the mirror phase originally anticipated; the alienated mastery of the instrumentalized body freezes the subject in a self-domination that ideologically, and in practice, appears as freedom, self-sufficiency, and autonomy. It is in this conjunction of the instrumentalized body and the imaginary body that the social agent achieves maturity, that is, the loss of free, self-developing activity.

Distinct from the body as image and as instrument is the erotogenic body, which psychoanalysis discovered to be complexly connected to the entire network of affective and symbolic ties among human beings. The theory of sexuality describes the differentiation of the body into erotogenic zones that follow their paths of excitation and gratification independently of one another. Freud conceived of these "component instincts"—the oral and anal drives, voyeurism, sadism, and so on—as making demands on the ego, which is then charged with either meeting those demands, through some "reality-altering" action, or averting them by means of repression. Such a conception misses the role of reification. The formation of the ego through the desexualization of reality is a historical and social process; the separation of the erotogenic body and reality has a specific form in bourgeois society. The subject's intention to satisfy the body must make a detour through exchange value; the response to the demands of the body is deferred, for the visible aim of laboring is the wage. The laborer converts the wage into food, clothing, shelter, and the objects of everyday life by means of a series of discrete exchanges of value (purchases). The gratification of the erotic drives is thereby not merely postponed, in the Freudian sense of delayed gratification. It is completely altered, for the subject's every action and transaction take place within a system of abstract equivalents. The entire circuit of production, exchange, and consumption is submitted to rational, quantitative calculation, making the wage equivalent to what it can buy, which is in turn equivalent to what the subject needs. Need itself is an abstraction, which is determined not by the body but by the wage itself. The need-code, as Baudrillard rightly calls it, superimposes itself on the erotogenic body, on activity, and on interaction. No universal distinction between work and sexuality can account for the subjective conflicts abstraction and calculation create. The modern subject's experience is divided between need, a realm of abstraction which is real, and desire, the concrete but unrealized realm of the possible.

6

Aesthetics of
Male Fantasy

From Psychoanalysis to Critical Hermeneutics

"Up till now we have left it to creative writers to depict for us the 'necessary conditions for loving' which govern people's choice of an object, and the way in which they bring the demands of their imagination into harmony with reality."[1] Thus begins the first of Freud's *Contributions to a Psychology of Love*. In choosing the term "psychology" for these three essays on sexuality and love, Freud underscores his intent to replace literary representations with a scientific presentation of clinical materials. Lacan often insists that psychoanalysis is not a psychology. But psychoanalytic theory can move beyond psychology only on the condition that the problematic of the *social* constitution of subjectivity and lived experience become the consistent framework within which the concerns of psychoanalysis are elaborated. As we have seen, no two terms require this framework more than *imagination* and *reality*.

In defining love as the subject's effort to harmonize imagination with reality, Freud touches on a thoroughly social problematic: the subject's relation to reality, the genesis and organization of fantasy, and the historical forms of the attempt to harmonize fantasy and reality within the sphere of intimate experience. The "necessary conditions for lov-

[1]Sigmund Freud, "A Special Type of Choice of Object Made by Men" (1910), *The Standard Edition of the Complete Psychological Works*, ed. and trans. James Strachey et al. (London: Hogarth, 1953–1974), XI, 165.

ing" are social, and love itself is a cultural form. Indeed, a critical hermeneutics will have to reassess Freud's sense of the resource and limits of literature to express the truth of love: "The writer can indeed draw on certain qualities which fit him to such a task: above all, on a sensitivity that enables him to perceive the hidden impulses in the minds of other people, and the courage to let his own unconscious speak. But there is one circumstance which lessens the evidential value of what he has to say. Writers are under the necessity to produce intellectual and aesthetic pleasure, as well as certain emotional effects."[2] Is this intellectual and aesthetic pleasure merely extraneous to the attempt, in love, to harmonize imagination and reality?

Through a reading of Goethe's *The Sorrows of Young Werther*, I will come to challenge Freud's methodological assumption that psychoanalysis can take up love as an object of inquiry once it has successfully brushed away the extraneous pleasure of the aesthetic: "These observations will, it may be hoped, serve to justify us in extending a strictly scientific treatment to the field of human love. Science is, after all, the most complete renunciation of the pleasure principle of which our mental activity is capable."[3] A socially critical hermeneutic will also have to confront the question of the relation between understanding and the negation or "renunciation" of the pleasure principle, but without separating the aesthetic from love's harmonizing of fantasy and reality. The question becomes, instead, the very connection between the fantasies that underlie the "necessary conditions for loving" and aesthetic form itself. Such an approach does not in fact abandon the Freudian project. For the concept of sublimation not only turns out to be the key though undeveloped category of Freud's thoughts on art, but also continually appears at the center of his theory of love. It is toward an interpretation of the historical and social forms of "sublimation" that we must aim.

By the same token, a critical hermeneutic of the cultural forms comprising "intimacy" cannot do without psychoanalysis. Yet the obstacle is clear. Historical reflection has never entered into psychoanalytic theory except in a deflected, partial way. As a social thinker, Freud developed his great theme of civilization and instincts without grasping the specific relationship between the "civilizing process" and the evolution of capitalist society. In the writings on sexuality and love, Freud

[2]Ibid.
[3]Ibid.

never wavered from his assumption that the modern world is incapable of abandoning the social norms of marriage and the family as the cornerstone of "civilized morality." This assumption is often regarded, narrowly and wrongly, as Freud's Victorian prejudice. It was, rather, an expression of his profound historical pessimism. Such pessimism may have been, and may remain, justified, but a theory cannot be tested according to its optimism or pessimism. It can be tested only in terms of its relation to the historical tendencies and countertendencies within society.

Freud himself theorized from the standpoint of the dominant tendencies of modern society—its moral precepts and behaviorial norms, its modes of creating and distributing wealth, its technical organization of violence, its systematic denial of human satisfactions. However much he raised his voice in protest against these tendencies, the theoretical standpoint stamped itself on psychoanalysis and affected its truth content. Freud's sexual theory became anchored in the notion that psychosexual maturation follows a path toward the "synthesis of all the component instincts under the primacy of the genitals and in the service of the reproductive function."[4] Critical theory, by contrast, allies itself with the countertendencies of modern society; theory takes on the task, in the words of the early Marx, of "the self-clarification (critical philosophy) of the *struggles* and *wishes* of the age."[5] One must indeed choose: does the intellectual labor of theory and interpretation proceed from the order and reality of the age, or from its struggles and wishes?

Freud proceeded from order and reality, in a tragic-realist mode. Lacan rejoins the project of critical theory in this context as a strange ally. Lacan's thought is in the ironic mode, meaning that it seeks to avoid the political consequences latent in Freudian theory and yet hides from the political consequences explicit in the alternative view. This ambivalence is particularly striking in *Le séminaire, Livre XI: Les quatre concepts fondamentaux de la psychanalyse.* Much of Seminar XI is devoted to a thoroughgoing reconceptualization of each element in Freud's sexual theory: the component instincts, love, narcissism, and sexual reproduction. At the same time, Lacan consistently pretends that Freud never really meant what is plainly written in the crucial essays "On Narcissism: An Introduction" (1914) and "Instincts and

[4]Freud, "Instincts and Their Vicissitudes" (1915), *S.E.,* XIV, 138.
[5]Karl Marx, letter to Ruge, September 1843, in *Early Writings,* trans. Rodney Livingstone and Gregor Benton (New York: Vintage, 1975), p. 209.

Their Vicissitudes" (1915). This rhetorical tactic does have a grain of truth, to the extent that Lacan unlocks the dialectical core of Freud's writings against many of their own most prominent and influential themes. More often, however, such maneuvers have encouraged a kind of psychoanalytic scholasticism rather than theoretical rigor, and they have obscured the consequences of the controversy which Lacan himself raised.

That controversy turns on Freud's definition of the heterosexual, genital aim of reproduction as what he called *die ganze Sexualstrebung* ("the sexual impulsion as a whole," in the *Standard Edition*). Lacan disputes the very existence of this supposed genital drive:

> The psychoanalytic experience teaches us...that the genital drive is submitted to the circulation of the Oedipus complex, to the elementary and other structures of kinship. This is what is called the field of culture—in an inadequate manner, since this field is presumed to be founded on a *no man's land* where genitality as such could subsist, whereas genitality is in fact broken up, not brought together, for nowhere in the subject can the *ganze Sexualstrebung* be grasped.[6]

No human being assumes a relation to the reproductive function of sexuality except through complex cultural mediations. Freud's own researches had shown that reproduction, heterosexuality, and genital sexuality are the last things anyone understands about sexuality. They are the result of a social learning process. "The paths of what one must do as a man or woman," Lacan says in Seminar XI "are completely left up to a drama, a scenario which is placed in the Other—what is strictly speaking the Oedipus complex."[7] Lacan's revision of Freud stops short of truly regrounding the psychoanalytic theory of sexuality in a cultural and social problematic, for the reason that he conceives of *culture* without reference to *society*.

Lacan's very tacitly stated suspicion of Lévi-Strauss's definition of the "field of culture" as a virtually autonomous system of signs and regulated exchanges reflects the psychoanalytic discovery that any subject's inscription in such a system of kinship relations, whether as the agent or the object of exchange, not only is susceptible to innumerable complicating effects but moreover never completely integrates sexuality

---

[6]Jacques Lacan, *Les quatre concepts fondamentaux de la psychanalyse: Le séminaire, Livre XI* (Paris: Seuil, 1973), p. 173.

[7]Ibid., p. 186.

into a regulated system of exchanges. All the deviations in experience from the reproductive-heterosexual aim indicate, in Lacan's view, something more than mere turbulence or "noise" in the system of culture. The subject's integration into the "elementary and other structures of kinship" and the disturbances that arise from this process are rooted together in the Oedipus complex itself. The Oedipus complex is as "pathogenic" as it is "normalizing." Now, this insight will yield no more than a restatement of "civilization and its discontents," unless Lacan's suspicion with regard to Lévi-Strauss is extended to any attempt, including Lacan's own, to grasp a cultural problematic only with reference to language and discourse. For the cultural mediations required for the subject to assume his or her sexual identity and sexual behavior are bound up with social institutions whose logic and function are tied to the total organization of society at a determinate historical moment, and bound up with those cultural codes, like the sex-gender system, which are the vehicle of economic as well as sexual domination.[8]

Lacan acknowledges this problematic only parenthetically, when he touches on a central means by which sexual domination imposes itself on experience (and on theory): *"What value does my desire have for you?*—the eternal question posed in the dialogue of lovers. But the supposed value, for example, of *feminine masochism,* as it's called, should be bracketed and seriously questioned. It belongs to this dialogue, which might well be defined at many points as a *masculine fantasy."*[9] Indeed, is not virtually the entire tradition of the discourse of love, love poetry, treatises on love, and so on, essentially a collection of male fantasies? Which is not to say that this discourse is a phantom. To the contrary, these cultural creations are themselves "intermediaries" in the experience of love—"galeotto fu il libro e chi lo scrisse" ("the go-between was the book and the one who wrote it"), Francesca tells Dante in the *Inferno* to explain how reading caused her to act on her passion for Paolo. Cultural forms and lived experience, fantasy and social domination, are intricately interwoven, and their interconnections have specific historical forms related to the actual organization of society.

[8]Cf. Gayle Rubin, "The Traffic in Women: Notes on the 'Political Economy' of Sex," in Reyna Reiter, ed., *Toward an Anthropology of Women* (New York: Monthly Review Press, 1975), pp. 157–210.
[9]Lacan, *Les quatre concepts,* pp. 175–176.

Although Lacan does not provide the needed aesthetic or sociological framework for such an inquiry, he does provide the philosophical thread in the precept *desire is the desire of the other*. He inflects this concept with a richly ambiguous range of meanings, principally: (1) I desire that my desire be recognized by another; (2) what I desire is the other's desire; and (3) I make the object of another's desire the object of my desire—this last process ranging from the phenomenon of rivalry to the internalization of collectively validated norms, traits, values, and so on. Desire is thus a play of subjectivities, of recognitions and satisfactions, of the body and speech. In an earlier, more Hegelian formulation, Lacan gave the dialectic of desire its fuller scope: "The satisfaction of human desire is possible only when mediated by the desire and labor of another."[10] The actual forms in which the dialectic of desire is played and lived are historical. These forms will open or close the play of satisfactions and recognitions in specific ways which must, in turn, be related to the institutional framework of society as it organizes the satisfaction of human desire through the desire and labor of others.

How, then, does the bourgeois form of love—male, heterosexual love with the aim of reproduction—structure the dialectic of desire? It is this question that jars the psychoanalytic discourse on love into historical reflection. Freud always theorized from the standpoint of male heterosexuality as it is formed in childhood within the restricted family and as it develops toward an adaptation to marriage and "civilized morality." In denouncing that standpoint, we need also to transform it into a critical self-reflection, an interpretation of the cultural and social forms that comprise the lived experience of male heterosexual love.

I will enlist Lacan—not without resistance!—in this critical task. Lacan's controversy with Freud in Seminar XI centers on the relation between love and narcissism, especially as Freud described it in "Instincts and Their Vicissitudes." Freud had termed the component instincts (or partial drives) *autoerotic*, by which he meant that the satisfaction of instincts involving the mouth, anus, and looking was narcissistic: "Originally, at the very beginning of mental life, the ego is cathected with instincts and is to some extent capable of satisfying them on itself. We call this condition 'narcissism' and this way of obtaining satisfaction 'autoerotic.' At this time the external world is

---

[10]Jacques Lacan, "L'agressivité en psychanalyse," *Ecrits* (Paris: Seuil, 1966), p. 121.

not cathected with interest (in the general sense) and is indifferent for the purposes of satisfaction."[11] Lacan, appealing to the easily available observation that even the newborn infant is avidly interested in its surroundings, rejects the equation of the autoerotic drives with narcissism. Instead, he gives the term *autoerotic* the sense of an impulse that operates on its own, independent of other impulses because localized on an erotogenic zone of the body (the mouth, the anus) and independent of any initial relation to the reproductive function of sexuality. Moreover, Lacan insists, the partial drive necessarily entails a relation to an external object (the breast, feces). The drive follows the circuit of an "out-and-back movement": it departs from and returns to a zone of the erotogenic body, having turned round an object. This interaction of the erotogenic body and objects manifests sexuality in its essential nonrelation to reproduction: "If the drive can be satisfied without having attained what, from the standpoint of the biological totalization of the sexual function, would be its satisfaction in the aim of reproduction, it is because the drive is partial, and has no other goal than this return through its circuit."[12]

The fictional-scientific construct of the "psychical apparatus" had led Freud to the hypothesis that the "external world"—including others—could be "indifferent for the purposes of satisfaction." The Lacanian dialectic of desire rejects this hypothesis, seeing the libidinal ground of intersubjectivity in the most elementary forms of the partial drives; the part-object required to satisfy these drives belongs to "the field of the Other," whether the mother's breast or the feces in their valence as a gift for another.

Freud followed out his assumption that the autoerotic drives are narcissistic by then distinguishing love for another (object-libido) from the narcissism of self-love (ego-libido): "The highest phase of development of which object-libido is capable is in the state of being in love."[13] Lacan, to the contrary, places loving as such within the framework of narcissism. Where Freud saw an active-passive opposition between loving and being loved, Lacan sees a narcissistic reflexivity: to love is to want to be loved. Lacan here attempts to resolve a series of ambiguities and inconsistencies that run through Freud's account of

---

[11]Freud, "Instincts and Their Vicissitudes," pp. 134–135.
[12]Lacan, *Les quatre concepts*, p. 163.
[13]Freud, "On Narcissism: An Introduction" (1914), *S.E.*, XIV, 76.

love in "On Narcissism" and "Instincts and Their Vicissitudes." The
heart of the problem is a passage from the latter essay:

> the word "to love" moves further and further into the sphere of the pure
> pleasure-relation of the ego to the object and finally becomes fixed to
> sexual objects in the narrower sense and to those which satisfy the needs
> of sublimated sexual instincts. The distinction between the ego-instincts
> [*Ichtriebe*] and the sexual instincts which we have imposed on our psy-
> chology is thus in conformity with the spirit of our language. The fact
> that we are not in the habit of saying of a single sexual instinct that it
> loves its object, but regard the relation of the ego to its sexual object as
> the most appropriate case in which to employ the word "love"—this
> fact teaches us that the word can only begin to be applied in this relation
> after there has been a synthesis of all the component instincts of sexuality
> under the primacy of the genitals and in the service of the reproductive
> function.[14]

This passage ends with the ill-founded conclusion that in love the partial
drives are synthesized into a reproductive heterosexual aim, but its
argument turns on Freud's enigmatic decision to associate love not
with the sexual instincts but with the ego-instincts or self-preservative
instincts, which are themselves not sexual at all. The pleasure that the
ego-instincts seek is the "homeostasis" of being satisfied with oneself.
   Let us restate the passage by treating its conclusion not as the necessary outcome of the dialectic of human desire, but rather as a particular experience whose possibility and preconditions Freud is trying
to explain. Let us also "gender" the ego and the object. Freud would
then say: in order for sexuality to be integrated into the reproductive
aim in a heterosexual marital relation, and in order for me to love the
woman in this relation, she must please me by making me satisfied
with myself. Goethe's young Werther will express the satisfaction he
feels in the first signs that Lotte loves him in just these terms, and with
no trace of irony:

> No, I do not deceive myself! In her dark eyes I have read a genuine
> sympathy for me and my destiny. Yes, I feel—and in this I can trust my
> heart—that she—oh, may I, can I express the Heaven that exists in these
> words?—that she loves me!
>   Loves me!—And how precious I become in my own eyes, how I—to

[14]Freud, "Instincts and Their Vicissitudes," pp. 137–138.

you as an understanding person I may say it—how I admire myself since she loves me.[15]

The Lacanian formula "to love is to want to be loved" thus defines love as narcissistic satisfaction obtained through a relation to another. Loving is "loving oneself through another."[16] This is not, however, an intersubjectivity founded on recognition of another. Rather, this form of love founds the relation of "self" and "other," man and woman, on the coordinates of what psychoanalysis calls the ideal ego and the ego ideal. In "On Narcissism," Freud's initial distinction between narcissistic self-love (ego-libido) and object love (object-libido) keeps slipping away whenever he notes men's tendency to see embodied in the woman they love elements or traits of the ego ideal:

> Since, with the object type (or attachment type), being in love occurs in virtue of the fulfillment of infantile conditions for loving, we may say that whatever fulfills that condition is idealized. The sexual ideal may enter into an interesting auxiliary relation to the ego ideal. It may be used for substitutive satisfaction where narcissistic satisfaction encounters real hindrances. In that case a person will love in conformity with the narcissistic type of object-choice, will love what he once was and no longer is, or else what possesses the excellences which he never had at all. The formula... runs thus: what possesses the excellence which the ego lacks for making it an ideal, is loved.[17]

Being in love is wanting to see oneself, through another, as being satisfactory from the viewpoint of this ideal.

This viewpoint is not the woman's judgment, but rather a cultural ideal which she is felt to embody. "The ego ideal," Freud writes in "On Narcissism," "opens up an important avenue for the understanding of group psychology. In addition to its individual side, the ideal has a social side; it is also the common ideal of a family, a class, a nation."[18] When Freud takes up these themes again in *Group Psychology and the Analysis of the Ego* (1921), especially in the important chapter entitled "Being in Love and Hypnosis," his accent falls heavily on the notion that in wanting to be loved a man seeks to satisfy the

---

[15] Johann Wolfgang von Goethe, *The Sorrows of Young Werther*, and *Novella*, trans. Elizabeth Mayer and Louise Bogan (New York: Vintage, 1973), p. 46.

[16] Lacan, *Les quatre concepts*, p. 177.

[17] Freud, "On Narcissism," pp. 100–101.

[18] Ibid., p. 101.

insufficient or threatened or damaged relation that he actually has to these binding ideals: "It is even obvious, in many forms of love-choice, that the object serves as a substitute for some unattained ego ideal of our own. We love it on account of the perfections which we have striven to reach for our own ego, and which we should now like to procure in this roundabout way as a means of satisfying our narcissism." Freud here goes so far as to say that in the most intense state of love the " 'devotion' of the ego to the object... is no longer to be distinguished from a sublimated devotion to an abstract idea."[19]

For Lacan, such a "roundabout way... of satisfying our narcissism" is the very essence of love. The ego ideal is "this sole signifier"—that is, this trait from the binding discourse of a family, class, or nation— "necessary to introduce a perspective placed somewhere in the Other from which the Other sees me in the form I like to be seen. The perspective of the ego ideal is that from which the subject will see himself, as one says, *as seen by another*—which will permit him to sustain himself in a dual relation that is satisfying for him from the standpoint of love."[20] In love, the subject's ideal image of himself (ideal ego) is satisfied by the love of another who embodies, for this subject, the ideal perspective (ego ideal) which he otherwise fails to measure up to. He wants the other, insofar as she embodies the ego ideal, to love his ideal image of himself—"How I admire myself since she loves me."

The ever-present irony in Lacan's remarks on the narcissism of love stems, in part at least, from the role of love in the therapeutic process of psychoanalysis. Transference love is the source of resistance to the unconscious in psychoanalysis. Lacan will claim that the transference is "the truth of love" in the sense that it manifests the dimension of deception in love. The path of analysis is toward the "liquidation" of the transference love. The liquidation of the transference "must be the liquidation of that deception by means of which the transference tends to work in the direction of a closing up of the unconscious. I have already explained the mechanism by referring to the narcissistic relation through which the subject turns himself into a lovable object. From his references to the one who ought to love him he tries to entice the Other into a mirage relation to convince this Other that he is worthy of love (*aimable*)."[21]

[19]Freud, *Group Psychology and the Analysis of the Ego, S.E.* XVIII, 112–113.
[20]Lacan, *Les quatre concepts*, p. 241.
[21]Ibid.

The transference love involves at the same time an idealization of the analyst, owing to his or her authority, prestige, and expertise. The subject approaches the analyst as a "subject who's supposed to know"—to know my desire and the meaning of what I say. Through this idealization, the subject will attribute to the analyst those traits of the ego ideal from whose perspective the subject wants to be viewed as worthy of love. (The tendency for the analytic transference to mobilize principally ideals archaically associated with the parents caused Freud to define the ego ideal as "the representative of our relation to our parents.")[22] The analytic situation sets out, through the subject's own speaking, in search of the unconscious; the transference ambiguously advances and hinders this search. In the words of Daniel Sibony, "The searching of the unconscious, its throbbing in speech, produces a love relation which alone sustains this searching: the transference—sustains it but also blocks it."[23] For I fail to recognize my desire in supposing it to be known. The analytic situation activates this unrecognized desire but at first leaves it unconscious; libido is *transferred* from the repressed material yet to be unveiled in the course of interpretation onto the figure of the analyst as an idealized object of love.

Interpretation, in Lacanian doctrine, is the libidinal subversion of this love, of this idealization, of the supposition that the Other knows what I desire. The subversion of the supposed knowledge transforms the speech relation itself. Wherever I give up telling the stories that prove I am worthy of love, I begin to construct the real history of my genesis. The request for love initially addressed to the analyst (the ideal) is supplanted by the subject's discovery of the libidinal impulses tied to his or her most basic fantasies. At this watershed the analysis breaks off: "What then becomes of those who have passed through the experience of this opaque relation to their origin, to the drive? How can someone who has made their way through the root fantasy then live the instinctual impulse? That's beyond analysis, and has never been broached."[24]

Lacan considers this question "beyond analysis" because it is an ethical question which the individual is able to pose only at the end of analysis: Do I want what I desire? The whole process of the analysis

[22]Freud, *The Ego and the Id* (1923), *S.E.*, XIX, 36.

[23]Daniel Sibony, "A propos du transfert," *Le nom et le corps* (Paris: Seuil, 1974), p. 180.

[24]Lacan, *Les quatre concepts*, pp. 245–246.

would be compromised if the analyst were to give counsel on this question. With the termination of analysis, this "ideal"—the traits, values, norms, and so on, that bind the individual's identity to the collectivity—will exert its claims anew. How the subject will live or not live the impulses disclosed in analysis in the face of these claims is easily ignored by analysts—it is, after all, none of their business.

Do I want what I desire?—this question also always takes a political, collective form, one that tends to disappear in the analytic process. Analysis steers clear of affirming or disputing the subject's ideal identifications. Indeed, they are perhaps implicitly reaffirmed because not opened to dispute. The claims of the so-called ego ideal have become visible in the analysis only with reference to the childhood relation to the parents, a relation that can seem to belong to the remote past. But the real scope of everything that requires me to want its love if I want my identity permeates the institutions and situations of social life. The dialectic of desire that psychoanalysis has discovered remains largely hidden and unheard within psychoanalysis itself. Daniel Sibony has seen in this a challenge to the self-limitations of psychoanalysis:

> "What, exactly, do you psychoanalyze?" One can of course reply: we analyze the individual's psyche (now that takes nerve): or, more "seriously": we analyze the patient's relation to the analyst insofar as it repeats a history, that of relations in the family. But there are many more sites of repetition, repetitions of other things, and many other props besides the analyst in his armchair. If psychoanalysis were to get up from the armchair, it would probably scatter and multiply—the unconscious is at work everywhere.... If psychoanalysis is now so little capable of hearing what is said—is shouted—in the political domain, though it is constantly intruding, this is perhaps not unrelated to the fact that psychoanalysis is considered a science, or a technique, whereas it is an open process of analysis-interpretation.[25]

A collective psychoanalysis?—Yes, though it cannot be invented whole-cloth, nor does it proceed directly from the clinical forms of group analysis which have seen their most significant development in the work of analysts such as R. D. Laing and Félix Guattari. Sibony's questioning is important first in redefining the limit of psychoanalysis in political terms. Psychoanalysis is the restricted, precollective form of the hermeneutics of subversion. So long as it eschews this self-

---

[25]Sibony, "Le transfini et la castration," *Le nom et le corps*, pp. 231–232.

understanding, its theory and practice will wander further from their sources of truth; psychoanalysis will continue to detach itself from the struggles and wishes of the age. This limit cannot be crossed in the manner of an "applied psychoanalysis," which has most often, even when it achieves important insights, merely carried a restricted interpretation into the wider domain of culture, whether religion, art, or literature.

A stronger demand for a collective psychoanalysis needs to be made in order that two related problematics come to the fore. First is the question of how the very processes of political formation and organization can develop their own self-understanding with reference to the dialectic of desire and the subversive hermeneutic of psychoanalysis. Every political process is caught up in the conflicts between desire and reality; between fantasies formed out of socially produced experiences of dissatisfaction, trauma, or loss and the critical cognition of social institutions; between those desires that urge individuals and collectivities toward self-activity and those instituted ideals to which human beings subject themselves in order to preserve their identity, security, self-respect. Politics has the task of discovering the subversive work of desire, and political organization stalls or regresses wherever it refuses the process of interpretation and replaces collective self-understanding with dogma.

The second problematic which pushes psychoanalysis toward a collective hermeneutic of subversion is the field of questions that we are exploring. Psychoanalysis is more than a methodological supplement to socially critical hermeneutics. It is first of all indispensable to the view that works of culture belong to a continuum of experience whose layers of interaction, fantasy, and cognition run through the whole history of an individual. Traditional theory uses the interpretation of cultural works to construct a "universe of meaning," a separate realm of universal, that is, socially binding meanings and values. Freud called the anchor-point that ties the subject's identity to these communal ideals the "ego ideal" or, later, the "super-ego." By the same token, these communal ideals arise from works and their interpretation; moreover, a subject's fantasies acquire a collective validity, a socially critical significance, only insofar as they become connected to cultural works and particularly to the forms of fantasy we call art. Consider again the two tasks I have proposed for critical hermeneutics: to bring forward from cultural heritages their power as concrete utopia; and, second, to pursue an always renewed counterinterpretation of the cultural tradition. It is

such counterinterpretations that a collective psychoanalysis should provide, undermining those meanings and symbolic constructions that
transfigure social domination into images of transcendence and establish communal ideals which rest on the real absence of community.

Let us now reconnect the psychoanalytic and social elements of our
reflection on love before turning to the aesthetic element. Psychoanalysis has addressed itself essentially to two forms of love, the transference
and male heterosexuality with an (implicit or explicit) reproductive
aim. In both these experiences of love, psychoanalysis discloses a number of paradoxes or ironies: to love is to want to be loved; loving is
loving onself through another; love is founded in the desexualized ego.
These paradoxes must be illuminated in terms of the material framework of capitalist social relations, including the organization of the
labor process, and not with reference to the mechanism of a "primitive
psychical apparatus." Freud's account of love is grounded in a formulation that I have restated thus: In male heterosexuality, being in
love is the one condition in which the subject's ego is capable of ap-
propriating the partial drives and integrating them into the *Ichtriebe*
(the self-preservative instincts) while satisfying the pleasure principle.
As I argued in the last chapter, the ego, defined as the seat of the
Ichtriebe, is not a primitive psychical agency; rather, it is the field of
perceptions, cognitions, and actions that are necessitated by the object
world of capitalism, one in which all objects, including other persons,
tend to become values to be acquired or instruments for the acquisition
of values, ultimately reducible to a field of economic calculation.

This "ego" then is socially contructed, and historically took form in
men socialized to the demands of the market economy. The desexualized, self-preserving ego is the product of the historical process that
"desexualizes" (disenchants) the social world. Capitalism at once establishes the rule of the autonomous economy, drains the social relations of the symbolic-affective bonds that characterize earlier social
formations, and creates the separated individual.

As all the themes of the capitalist work ethic suggest, the subject
experiences a permanent rift and conflict between the practices of self-
preservation and the demands of the erotogenic body. Psychoanalysis
represents this conflict as the ego's defensive struggle against the partial
drives, whose upsurge is a source of unpleasure. The concept of the
"ego"—not to be confused with the subject—names the separation of
the erotogenic body from a reified reality, or more precisely, the dis-
ciplining of the body required to make it an instrument of production

at the expense of its erotogeneity. This ego now lets itself be invested with the demands of the erotogenic body (the drives) primarily within a space or site of experience separated from the practical domain of labor and value: the intimate sphere of heterosexual love. It is this split within the private sphere, between economic instrumentality and intimacy, that allows the "integration" of the sexual instincts and the *Ichtriebe*.

The second of Freud's conditions for love is that this integration of the sexual drives into the organized interests of the ego be felt as pleasurable in the sense of providing a source of self-satisfaction. Both Freud and Lacan, by different paths, locate this self-satisfaction in the male subject's experience that in being loved by a woman his ideal image of himself proves satisfactory from the viewpoint of some set of communal ideals which are projected in her—which she, in her person, represents. What is this ideal image of the self? Why does it need confirmation by an idealized Other? How does a woman come to represent those communal ideals? These questions should remind us that the "dialectic of desire" is never a purely psychic or linguistic process. Bourgeois love gives a particular *form* to the dialectic of desire, opening and closing its possibilities in ways that become visible only through interpretation.

The separated male individual's economic life imposes on him a real isolation, which is ideologically represented as self-sufficiency. There is a compulsion to identify with myself in my role as a producer or entrepreneur. There is in this experience not only alienation, as I attempt to identify with myself and see myself in my social role as a thing and a calculator of things; there are also experiences of damage, from the fatigued and broken body of the worker to the wounded self-respect of the entrepreneur subjected to the vicissitudes of the market. Intimacy becomes the sphere in which the male subject seeks not only to repair the damaged body and self but to have the self's fragile, imaginary sufficiency confirmed by the love of an Other. And why an idealized Other? I have been developing the hypothesis that capitalism empties social labor of symbolic-affective bonds, and that those bonds then reappear in other, internalized sites of experience—intimacy, the "psyche," culture in its affirmative character. The communal bonds have become disconnected from traditional societies' ritual, festive, mythic, and religious practices. These bonds are internalized, and their symbols (the ideals) are personified by actual persons within the increasingly isolated and intensified sphere of affective life. There the male self seeks to confirm its imaginary self-sufficiency and its tie to the community through the love of a woman. It is thus that loving as *loving oneself through another* enters into the closest connection with *male fantasy*.

Werther: The Lover's Discourse

Contrary to Freud's search for a science of love, the aesthetic forms in which male fantasy is elaborated cannot be made extraneous to the experience of love. Freud, with occasional flashes of awareness, grounded his theory on the historically specific form of love which is male heterosexuality as it arises within the restricted family. The attempt in love to bring imagination into harmony with reality must be *read* in relation to the dialectics of literary form itself. The problem we now take up in turning to Goethe's *Sorrows of Young Werther* is interpretive, not metapsychological. It is a question of grasping culture as a continuum of experiences, the layering of interactions and symbolic practices that link the forms of individual experience to the whole of society and its history. Merleau-Ponty stated the problem as follows:

> The individual drama takes place among *roles* which are already inscribed in the total institutional structure, so that from the beginning of his [sic] life the child proceeds—simply by perceiving the attentions paid to him and the utensils surrounding him—to a deciphering of meanings which from the outset generalizes his own drama into a drama of his culture. And yet it is the whole symbolic consciousness which in the last analysis elaborates what the child lives or does not live, suffers or does not suffer, feels or does not feel. Consequently there is not a single detail of his most individual history which does not contribute to that personal significance that he will manifest... when he finally comes to the point of reversing the relationship and slipping into the meanings of his speech and behavior, converting even the most secret aspects of his experience into culture.[26]

Goethe's influence pervaded Freud's thought. Beyond providing a storehouse of poetic sayings or the occasion to test psychoanalytic concepts on the poet's rich biography, Goethe's literary practice was formative for psychoanalytic theory as such. Psychoanalysis too is a cultural practice, the language practice of the "talking cure," and emerges from the same configurations of lived experience that are the

---

[26]Maurice Merleau-Ponty, "The Philosopher and Sociology," *Signs*, trans. Richard C. McCleary (Evanston: Northwestern University Press, 1964), p. 112.

raw material of literature. The cultural tradition that embraces Goethe and Freud is, however, also marked by significant historical discontinuities. Written in 1774, *The Sorrows of Young Werther* announces the revolutionary claims of bourgeois humanism—the individual's right to the pursuit of happiness, the free development of the personality, and the promise of fulfillment in individual love. Freud will encounter in the clinic of the early twentieth century all the unhappiness and disorder to which the personality is prey in the bourgeois process of socialization, its symptoms, inhibitions, and anxieties rather than its free development, the "universal debasement" rather than the promise of erotic life.

From Goethe to Freud is not, however, merely a history of lost innocence or gradual decline. It is rather the history of the contradictions of the social bond in capitalist society, contradictions that were being formed from the outset. Lukács's reading of *The Sorrows of Young Werther* in *Goethe and His Age* locates this novel's power to announce the promise of individuality and love while at the same time disclosing the betrayal of that promise in the new society as well as the old. "Young Goethe," Lukács writes,

> did see a direct and essential obstacle to the development of the human personality in the feudal stratification and separation of the social classes [*Stände*] and correspondingly criticized this social order with sharp satire. But at the same time, he saw that bourgeois society itself, the evolution of which so vehemently posed the problem of personality, incessantly hinders the development of personality. The same laws, institutions, etc. which serve the development of personality in the narrow class sense of the bourgeoisie and which generate the freedom of *laisser faire* are simultaneously destroyers of the real development of personality.[27]

So, too, Lukács sees in the tragedy of Werther's unfulfilled love a double-edged critique of the feudal order and of a bourgeois order yet in the earliest stages of its development. On the one hand, "Goethe made Werther's love for Lotte into an artistically heightened expression of the hero's popular, anti-feudal way of life."[28] On the other hand, Werther's tragedy goes to the heart of the conflict between the bourgeoisie's pursuit of happiness and its own institutions:

[27]Georg Lukács, *Goethe and His Age*, trans. Robert Anchor (New York: Grosset & Dunlap, 1969), pp. 39–40.
[28]Ibid., p. 46.

Lotte also loved Werther and . . . became conscious of this love through the explosion of his passion. But this is exactly what brings about the catastrophe. Lotte is a bourgeois woman who instinctively holds on to her marriage with a capable and respected man and draws back from her own feelings. Thus the tragedy of Werther is not only the tragedy of unhappy love, but the perfect expression of the inner contradiction of bourgeois marriage: based on individual love, with which it emerged historically, bourgeois marriage, by virtue of its socio-economic character, stands in insoluble contradiction to individual love.[29]

The "necessary conditions for loving" can already be discerned in the themes and maxims that appear in Werther's letters before his first sight of Lotte. His coming to a small town near the village of Wahlheim is a kind of premeditated flight: "How happy I am to have come away!" he writes in his first letter to Wilhelm. Werther has in part escaped the pain and guilt of an event whose real significance remains vague in the allusive account of it:

Poor Leonora! And yet I was blameless. Was it my fault that, while the capricious charms of her sister provided me with a pleasant entertainment, her poor heart built up a passion for me? Still—am I altogether blameless? Did I not encourage her perfectly genuine and naive expressions which so often made us laugh, although they were anything but amusing? Did I not—but oh, what is man that he dares so complain of himself![30]

Unable to sort out his responsibility in this disproportion between the authenticity of Leonora's feeling and his own entertainment and amusement, Werther has fled in search of the authenticity of his own feeling. He reports that "the solitude in this heavenly place is sweet balm to my soul" (p. 4), and that "wonderful serenity fills my whole being, like these lovely mornings which I enjoy with all my heart" (p. 5). That Werther's flight is in fact a search, a project, a pursuit, is first articulated in the form of his protest against the predominant patterns and demands of practical existence. Escape has taken the form of securing free time, a freedom he sees everywhere denied and met with anxiety:

There is a certain monotony about mankind. Most people toil during the greater part of their lives in order to live, and the slender span of

<hr />

[29]Ibid.
[30]Goethe, *The Sorrows of Young Werther*, p. 3. References will hereafter be cited in the text.

free time that remains worries them so much that they try by every means to get rid of it. [P. 9]

Werther's rejection of the practical, material demands of society not only advances the bourgeois right to worldly happiness against the feudal conception of the curse of labor, but already protests the capitalist form of exchange in which self-preservation becomes a wholly abstract need:

> When I see the limitations which imprison the active and speculative faculties of man; when I see how all human activity is directed toward procuring satisfaction for needs that have no other purpose than prolonging our miserable existence; . . .

The social limiting of human activity and the human faculties inverts the conditions of subjectivity and objectivity; adherence to outer reality acquires the false glow of the daydream while the fullness of a world cannot be sought, Werther believes, except in the inner realm of the self:

> when I see, moreover, how any comfort we may derive from certain points of inquiry is merely a dream-like resignation, in which we paint our prison walls with gaily colored figures and luminous prospects—all this, Wilhelm, leaves me speechless. I withdraw into my inner self and there discover a world. [Pp. 11–12]

The active attempt to realize this inner world defines Werther's project. Being in love will become Werther's surest evidence that he is yet faithful to the pursuit of happiness in the sphere of inwardness and intimacy. When Wilhelm first suggests that he leave Wahlheim and resume an occupation, Werther will retort with a maxim affirming inner over outer necessity: "As everything in the world amounts after all to nothing to speak of, a person who drudges for the sake of others, for money or honors or what not, without following his own ambition, his own need, is always a fool" (p. 49).

Werther can turn toward the promise of freely developing individuality and of happiness only as he turns away from the "philistine" demand that he become "a useful member of society" (p. 15). While Lukács rightly saw in this attitude the emphatic expression of the contradictions of bourgeois experience, the contradictions are nonetheless expressed in the language of bourgeois ideology. Goethe thematizes Werther's conflict as the opposition between the "inner" and the "outer," ultimately between the *individual* and *society*. Lukács can so effortlessly give a Marxist cast to Goethe's themes because he believes that a fundamental continuity unites bourgeois culture and socialist society, as though a socialist transformation of the "outer" realm (the economy, class relations) would redeem the "inner" realm unchanged, as though the transformation of society would merely free the bourgeois form of individuality from its external constraints.

But as I have tried to show with respect to *the economy and the symbolic* and *the social constitution of subjectivity,* capitalist social relations are not external to the forms of individuality. Capitalism engenders its own prevailing form of individuality. The resulting concept and experience of individuality have been inextricably tied to the social formation of the separated, private individual. The capitalist division of labor "individualizes" human beings through the material organization of the labor process. Commodity production, as Nicos Poulantzas points out, requires this "individualization": "Through being totally dispossessed of the means of labor, the direct producer emerges as the 'free' and 'naked' worker, cut off from the personal, statutory and territorial bonds that actually constituted him in medieval society. Such dispossession therefore imprints a determinate structure on his labor: 'Only products of mutually independent acts of labor, performed in isolation, can confront each other as commodities.' "[31]

The individual's everyday life is now divided anew between work and leisure—time experienced as necessary and time experienced as free—, but the thematization of this division as one between the outer and the inner veils the fact that both realms are founded upon individuality in its capitalist form: separated, private individuality. Neither the "outer" nor the "inner" exists except in their relation to one another as they are "unified" in the separated individual, whose own existence is henceforth divided. As work is emptied of the symbolic-affective ties that had previously taken the feudal form of "personal, statutory and territorial bonds," the site of such ties, of the symbolic-affective relation to others, is recreated in the form of the so-called intimate sphere of bourgeois life. The intimate sphere is inadequately understood as an "inner realm." Grounded in heterosexual love, marriage, and the family, "intimacy" is the historical product of the evolution of society. It

[31]Nicos Poulantzas, *State, Power, Socialism,* trans. Patrick Camiller (London: New Left Books, 1978), p. 64.

is also therefore a site of cultural practices—everyday symbolic practices, forms of interaction, discourses, and so on.

The symbolic ties that feudalism embodied in the material relation of lord and vassal do not simply disappear. The autonomous economy of capitalism may drain mythic and religious ties from the labor process and from social relations, but it does not destroy them. Myth and religion are displaced to the intimate sphere of the separated individual's experience. Being in love inherits the symbolic-affective ties of the vanishing society and reinscribes them on the scene of intimacy as history erases them from the social world as a whole.

An entire language of religious devotion organizes Werther's discourse on love. A few days after he first meets Lotte, Werther writes to Wilhelm: "My days are as blissful as those which God reserves for his saints; and, whatever may happen to me, I shall never be able to say that I have not experienced the purest joys of life" (p. 32). "Had I known, in choosing Wahlheim as the goal of my walks, that it lies so near to heaven!" (ibid.). "She is sacred to me," he writes a few days later. "She plays a melody on her clavicord with the touch of an angel, so simple, so ethereal!" (p. 47). Her voice is as angelic as her music for Werther, who "delights" in "the heavenly expressiveness of what she says" (p. 69).

These phrases are more than "literary conventions," especially in a novel that so vehemently opposes conventionality in aesthetics. The love poetry of the literary tradition needs to be viewed in relation to the social process of transforming the symbolic into the materials of intimacy. At the beginning of the Italian Renaissance, Petrarch's writing registers the tear that is already separating religion from material production. The relationship between lord and vassal is, in this poetry, *interiorized* and *heterosexualized;* it becomes the symbol of the relation between Laura (the lord) and the poet (the vassal). The woman projected in this literary tradition becomes the repository of the symbolic-affective networks that had integrated the old society. Whereas court poets used heightened descriptions of their beloved essentially to display their own rhetorical skills, hyperbole becomes for the bourgeois lover the figure of actual experience. Lotte's slightest actions stir a religious awe in Werther, as when she has her youngest sister wash away an unwanted kiss that Werther had given her: "—I tell you, Wilhelm, never did I attend a ceremony of baptism with more reverence; and when Lotte came up the steps again, I would gladly have knelt before her, as before a prophet who has washed away with holy water the crimes of a nation" (p. 42).

Goethe explicitly reflected on the difference between aristocrat and bourgeois through the voice of his protagonist in *Wilhelm Meisters Lehrjahre:*

> If the nobleman, through the presentation of his person, manifests everything, the bourgeois, through his personality, gives and ought to give nothing. The former may and ought to appear; the latter ought only to be, and what he wants to appear is ridiculous and in poor taste. The former ought to do and effect, the latter accomplish and produce; he ought to train particular abilities in order to become useful, and it is already assumed that there is no harmony in his being, nor may there be any, for in order to become useful in one way he must neglect everything else.[32]

The bourgeois's social being resides solely in his capacity for productivity and is, therefore, without symbolic significance. The nobleman, by contrast, represents or symbolizes, in his very person, what he *is* with respect to power and social standing; he enjoys this unity between symbolic appearance and social being, a unity that the bourgeois cannot exhibit except through philistine and mannered pretentions. Jürgen Habermas, in his very important *Strukturwandel der Öffentlichkeit*, has seen in this difference in the relation of personality to publicness the key to the transformation of the public sphere in the early bourgeois period.[33] The "representative public sphere" of feudalism, in which the lord's very appearance or presence demarcated his actual power within social relations, is progressively replaced by a bourgeois public sphere in which political and cultural opinion is formed through open discussion among private individuals. The aristocrat was in his person a public entity, whereas the bourgeois public is an aggregate of private individuals.

My argument is that the feudal form of publicness does not simply evaporate but is reinscribed in the intimate sphere of the private individual. Harmony of being, self-presentation, and the symbolic significance of the person now reappear in the bourgeois's vision of the woman he loves. Werther describes the first time he meets Lotte:

---

[32]Quoted in Jürgen Habermas, *Strukturwandel der Öffentlichkeit: Untersuchungen zu einer Kategorie der bürgerlichen Gesellschaft* (Neuwied and Berlin: Luchterhand, 1962), p.27.

[33]Ibid., pp. 13–41.

I paid her an insignificant compliment while my soul was taking in *her whole appearance, her voice, the grace of her bearing;* and I had just enough time to recover from my surprise when she ran to her room to fetch her gloves and fan. [P. 23]

Werther thus endows Lotte's being with the symbolic significance that his own being necessarily lacks. The intimate sphere of heterosexual love in this way inherits the symbolic-affective ties that organized the social and public world of feudalism. The symbolic residue of the social relations uprooted in the development of capitalism survives in the structures of feeling and forms of interaction that organize the private individual's "inner life."

The aura of unreality that surrounds the woman in traditional love poetry and in the romantic novel marks the effort in love to harmonize the imagination (of the poet) and the reality (of a woman). Goethe's novel concatenates a series of moments that prepare for Werther's falling in love. The youth first discusses love in one of the first letters to Wilhelm. He describes the love experience by way of analogy in his argument for a view of art that opposes rules and convention. Love here takes on its value as a protest against the calculative rationality of bourgeois existence:

Any rule is likely to destroy both the true feeling of Nature and its expression, whatever people may say to the contrary. You will object that this statement is too severe, and that rules only restrain and prune the over-luxuriant vine, etc. My dear friend! Shall I give you an analogy? It is the same with love. A young man's heart is entirely attached to a girl; he spends every hour of the day with her, wastes all his strength, all his fortune, in order to prove to her at every moment that he is wholly devoted to her. Should a philistine then enter the picture, a man of some responsible position, and say to him: "My dear young man, it is natural to love, but you must love only in a sensible way. Organize your day; some hours for work and some—the hours of relaxation—for your sweetheart. Calculate your means and it is perfectly permissible to use whatever is left over and beyond your personal needs to buy her a present of some sort, only not too frequently—perhaps for her birthday or a similar occasion."—Should the young fellow follow this advice, he will certainly turn into a useful member of society . . . ; but his love is done with, and if he is an artist, his art as well. [Pp. 14–15]

Love is a capacity that awaits a woman to release it, and indeed Werther will fall in love at first sight. The event is prepared. Werther has been told of Lotte by two young people whom he is accompanying to a country dance. Werther has "asked a good, pretty, but otherwise uninteresting girl to be my partner," and it is from her and her cousin that he learns of Lotte just before they meet:

> "You will meet a beautiful girl," my partner said while we were driving through a broad clearing of the forest toward the hunting lodge. "Be careful that you do not fall in love with her!" her cousin added.—"What do you mean?" I said.—"She is already engaged," was her answer, "and to a very worthy man who is not here at present." [Pp. 21–22]

In the preceding letter Werther had given an account of meeting "a young peasant" whose descriptions of the widow for whom he works had caused Werther to "guess that he was heart and soul devoted to her." The letter exemplifies an essential aspect of the male discourse on love; through the discourse of the love experience men recognize themselves and one another as "cultivated" or "civilized," cultivation here having, in keeping with Goethe's themes, the sense of the developed forms of inner feeling rather than conventions of behavior. Werther is so struck with the authenticity of the peasant's feeling that he wants to preserve only the fiction of the woman who is thus loved: "It is better that I see her through the eyes of her lover; she might not appear to my own eyes, in reality, as I now see her, and why should I destroy the lovely image I already possess?" (p. 20).

These two anecdotes prepare for Werther's first sight of Lotte. He has been moved by the value, indeed the cultural value, of another man's love, and he has learned that he will meet a beautiful woman who is engaged. The first moment he sees Lotte is presented in a vision or tableau which obviously resonates in Werther's experience but whose precise meaning remains indistinct. He is indeed struck not with Lotte's beauty—"a handsome young girl of medium height"—but with the view of her in her role as mother to her brothers and sisters, for whom she has cared since her mother's death:

> When I had gone up the outer staircase and entered the house, I saw the most charming scene I had ever in my life beheld. In the entrance hall six children, between the ages of eleven and two, were swarming around a handsome young girl of medium height, who wore a simple white dress with pink bows on her arms and breast. She was holding a loaf of dark bread and cutting one slice apiece for each of the children

around her, in proportion to age and appetite, dealing it out so kindly, and each child cried out "Thank you!" so artlessly, after having stretched out two tiny hands as high as possible before the slice was cut. [P. 22]

The vision of a maternal love that awakens no rivalries, this brief utopia of family life, shows Lotte in her knowledge of every child's wants and her capacity to fulfill them.

The relation between the meaning realized in this scene and the lived experience of childhood, the resonance between the aesthetic and the infantile, here permits of a conjecture or "construction" with reference to Goethe's own biography. It also illustrates the kind of transition from personal significance to cultural meaning that Merleau-Ponty identifies. The biographical material comes from Freud's essay "A Childhood Recollection from *Dichtung und Wahrheit.*" Freud concerns himself with the one episode from early childhood—an incident of naughtiness—which Goethe recalls in these autobiographical reflections. Goethe himself had been "born as though dead," and he and his sister Cornelia were the only children in a large family to survive childhood. Freud's main argument, occasioned by certain clinical parallels, simply interprets Goethe's naughty action—throwing plates through a window and watching them crash on the street below—as expressing the jealous wish to be rid of his newborn brother Hermann Jakob, who was born when Johann Wolfgang was three-and-a-quarter. Goethe's own recollection of Hermann Jakob in *Dichtung und Wahrheit* is limited to a single reference in the context of family illness: "He was a delicate child, quiet and self-willed, and we never had much to do with each other. Besides, he hardly survived the years of infancy."[34] He actually lived to the age of six, when Goethe was nine, and Goethe's mother had given the following account of Johann Wolfgang's reaction to his brother's death: " 'It struck her as very extraordinary that he shed no tears at the death of his younger brother Jakob who was his playfellow; he seemed on the contrary to feel annoyance at the grief of his parents and sisters. When later on, his mother asked the young rebel if he had not been fond of his brother, he ran into his room and brought from under the bed a heap of papers on which lessons and little stories were written, saying that he had done all this to teach his

---

[34]Quoted in Freud, "A Childhood Recollection from *Dichtung und Wahrheit*" (1917), *S.E.*, XVII, 151 n.
    [35]Ibid., pp. 151–152.

brother.' "[35] In Freud's interpretation, the recollection of naughtiness, recounted with a sense of its meaninglessness and inconsequence, is the memory that expresses and screens what the autobiographer no longer recalls about his relation to his brother; thus, Freud translates the screen memory: "It would run thus: 'I was a child of fortune: destiny preserved my life, although I came into the world as though dead. Even more, destiny removed my brother, so that I did not have to share my mother's love with him.' "[36]

Freud is so intent on identifying Hermann Jakob as the object of rivalry that he leaves uninterpreted the recurrences of death in Goethe's childhood, though he meticulously provides all the information. The resonances with the tableau of maternal love in *The Sorrows of Young Werther* are striking. Illness turned the growth of this family into a frightful rhythm of birth and death, the appearance and disappearance of children. Johann Wolfgang and Cornelia, the two eldest, have first one sibling, then two, then one, then none, then one, then none. The last sibling dies when Goethe himself is eleven—the age of the oldest child in the family scene in the novel. There had been altogether six children born to Goethe's mother, just as there are six children being tended by Lotte (though elsewhere in the novel it is mentioned that there are actually two more children in the family). There is no prospect of rivalry over the sharing of Lotte's love, because she is presented as knowing each child's desire, each share, "cutting one slice apiece . . . in proportion to age and appetite."

Encountering this vision, Werther falls in love. Lotte's love will give him an experience of happiness, but happiness first appears in this love relation as the happiness of the Other. Indeed, Lotte's happiness and the images of her happiness are essential "conditions for loving" her. During their very first conversation, on the way to the dance, Lotte tells Werther of the pleasure she gets from reading, a pleasure in which fiction and reality are the same:

> "And the author whom I like most of all is the one who takes me into my own world, where everything happens as it does around me, and whose story, nevertheless, becomes to me interesting and as touching as my life at home, which is certainly not a paradise but is, on the whole, a source of inexpressible happiness to me."
> I tried to hide my emotion at these words. [P. 25]

[36]Ibid., p. 156.

What is the value of this happiness in Werther's eyes? Lotte is continually represented as someone whose inner life and outer life are in harmony. She derives all her satisfactions from what she does, which is always what she does for others, the children, her father, the neighbors, and so on. The wholeness that she embodies for Werther is exactly what the social conditions of his own existence deny him. Werther has set out in search of happiness and meaning wholly within the self, a project that ambiguously signifies both a protest against merely outward actions and compulsions and a desperate flight from the dissatisfactions of practical existence. Lotte represents to Werther a being whose outward appearances and actions manifest her inner life. Her happiness is the image of what he is not, and in relation to him she comes to fulfill the role of the one who has the power to heal the rift in his own being: "What Lotte's presence must mean to a sick person I can feel in my own heart, which is worse off than many a one that pines on a sickbed" (p. 35). She possesses a kind of magic which Werther compares to the light in a magic lantern or the luminous effect of the sun on a Bologna stone. Her presence heals those divisions between the inner world and the outer world that haunt him, that cause disenchanted reality to seem like an aimless collective dream as against what he discovers within himself and then break up this inner world because he cannot bring it to realization.

> She plays a melody on her clavicord with the touch of an angel, so simple, so ethereal! It is her favorite tune, and I am cured of all pain, confusion, and melancholy the moment she strikes the first note.
> Not one word about the magic power of music in antiquity seems to me improbable when I am under the spell of her simple melody. And how well she knows when to play it, at the moment when I feel like blowing out my brains. The confusion and darkness of my soul are then dispersed and I can breathe more freely again. [P. 47]

Werther experiences her knowledge of his wants and the healing power of her happiness. It is in this play of his deficiency and her wholeness, his confusion and her knowledge, that he feels himself loved; he there finds the self-satisfaction that he calls his own happiness: "In her dark eyes I read a genuine sympathy for me and my destiny. Yes I feel ... that she loves me! ... And how precious I become in my own eyes" (p. 46). This love, in satisfying him, disperses what he only vaguely recognizes as his own desire: "She is sacred to me. Any desire is silenced in her presence" (p. 47).

Werther's happiness lasts only during the brief interval until Albert returns. With Albert's arrival, Werther's feeling for Lotte is reinscribed within the drama of rivalry. Only from within this drama does Werther glimpse the sexual aspect of his love, and sexuality now becomes visible for the first time in the form of possession and of the rival's claims on Lotte:

> He [Albert] feels deeply, and he knows what he possesses in Lotte. . . .
> He thinks me a person of sensitive intelligence; and my devotion to Lotte, my warm enthusiasm for everything she does, increases his triumph, and he loves her all the more. . . . My happiness with Lotte is gone. Shall I call this folly or delusion? What are names! The situation itself is evident. I knew everything I now know before Albert returned; I knew that I could not make claims upon her, nor did I make any; so far, that is, as it is possible for one not to feel desire in the presence of such sweetness. And yet the idiot now stares with wide eyes because the other man really arrives and carries off the girl. [P. 52]

Werther becomes fully aware of his desire only at the extreme point of his sorrow over losing Lotte, when he begins to dream of passion and "grope for her and suddenly find myself fully awake, a torrent of tears bursts from my oppressed heart, and I weep bitterly in view of a hopeless future." Throughout Part One of the novel, Werther feels the rivalry as defeat. When Wilhelm writes advising him to "carry the matter through" if he has hopes of winning Lotte or else "get rid of an unfortunate passion," Werther's response expresses how the love that had been a source of healing has been transformed into illness: "And does not the disease, at the very same time that it burns up his strength, also destroy the courage he needs to free himself from it?" (p. 67).

A month later, in September, Werther resolves to leave and take a position at court. The dissatisfactions of work and his experience of humiliation as a bourgeois amid the hierarchical conventionalized life of the aristocracy cause him to return in June. In the interim, Lotte and Albert have married. Werther now enters the drama of rivalry, at least in his letters and fantasies, with renewed bitterness and pain: "She would have been happier," he writes Wilhelm, "with me than with him. Oh, he is not the man to satisfy all the needs of her heart" (p. 100). In his diary, he writes, "Sometimes I cannot understand how another *can*, how he *dare* love her, since I alone love her completely and devotedly, knowing only her, and have nothing in the world but her!" (p. 102). There is the growing intimation that the rivalry of Albert and Werther is lethal as Werther's fantasies oscillate between images of Albert's death—"When I become lost in dreams I cannot avoid thinking, 'what if Albert should die? You would! She would—' " (p. 101)—and images of his own death.

As Werther's attentions to Lotte begin to strain Albert, the men's rivalry most often taking the form of increasingly heated disputes over the nature of human experience, passion, and the rule of law, Werther comes to believe that "he had destroyed the harmonious relationship between Albert and his wife, and he reproached himself, at the same time, that he mixed this reproach with secret indignation against the husband" (p. 127).[37] At the height of his tensions with Albert and his sorrow at the loss of Lotte, Werther's full realization that his passion is sexual overwhelms him. On December 14, he writes to Wilhelm:

> What is this, what has happened to me, dear friend? I am alarmed at myself. Is not my love for her the most sacred, the purest, the most brotherly love? Have I ever felt any culpable desire in my soul? But I will not protest!—And now—dreams! Oh, how right were the instincts of those peoples who attributed such contradictory effects to unknown powers! Last night—I tremble to confess it—I held her in my arms, close to the breast, and covered her love-murmuring lips with endless kisses; my eyes sank into the intoxication of hers. Dear God! Am I culpable that I even now feel a supreme happiness in again living through those glowing moments of joy in all their intensity? Lotte! Lotte!—And this is the end! My mind is in a daze.... [P. 135]

The narrative has made a sequence of the different moments in the love relation that ties Werther to Lotte. In the first movement: Falling in love at the sight of Lotte's happiness and care, Werther finds his own happiness in being loved by her, in the form of the self-satisfaction that comes from the healing effect of her (supposed) knowledge of his wants and his destiny. In the second movement: Werther loses Lotte in the drama of rivalry. In the third movement: Werther experiences his sexual passion as a destructive, yet irresistible force carrying with it the ambivalences of guilt, aggression, indignation, self-destructiveness. Happiness, then rivalry and loss, then the violent upsurge of sexuality—this, then, constitutes the narrative sequence which brings us to the verge of the novel's denouement.

---

[37]This passage is in the voice of the (improbably omniscient) third-person narrator.

Narrative Form and the Dialectic of Desire

The narrativization of desire calls for interpretation. *The satisfaction of human desire is possible only when mediated by the labor and desire of another.* How then has the narrative given form to the dialectic of desire, a form through which this dialectic becomes meaningful in the cultural sphere? Put another way, what are the forms of mediation that become visible in the work's narration of satisfactions and non-satisfactions?

The Sorrows of Young Werther forms the dialectic of desire in a "gendered" play of subjectivities. In the Lacanian dialectic, desire is a lack (*manque*) that manifests itself either as a "failing-to-be" (*manque-à-être*) or as a "wanting-to-have" (*manque-à-avoir*).[38] The novel is imprinted with historical modes of being and having. Through the first three movements of the narrative, Lotte embodies *an absence of desire*. In the first movement, she is the very image of happiness, a fulfilled being whose value for Werther lies just in this absence of want; in the second movement, she is the prize in the rivalrous conflict between Werther and Albert, being what Albert possesses and what Werther loses. Werther indeed loses what he never "had," since he recognizes his desire, this wanting-to-have Lotte, only after he sees her possessed by Albert. Much of the power of the novel—or its romantic improbability, to more ironic eyes—stems from the fact that Werther does not enter into the two folds of his desire—the failing-to-be and the wanting-to-have—until Lotte already belongs to Albert. Only in the third movement of the narrative does Werther face the completed form of his desire, the conjunction of being and having: what she *is* will satisfy me on the condition that I *have* her. It is quite clear in the drama of rivalry that Werther discovers his sexual desire only in seeing it in the desire of the other, that is, in Albert's wanting-to-have Lotte. But it is necessary to insist on the form taken by the other slope of desire, the failing-to-be, for here Werther's desire rests on his perception of an absence of the desire of the other. That is Lotte's happiness.

[38]The ambiguity of the term *manque*, and of the appropriate English equivalents, should alert us not to simplify or rigidify this conception into an abstract polarity or opposition between "being" and "having." As I hope the following analysis shows, the forms of "being" and "having"—and the forms of the "lack" of being or having—are in fact the product of cultural valuations and symbolizations and social relations and interactions that could not be accounted for by means of any such abstract distinction merely between two modes or types of "desire."

Indeed, for both men Lotte's value lies in her being the *subject of love* and the *object of desire;* she is loved for the happiness she appears to possess. The rivals want to know nothing of her desire, they want only to be assured of her love. For Albert, her happiness has the pragmatic value acquired in the marital relation, in that he needs her to care for him; the first expression of his displeasure with her occurs when he finds out that she has not completed "some errands he had wanted her to do for him." For Werther, Lotte's happiness, as we have seen, has had the nearly metaphysical value of being able to repair the divisions of his own being (that is, his failing-to-be).

What is the nature of Lotte's happiness? It is represented—not only by Werther's letters but also by Goethe's placement of her in the novel— as a given, a virtually natural fact of her existence. The duties that she has acquired through her "natural" family ties accord completely with her personal qualities and capacities. Even her engagement to Albert is essentially an expression of the most basic continuity in her life, her tie to her mother; Werther first learns of the mother's dying wish from Albert:

> When he tells me of Lotte's kindly mother; how on her deathbed she entrusted Lotte with the care of her household and her children, and Lotte herself to Albert's care; how from that day on Lotte had been animated by an entirely new spirit; how she had conscientiously taken over the house and become a real mother to the children; how not one moment of her time had been spent without tasks and active love, and yet she kept her former cheerfulness and lightness of heart.—[P. 55]

During Werther's last evening with Lotte and Albert before he left to take up his position at the court, Lotte had recollected her mother's dying look as she and Albert stood over her: " 'How she looked at you and at me, her mind relieved and at rest, knowing that we would be happy, be happy together' " (p. 75). We can again discern the relation between the bourgeois conception of womanhood and the values and symbolisms of the destroyed feudal order. Lotte represents, is represented as living, the idealized "organic community" of precapitalist society. She embodies the continuity of family bonds and of satisfactions deriving directly from the labor process—the latter being a key element in the bourgeois romanticization of housework, childcare, nursing the sick and elderly, and so on. There is, moreover, a religious resonance in Lotte's experience; her happiness comes from doing the Other's will, her mothering and her marriage being the fulfillment of her dying mother's wish. Her happiness is the absence of discord between her own activity and this will of the Other. The religious connotations are more than a metaphorical residue. Historically, intimacy inherits the destroyed but unsuperseded religious symbols of the old order; and within the narrative, the religious register of Lotte's happiness will eventually form the basis of Werther's last fantasies.

There is a dissymmetry in the novel's determination of happiness. For Werther, happiness is an aim and a right. He has set out, militantly and in the style of revolutionary humanism, in pursuit of happiness. He declares it to be an inalienable right and its only possible path that of his desire or the wants of his heart. His initial experience of happiness in fact rested upon the nonrecognition of his desire. In Freud's phrasing, Werther at first loves where he does not desire and where he desires he cannot love. In the novel, this "cannot" expresses not the emotional or sexual dysfunctions manifested clinically, but rather the force of a taboo, which of course Freud had found at the base of the clinical manifestations of "debasement." In the novel, the clearer the taboo becomes—with Albert's return and then the marriage—the more love and desire unite in Werther. He will revive the demand for happiness in the final movement of the novel, even as he sees that he cannot achieve happiness; two of the novel's greatest themes are then brought together, the right to the pursuit of happiness and the moral right to suicide.

With Lotte, on the other hand, happiness is a given condition and an obligation. "Be happy!" she is told, first by the voice and memory of her mother and then, in a different register, by Werther and Albert, for their devoted love requires her happiness. I have, therefore, defined her happiness as an absence of desire, a not-failing-to-be. The distinction or difference between these two forms of happiness—happiness as aim and right, happiness as condition and obligation—is a mark of domination. Werther posits his freedom in the pursuit of happiness, but to do so he obligates another to happiness. He silences her desire. In a paradox that cannot, I believe, be resolved with reference to the paradoxical identity of taboo and transgression, Werther cannot have Lotte's love unless she can risk her own happiness.

The novel's denouement begins as Lotte's happiness, her condition of being satisfied in her obligations, is put in jeopardy—by her desire. The scene is a few days before Christmas. Albert has demanded that Lotte see less of Werther, following a quarrel which Werther has with Albert and Lotte's father and in which he passionately defends and

seeks forgiveness for his friend the young peasant, who has murdered
the woman he loved (the widow) because she planned to marry someone else. Lotte has undertaken to honor Albert's request by limiting
Werther's visits:

> Now she sat at home alone—none of her family was with her—and
> she gave herself up to her thoughts, which quietly moved over her cir-
> cumstances. She saw herself united forever to her husband whose love
> and loyalty she knew, to whom she was deeply devoted and whose
> calmness of disposition and whose trustworthiness seemed to be intended
> by Providence for a good wife to build on it her life's happiness; she
> keenly realized how much he would always mean to her and to her
> children. On the other hand, Werther had become very dear to her heart;
> from the beginning of their acquaintance the harmony of their minds
> had showed itself in the most pleasant way, and continued friendly
> relations with him as well as their many mutual experiences had made
> a lasting impression on her heart. She had become accustomed to share
> with him everything of interest she felt or thought; and his departure
> threatened to create a great gap in her existence which could not be filled
> again. Oh, if only she had the power to transform him this very moment
> into a brother, how happy she would be!—had she only been fortunate
> enough to marry him off to one of her friends, or could she be allowed
> to hope that his friendship with Albert might be completely restored!
>
> She passed all her friends in review, one after the other, but found
> flaw with each and could not think of one girl to whom she would not
> have begrudged Werther.
>
> As she pondered on all this, she felt for the first time, keenly if sub-
> consciously, that in her heart of hearts she secretly wished to keep him
> for herself, at the same time saying that she could not, should not keep
> him; her innocent noble nature, usually so light and resourceful, felt the
> weight of a melancholy that sees all hope for happiness barred. Her heart
> was oppressed and a dark mist lay upon her eyes. [Pp. 143–144]

The woman's desire enters the narrative to announce disaster. Why?
Lukács responded too quickly to Lotte's ultimate choice of the morality
of marriage over authentic passion. Her desire—its recognition by herself and by Werther, and its concealment from Albert—indeed touches
off the catastrophe of the story. But let us take the elements one at a
time. Werther returns to Lotte's that same evening, though she had
pleaded with him to stay away until Christmas Eve. She composes
herself, and they sit down as Werther begins to read a long, tumultuous
passage from Ossian. Lotte and then Werther begin to weep: "Both
were in a terrible emotional state. They felt their own misery in the

fate of the noble Gaels, felt it together and their tears mingled. Werther's lips and eyes burned on Lotte's arm, and a shudder ran through her body" (p. 153). The novel's catastrophe begins to unfold when Lotte's desire speaks, through her body. Werther attempts to continue the reading but is overwhelmed by a passage forecasting death: "A tumult rose in her; she took his hands, pressed them against her breast and, bending toward him with a mournful glance, their glowing cheeks touched" (p. 154). Werther begins kissing her, she pushes him away. "She quickly got up and said in a terrible confusion, torn between love and indignation, 'This was the last time, Werther! You will not see me again.' And with a look full of love for the unhappy man, she rushed into the next room and locked the door behind her." The next evening, when Albert has returned, Werther's servant comes with a request from Werther to borrow Albert's pistols. Lotte knows his purpose, and faces the choice of telling Albert "the whole truth about last night's event, as well as her own guilt and her forebodings." She chooses to remain silent and hands over the pistols. There continues to be no discourse and no love relation in which her desire may be spoken; her desire has shuddered through her body in the brief instant that marked her loss of happiness.

Her desire and her loss of happiness will immediately become transcribed into Werther's discourse of love, in the form of the two fantasies that prepare his act of suicide. The first fantasy, coming before his final evening with Lotte and after he senses the discord that he has created between her and Albert, contemplates suicide as a sacrifice of himself for Lotte's sake, an effort to restore her happiness. He writes in a letter addressed to her and found after his death:

> It is not despair; it is the certainty that I have suffered enough, and that I am sacrificing myself for you. Yes, Lotte! Why should I hide it from you? One of the three of us must go, and I am to be that one! O my dearest, my wounded heart has been haunted by a terrible demon— often. To murder your husband! Or you! Or myself! Well, so be it! [P. 141]

The fantasy of self-sacrifice represents the rescue of the woman from danger. In his last moments Werther revives the image of self-sacrifice and rescue: "Had I been granted the happiness to die for *you!*, Lotte, to sacrifice myself for *you!* I would die bravely, I would die cheerfully, if I could restore to you the peace and happiness of your life" (p. 165).

The heroic sacrifice, the willingness to die for Lotte's happiness, is transformed after the passion of their last night together. Werther knows that she loves him, and he knows from his servant that she has handed over the pistols. The fantasy of sacrificing himself for her sake is transformed into a fantasy of devoted victimage in which she is murdering him:

> They have passed through your hands; you have wiped the dust from them. I kiss them a thousand times because you have touched them; and you, Heavenly Spirit, approve of my decision! And you, Lotte, offer me the weapon—you from whose hands I wished to receive death, and ah! not receive it. [P. 162]

By means of the two fantasies Werther attempts to find the meaning of his desire in the desire of the other. But these final impassioned male fantasies once again eclipse Lotte's desire even as they represent Werther's final attempt to preserve his love for her. In the first fantasy, self-sacrifice is to restore Lotte to the happiness on which his own love for her depends. And in the second fantasy, Werther's devoted victimage causes the conflict which has erupted within Lotte—not only that between her passion and her morality, but more fundamentally that between desire and the obligation to happiness—to be heard by Werther as *she desires me dead.* Werther, that is, finds meaning in his destiny only insofar as his death can be at once Lotte's desire and his own expression of love.

Werther's last moments evoke the defiance and the desire of the revolutionary bourgeois—give me liberty or give me death. His final image of love liberated from societal constraint would project love beyond the roles and institutions of marriage and morality:

> She loves me! This arm held her, these lips have trembled on her lips, this mouth has stammered against hers. She is mine! You are mine, Lotte, forever!
> And what does it mean that Albert is your husband? That may be for this world—and in this world it is sin that I love you, that I should like to snatch you from his arms into mine. Sin? Very well, and I am punishing myself for it; for this sin, which I have tasted in all its rapture, which gave me life-giving balm and strength. From now on you are mine! mine, Lotte! I go before you. I go to my Father, to your Father. I shall put my sorrow before Him, and He will comfort me until you come; and I shall fly to meet you and clasp you and stay with you before the Infinite Being in an eternal embrace. . . . we shall see one another again, see your

mother. I shall see her, find her and ah! pour out my heart to her, your mother, your very image. [Pp. 157–158]

The return of religious expectation in the collapse of the worldly pursuit of happiness marks a historic impasse, and not merely the frenzy or delusion of the young Werther. Nor is it an impasse that we have yet lived through. Werther revives his claim or demand for individual happiness and for the liberation of his love by repudiating the moral order of bourgeois society. The repudiation does not, however, express itself politically; indeed, nowhere does the image of political transformation, including those alive in Goethe's own time, appear within the novel or within Werther's fantasies. Instead, it expresses itself in two "compromise formations": (1) Werther rejects the morality of marriage, which calls his desire a sin, and he repudiates the meaningfulness of Albert's role as a husband who possesses Lotte. Morality and social role are, for Werther, mere external constraints, meaningless barriers to the law of the heart. But when Werther affirms the higher truth of the inner realm of individuality, he takes into himself this same morality and this very role: he will take possession of Lotte eternally, and he will die to punish himself for his sin. (2) Werther has chosen to die as a protest in the name of his freedom, preferring death to unliberated love. But the figure of freedom he assumes in dying, through the two suicide fantasies, is yet founded on the moment of unfreedom that defines love as male fantasy: namely, the denial of Lotte's desire, the refusal of the play of the desire of the other in all its negativity and conflict. Not only would Werther rescue Lotte from unhappiness but he would restore her happiness in its original form, her obligation to happiness: indeed, Werther seeks the blessing of the Other whose will Lotte does: "We shall be! we shall see one another again, see your mother. I shall see her; find her and ah! pour out my heart to her, your mother, your very image." The male discourse of love once again closes the dialectic of desire.

Werther's last days are his ultimate attempt to preserve the inner realm and find there his freedom. The fantasies that prepare his act of suicide are inner fantasies of the self's heroism. His decision to die was made several days before his last encounter with Lotte, and the context defines the crisis from which he could not escape. His friend the young peasant has murdered the widow to whom he had been so devoted because she, after her brother had dismissed the young peasant, planned to marry his replacement. Werther rushes to the scene in hopes of talking to the young man, who can only tell him, " 'No one is going to have her; she will have no one!' " Werther is completely shaken but resolved to defend the young man and returns to make a case before Lotte's father, the bailiff: "he was overcome by compassion and moved by an irresistible desire to save this man, whose predicament he felt deeply. He considered him, even as a criminal, to be free of real guilt, and he identified himself so completely with him that he was certain to be able to also convince others" (pp. 129–130). Albert is there too. The dispute that Werther has with them cuts to the quick of a social order that is founded at once upon the sovereign truth of the individual and the sovereign power of the state:

> When he entered the house, he found that Albert had arrived; this dampened his spirits for a moment but he managed after a while, to control himself and began to impress his opinions on the bailiff with much warmth. The latter shook his head repeatedly, and although Werther with the greatest brilliance, passion and truth put forward every-thing a human being could say to exculpate another human being, the bailiff remained unmoved, as one can easily understand. He did not even allow our friend to finish his discourse but eagerly contradicted him and reproached him for defending an assassin. He pointed out that in this way every law would be annulled, the whole security of the state en-dangered; and besides, he added, he himself would not be able to do anything in a case like this without taking upon himself the heaviest responsibility. Everything would have to be done in the legal way, and according to instructions.
>
> ...Albert, who had finally joined in the discussion, sided with the older man. Werther was overruled and left in a terrible state of suffering after the bailiff had said to him several times: "No, there is no help for him."
>
> How deeply these words must have struck him we can see from a note found among his papers, undoubtedly written that same day:
>
> "There is no help for you, unfortunate man! I see only too well that there is no help for us!" [Pp. 130–131]

The crime of passion—in which "love and loyalty, the most beautiful of human emotions, had turned into violence and murder" (p. 129)—confronts bourgeois society with the question of the basis of the social bond. Is the coherence of the community founded on its capacity to recognize itself in the criminal, or in its power to exclude him from the community? Werther recognizes himself in the young peasant, and his argument represents his effort, as Hegel read the figure of Werther, to impose the law of the heart on reality against the ruling order. The bailiff and Albert, voices of the ruling order and of duty, condemn the man; they do not see themselves in him. Exclusion from the community requires just this nonrecognition of one human being by another. The argument causes Werther to feel his own nonrecognition by the Other and exclusion from the community here represented by the bailiff and Albert, Lotte's father and her husband.

Werther's suicide is more than desperate defiance in the face of a social order that refuses his happiness. The individuality that founds his tie to humanity has proved irreconcilable with life in the historical community. To preserve this inner realm he renounces the social bond. Werther's is an emphatic experience of the historical conditions in which the inner self is at once the necessary and the impossible path to happiness. Death is not merely the consequence of Werther's revolt. Rather, Werther can preserve his *consciousness* of his freedom, his love, and the meaning of his existence only in the act of suicide. That moment cannot be lived but only contemplated, and the novel gives this contemplation two distinct forms, the fantasmal and the aesthetic, that is, Werther's fantasies and the aesthetic contemplation which the novel as a whole invites.

The aesthetic of "affirmative culture" requires that the experience of the work of art resolve itself in an attitude of contemplation. Is this contemplative attitude achieved as the result of the work itself or of historical categories of aesthetic reception? This question animates the rich discussion of aesthetics in the age of Goethe, without ever being posed as such. That the categories of aesthetic reception are themselves historical is vibrantly demonstrated in this period when the categories were being defined, debated, and redefined in an attempt to establish their universality.

What is most striking, for example, in Schiller's relation to Goethe is the way the inner form of contemporary literature and the process of forming the categories of reception act on one another. The search for the a priori categories of aesthetic judgment shows that these categories were anything but given. Even in Kant the universality of the aesthetic judgment is based not on the fact of a shared judgment of taste but rather on the claim that others should share the individual's judgment. In Schiller, the idea of aesthetic education points to the necessity of a process of cultivation through which the individual develops the "capacity for feeling" and the "capacity for reason," which turn out to be the impulses whose reconciliation is aesthetic experience. Not only was Schiller himself engaged in the making of aesthetic categories, but he called upon the aesthetic, in the sense of artistic creation and of aesthetic reception, to solve a whole series of antinomies that continually interrupt the bourgeois individual's pursuit of self-realization, antinomies, that is, which divide the individual from himself: reason and sense, freedom and nature, duty and spontaneity, and so on. Schiller looked to art to reconcile these antinomies, which for him "are not by nature mutually opposed, and if nevertheless they appear to be, they have only become so by a willing transgression of Nature, by misunderstanding themselves and confounding their spheres."[39] This "willing transgression of Nature" is nothing less than the history of humanity from the Greeks to Schiller's own time; the contemporary world was for Schiller the offspring of this transgression and yet the prospective heir of the ancient world. In this perspective, culture itself was not a given but rather the task of "providing the receptive faculty with the most multifarious contacts with the world, and as regards feeling, pushing passivity to its fullest extent" while at the same time "securing for the determining faculty the fullest independence from the receptive, and as regards reason, pushing activity to its fullest extent. Where both qualities are united, Man [sic] will combine the greatest fullness of existence with the utmost self-dependence and freedom, and instead of abandoning himself to the world he will rather draw it into himself with the whole infinity of its phenomena, and subject it to the unity of his reason."[40]

The aesthetic education was to direct the cultural task of combining the receptivity of the senses and the activity of reason in the formation of the individual's personality or character. Just as writing is the act of individual genius, reading is the interaction, within the individual, of the movement of the work and the cultivation of categories of aesthetic reception. What then is the logic of this interaction, and how are we to grasp its historical determinations? Schiller's reading of *The Sorrows of Young Werther* in *Naive and Sentimental Poetry* (1795–1796) shows this interaction in the very process of its construction. The "naive" and the "sentimental" express an opposition between artistic types (works as well as artists), the one adhering to sensuous reality and the other to the ideal. But the opposition also distinguishes the ancient, where the harmonious nature of reality afforded poetry

[39]Friedrich Schiller, *On the Aesthetic Education of Man in a Series of Letters*, trans. Reginald Snell (New York: Frederick Ungar, 1965), p. 68.
[40]Ibid.

the ability to hold to sensuous reality, and the modern, in which the loss of just this harmony stirs poetry to recover nature through "the representation of the ideal." "The naive poet *is* nature," adhering to the sensuous, already unified reality of the world; the sentimental poet "*seeks* her," for "even if man should separate himself by the freedom of his fantasy and his understanding from the simplicity, truth and necessity of nature, yet not only does the way back to her remain open always, but also a powerful and ineradicable impulse, the moral, drives him ceaselessly back to her, and it is precisely with this impulse that the poetic faculty stands in the most intimate relationship."[41]

Goethe initially presents Schiller with a problem, and then a solution, in the working out of these categories. For Goethe embodies the naive poet in the modern world. Goethe adheres to the sensuous reality of a world that is divided, not unified, more the obstacle to fulfillment than the source of it. It is Werther—"this dangerous extreme of the sentimental personality"—who provides Goethe's work with the stamp of modernity. Schiller's reading of the novel is an investigation into "how the naive poetic spirit proceeds with a sentimental theme":

> This task appears to be completely new and of a quite unique difficulty, for in the ancient and naive world a *theme* of this kind did not occur, whereas in the modern the *poet* would be lacking. Nevertheless, genius has accepted this task also and has resolved it in an admirably felicitous manner. A personality who embraces the ideal with burning feeling and abandons actuality in order to contend with an insubstantial infinitude, who seeks constantly outside himself for that which he continually destroys within himself, to whom only his dreams are the real, his experience perennial limitations, who in the end sees in his own existence only a limitation, and, as is reasonable, tears this down in order to penetrate the true reality—this dangerous extreme of the sentimental personality has become the theme of a poet in whom nature functions more faithfully and purely than any other, and who among modern poets, is perhaps least removed from the sensuous truth of things.
> It is interesting to note with what fortunate instinct everything that nourishes the sentimental character is concentrated in *Werther:* fanatically unhappy love, sensitivity to nature, feeling for religion, a spirit of philosophical contemplation; finally, so that nothing shall be forgotten, the gloomy, formless, melancholic Ossianic world. If one takes account of how little recommendation, even in how hostile a manner actuality is contrasted with it, and how everything external unites to drive the

---

[41]Friedrich von Schiller, *Naive and Sentimental Poetry,* and *On the Sublime,* trans. Julius A. Elias (New York: Frederick Ungar, 1966), p. 110.

tortured youth back into his world of ideals, then one sees no possibility how such a character could have saved himself from such a cycle.[42]

Through the emphatic experience of Werther, Schiller sees emerge an authentic figure of modern individuality, the sentimental personality. Goethe's writing, on the other hand, is naive to the extent that it shows the sentimental personality confronted with an actuality or external reality that destroys any saving self-realization. Modern individuality falls to ruin in the face of modern reality. Schiller's reading, while tacitly containing just this conclusion, elides any *political break* with social reality but looks instead to the aesthetically cultivated individual's character as the only possible path to resolving the antinomies of bourgeois existence.

Schiller's *On the Aesthetic Education of Man* expresses the elision of the political as an absence of faith in the German state's capacity to be the instrument of cultural development: "All improvement in the political sphere is to proceed from the ennobling of character—but how, under the influence of a barbarous constitution, can the character become ennobled? We should need for this end, to seek out some other instrument which the State does not afford us, and with it open well-springs which will keep pure and clear throughout every political corruption. . . . This instrument is the Fine Arts, and these well-springs are opened up in their immortal example."[43] But Schiller's critique of the German state, at the very time of the French Revolution, refused to comprehend that a political break with the feudal state was necessary to the self-development of the bourgeoisie. The aesthetic education not only detaches itself from political processes, it becomes a substitute for them. Oskar Negt has discussed *the deflected concept of revolution* in German literature and philosophy from Luther to Goethe and Schiller; "bourgeois German intellectuals . . . have . . . divided the revolution into a *political* component, equated with conspiracy, insurrection, and crime, and an *intellectual-cultural* element in which historical traditions are preserved and transmitted."[44] Failing to experience political revolution as a means of class formation, the German bourgeoisie, Negt argues, tried to resolve its identity problem first through cultural and

[42]Ibid., pp. 137–138.
[43]Schiller, *On the Aesthetic Education*, pp. 50–51.
[44]Oskar Negt, "The Misery of Bourgeois Democracy in Germany," *Telos* 38 (Winter 1978), 114.

philosophical forms detached from politics and then through bureaucracy as its "most stable substitute for identity."

The aesthetic that Schiller works out through his reading of *Werther* refines the categories that remove cultural expression from revolutionary politics. Rather than deriving a sense of revolt from the confrontation between Werther's sensibility and reality, Schiller finds in the "admirably felicitous manner" of the novel's construction an aesthetic unity of the naive and the sentimental which can take the place of a lived unity. This aesthetic unity, I will argue, is purely formal; or, more precisely, the aesthetic apprehension of a unity where real unity is lacking is conditioned by a purely formal movement of the work, namely, its organization of the interplay of metonymy and metaphor and of *énoncé* and *énonciation*.

Threading the narrative of Werther's life is a purely formal play of metonymy and metaphor. The metonymical sequences include both the main narrative: *falling in love / leaving / returning*, and the various subplots: *Lotte's engagement / marriage / unhappiness // the peasant's love story / his dismissal / his murder of the lady // the story of little Hans / his death and the family's financial ruin*, and so on. Each subplot's sequence is completed by an event which assembles the metonymical elements into a perceptible unity or unit: Lotte's unhappiness, the peasant's arrest, Hans's death. The completed units are the metaphors that in turn, at the next highest level of the narrative's organization, are themselves metonymically strung together until they are assembled and completed in Werther's death. His death binds each sequence into a kind of final metaphor, a process which can be seen in the fact that Werther, as well as the reader, will read in the completed subplots his own destiny. It is this metonymical-metaphorical organization which supports Schiller's insight that "one sees no possibility how such a character could have saved himself from such a cycle."

The second aspect of the work's formal movement likewise supports the movement of reading toward its endpoint in contemplation. From the outset of the novel, the voice of its *énonciation*, that is, of the speaking or writing that complexly relates and relates to the narrated events or *énoncé*, is that of Werther. But this voice disappears and in its place is heard the "authorial" voice which takes command of the *énonciation*. It is this latter voice that Schiller can define as the "naive poet" who treats a "sentimental theme." The "sentimental" loses its own speech and becomes theme; that is, the *énonciation* which is Werther's speaking falls to the level of *énoncé*, the narrative's subject matter or theme. There are two ways to map this movement. First of all, the transposition is embodied by what is a relatively awkward technique from the standpoint of the finely honed third-person narration and *style indirect libre* that will develop in the nineteenth-century novel: namely, the sudden appearance, in the second half of Part Two, of a narrator-editor who tells the story of Werther's last days and introduces the kind of "distance" that will eventually become the hallmark of realism. Quite literally, Werther disappears from the *énociation,* his letters and diary entries becoming citations reported by another voice. Second, and more significant, the suicide is the event in relation to which the structure of voice goes through its ultimate permutation. As I have argued, the act of suicide becomes Werther's only means of preserving his consciousness of freedom, of love, of the meaning of his existence, but in suicide act and consciousness cannot coincide. The act can only be contemplated—fantasmally or aesthetically, that is, in anticipation or in retrospect. Werther's disappearance from the *énonciation* can be more exactingly mapped in the very moment he articulates, through his suicide fantasies, the meaning of his death and with it the meaningful shape of his life as a destiny, for the meaning expressed in these fantasies is not retained within the completed narrative. The narrative does not validate Werther's religious expectation of happiness before God but depicts his death-agony with brutal matter-of-factness; nor does it avow the fantasy of rescue but rather reports that the night Werther is buried, "Lotte's life was in danger." The possibility of aesthetic contemplation is achieved in this moment where Werther's death at once completes the text's metonymical-metaphorical organization and marks the transposition of the narrative voice from Werther himself to an "author."

This movement of the text sustains the movement of Schiller's reading, providing it not only with its aesthetic categories, the *naive* and the *sentimental,* but with their relation: *naive poet / sentimental theme.* It is the purely formal completeness or closure of the narrative (its "admirably felicitous manner") which produces the aesthetic pleasure that permits the lived conflict between freedom and reality to be transfigured into the aesthetic unity of sentimental and naive. Goethe stated his understanding of the cultural task of art in the novel's prefatory note:

> You cannot withhold your admiration and love for [poor Werther's] character, any more than your tears for his fate.

And you, noble soul who feels the same longing that he felt, take comfort from his suffering, and let this little book be your friend, when because of destiny or some fault of your own you cannot find a nearer and dearer one.

In the age of Goethe, aesthetic experience and artistic practices are called upon to resolve the most basic contradictions within subjectivity and within the social bond. *The Sorrows of Young Werther* unveils the impossibility for individual inwardness to live its freedom and its love in the very society that produces this individuality and these aspirations. Yet the work is at the same time compelled to furnish a form of aesthetic experience which will sustain the individual's cultivation of an inner realm of freedom. The element of revolt heard in Werther's speech is deflected from its possible political elaborations and is transformed into an object of contemplation. It is in the achievement of this contemplation that Schiller and Goethe, through the ideologically linked processes of constructing literary form and categories of literary reception, establish cultural experience in its "affirmative character."

Conclusion: Heritage
and Hegemony

I have sifted through a number of theoretical and methodological problems that the project of "critical hermeneutics" inherits from the intellectual traditions of Marxism and psychoanalysis and have
counterposed this project to "traditional hermeneutics." I have also
tried to clarify the cultural-political aim of critical hermeneutics:
namely, to construct the cultural heritages of a classless society. It is
that aim which ties this project to the "background" problematic and
submerged critical-utopian discourse of Marxism. Against Marx, I have
argued that the classless society is a utopian commitment that cannot
be grounded in a faith in inevitable historical processes or in the intrinsic
consciousness of any social class or social group. The extent to which
this utopian vision illuminates the sufferings, deprivations, and injustices inflicted by capitalist society is a matter of cultural revaluation
and moral-political persuasion. By the same token, I have argued that
the radically egalitarian society to be envisioned must itself be a political
community and not the supersession of politics, that is, of the demo-
cratically secured space for conflict and debate regarding the values,
aims, and aspirations of the society. Against various positions developed by Gadamer, Habermas, and others, I have argued that the cultural heritages of the modern world are plural, not "universal"; that
they are constructed, not preserved-transmitted in the form of a self-
same tradition or a core of invariable meanings; and that such constructions are the site of the conflict of interpretations.

What then of the apparent paradox in the notion of the cultural heritages of a classless society, of the "heritages" of the "future"? This is not really a paradox, but rather a way of grasping the dynamic of a critical-utopian interpretation of cultural practices and traditions. It means to suggest that our critical relation to our own society is shaped by how we at once undertake to understand the past and take responsibility for the future. Critical hermeneutics thus introduces both a critical and an anticipatory moment into the process of cultural preservation-transmission. The critical moment aims at the forms of domination which imprint the production and reception of culture, past and present; the anticipatory moment seeks to clarify social changes the need for which is articulated in the symbolic domain of culture and the realization of which lies in the direction of political self-organization and action. The interpretive procedures required for such a project are therefore located at the juncture between cultural heritages and social critique. And since that juncture is always situational, the construction of the future's cultural past is itself contextual and variable, justified neither by the immanence of meaning nor by the goal of history.

My intent in the studies of Blake and Goethe has been to work through, and reflect upon, such interpretive procedures with regard to just one cultural field relevant to critical hermeneutics—specifically, the field constituted by the Western cultural tradition as it has been constructed or preserved-transmitted by traditional hermeneutics. The task has been two-edged and hence reflects both the reactive and the innovative moments of critical hermeneutics. On the one hand, a *negative* hermeneutic of the constructed tradition aims at disturbing the illusions of univocality and continuity which traditional hermeneutics gives to the so-called canon. And, on the other hand, a *reconstructive* hermeneutic develops a kind of counterinterpretation that preserves those transmitted texts by disclosing not only their promise of civilization but also their inherence in barbarism. The relevance and value of Blake's and Goethe's work has, therefore, had to be tested in the interpretive process, not presupposed by the fact that these works and authors have been accorded—or have achieved—canonical status. Indeed, all that we have been assured of in advance is that the form in which these texts have been preserved-transmitted is inseparable from the project of "affirmative culture," and hence the legitimation of domination.

The Western tradition is not the only or the privileged cultural field of critical hermeneutics. There are two other such fields from which a socially critical hermeneutics constructs heritages and draws the values and meanings relevant to both the critique of contemporary society and its utopian aspirations. While these fields frequently overlap and need to be continually related to one another anew, they do not form a monological horizon of universal meanings and values.

The first might be called, with Walter Benjamin, Ernst Bloch, and E. P. Thompson in mind, the discontinuous heritage of revolt—the symbolizations and representations of those who have been vanquished in the social struggles of the past. Slaves, peasants, and workers as well as women and oppressed peoples have developed cultural practices and traditions in which can be read their resistance to domination and their historically defeated attempts to oppose injustice and oppression. To preserve those heritages, indeed to recover them from beneath the rubble created by the victors, is to transmit an understanding of what Bloch called humanity's unfinished tasks.

Second, there are the cultural practices through which the social movements and oppressed peoples of the contemporary world mold their social identities and elaborate their specific forms of resistance and opposition in response to modern forms of domination, that is, institutionalized exploitation, coercion, and nonreciprocity. This "field" is in fact as variegated as the struggles of women, Third World populations, gays, youth, and popular movements struggling over specific rights and freedoms, the environment, militarism, living conditions, and so on. It is here that critical theory has the task of opening, and opening itself to, the *dialogue* of contemporary culture. Those practices of contemporary culture which are marginalized and typically declared merely particular as opposed to universal can be all the more effectively given their voice as we relativize and reinterpret the Western tradition, which has staked its claim to universality. It is also the responsibility of critical social theory and socially critical cultural theory, whose intellectual and aesthetic formation is so closely bound up with the Western tradition, to recognize how significantly the cultural practices of social movements today provide the real motive and leverage of social critique.

Throughout this work, I have used the term *domination* in the following sense: the socially organized forms of exploitation, coercion, and nonreciprocity which structure the uses that one individual or group makes of another for the satisfaction of its own need. The capacity of human beings to serve as wealth for one another is not itself the defining feature of domination. Following a premise to be found in Marx and in Freud, I have considered such interdependence an essential aspect of social life in the sense that all human satisfactions require the mediation of the labor and desire of others. However, that individuals or groups are made to serve as wealth, as the source of others' satisfactions, without controlling the products of their own labors or enjoying the recognition of their own desires—this is the condition of domination. It follows from these definitions that domination has not only the economic aspect which has been central to Marxist theory but also a moral-political aspect. Social relations are not only relations of production, the division of labor, the distribution of surplus wealth, and so on; they are at the same time interhuman relations conducted through interactions whose coerciveness or non-reciprocity can be expressed or disguised, challenged or defended, by the participants themselves. I have tried to clarify this perspective, and its capacity to orient our self-understanding of cultural interpretation, through a range of problematics.

First of all, I have taken up and extended Habermas's discourse-ethic as a means of theorizing the tension that is built into discursively or symbolically mediated interactions. On the one hand, discursive practices are a society's means of legitimating its prevailing forms of domination. On the other hand, there is inscribed in the pragmatics of communication what might be called the *promise* of uncoerced mutual understanding and mutual recognition among the participants. In Habermas's phrase, the intersubjectivity of understanding holds "the possibility of agreement without constraint and recognition without force." The potential for uncoerced mutual understanding and recognition in any given set of language practices is, however, constrained by the social relations of domination in which those practices function. It is for this reason that Habermas has called the legitimation of domination systematically distorted communication or a violation of the "ideal speech situation." But it is for this same reason that I have rejected Habermas's adaptation of key aspects of Gadamerian hermeneutics and argued instead that the hermeneutical experience of cultural traditions is, like any other form of social communication, saturated with the struggle between legitimation and resistance, contestation, or critique.

Second, I have attempted to trace how Marx's initial insight into culture as a set of material-social practices and, therefore, practices whose participants can contest and revaluate according to established or innovated standards of enrichment, noncoerciveness, or reciprocity was lost in his transposition of the cultural problematic into a question of consciousness and ultimately class consciousness. As regards literature and art, this inaugural conception of culture in the Marxist tradition has given rise to two contrary tendencies: either to reduce artistic practices to a "reflection" or function of an ideology whose terms are externally determined by the relations of production (a tendency most fully represented by Lukács) or, like Marcuse, Adorno, and Habermas, to privilege art and aesthetic experience as those social practices most removed from, and hence least tainted by, social relations of domination. Both perspectives share with the original paradigm an assumption that artistic practice and aesthetic experience are not themselves, as material-social practices, permeated by moral-political relations or by power.

Given that the literary texts I have discussed in depth belong to the constructed tradition of traditional hermeneutics, I have worked through my criticism of the Marxian paradigm in the form of a negative-reconstructive interpretation of Blake and Goethe. In this context, though, the narrowing of the focus to artworks has been a kind of litmus test for the broader sorts of questions regarding cultural theory.

Gadamer sees the need for interpretation as arising from the situation in which the mutual understanding promised directly in aesthetic experience has been disturbed, paradigmatically by the passage of time. The supposed "timelessness" of the artwork prompts a countermovement to this interruption of understanding and sustains the hermeneutical process of repairing. Critical hermeneutics sets the terms of the problem differently. For there is another sense in which the intersubjectivity of understanding is broken or disturbed, namely, by those systematically distorted processes of communication which condition a text's production and its reception within specific social relations of domination. Mutual understanding is disturbed not only by the passage of time from the moment of artistic production to that of aesthetic reception. Within either of these two moments, the potential for mutual understanding is blocked to the degree that the production or reception of the text is constrained by the effects of domination.

Aesthetic communication does indeed promise such mutuality. But its realization is neither a given of aesthetic experience nor the assured outcome of the interpretive process. The nonrealization of mutual understanding is ingrained in aesthetic experience just as deeply as is the promise of mutual understanding. Because of this tension, socially crit-

ical interpretations are situational and strategic. The interpreter encounters the transmitted text as a mediation between the historical
context of its production and that of its reception. The text is informed
by, and gives a formed response to, the modes of domination which
structure the social context of its production. By the same token, the
forms of domination which structure the social context of reception
come into play in the interpretive process, critically or uncritically
according to the interpreters' social commitments and interests. For
traditional hermeneutics, the communicative power of the artwork is
taken as a signal that its meaning bridges the temporal distance between
text and interpreters and transcends the historical differences between
their respective societies. For critical hermeneutics, the communicative
promise of aesthetic experience indeed engages the text in a countermovement to domination, but without thereby releasing the interpreters
from the tasks of ideological critique and historicizing analysis, including the task of measuring the distance and historical difference
between societies.

Let me formulate the problem in terms that will still resonate with
Gadamer. Insofar as the transmitted text comes to address new interpreters, it occasions or invites a communicative experience that is no
longer contained within the horizon of the text's original context or
the closed circle of its original audience. As soon as the text comes to
address interpreters who are differently situated historically and socially, its promise of uncoerced mutual understanding undergoes a
change. The text now makes a claim to validity that was not immanent
in its original context. The new *claim* to validity comes from the specific,
historically contingent *demands* for validity on the part of the interpreters—demands shaped by contemporary forms of resistance and
opposition to domination and to the systematic distortions of communication which legitimate domination. The artwork's excess of address carries it into a communicative context which, retroactively,
determines anew the content of its promise of uncoerced understanding
and recognition. It should not, therefore, be paradoxical to assert that
such changing claims to validity *become immanent* in the text, even as
they were not immanent in its original context.

As a consequence, the internal organization of the text is volatilized.
"Unity of meaning" ceases to be a viable postulate once we recognize
that the inner logic of the transmitted text is shaped by the interplay
between, on the one hand, its changeable claim to validity or promise
of uncoerced understanding and recognition and, on the other hand,

the historically contingent social constraints at play in its production- and reception-contexts and, by implication, in the process by which it has been historically preserved-transmitted down to the present. Even as we relate part and whole heuristically in the interpretive process, we have no grounds for assuming in advance that the relation of part-whole in a text will turn out to be a relation of unity. Given the dialectic of communicative promise and social constraint, the economy of a text's significations and the interaction of its form and meaning are more likely to be unresolved, even contradictory. Critical theory also has to assume an attitude of "hermeneutical suspicion" with regard to the related assumption of Gadamerian method, namely, that an ultimate unity of part-whole relations lies in the power of the constructed cultural tradition to furnish a universe of meaning which masters textuality by sifting the significations of texts into a continuous, unified, and putatively universal monologue.

Once these assumptions are suspended, the sequence of hermeneutical processes: fore-understanding / interpretation / appropriation / application, loses the tautological structure of seamlessly interconnected moments. Rather, the "slashes" mark the joints that have to be connected or broken in the critical-hermeneutical process in accordance with the concrete exigencies of the interpretive situation. If fore-understanding is no longer guided by the presupposition of the unity of part-whole, then the explicitly elaborated interpretation is no longer assured of lifting the fore-understanding of a given text to the level of a confirmed critical judgment. The outcome of such a process becomes an open question. Which elements of our overdetermined fore-understanding are rejected and which are retained—indeed, even which elements are made explicit and scrutinized—are questions decidable only in the self-reflective moments of actual interpretations. They have to be answered and justified in relation to interpretive aims that are not purely text-immanent in the traditional or Gadamerian sense.

Similarly, the sequence interpretation / appropriation / application does not have, within the procedures of a socially critical hermeneutics, the circular movement that Gadamer traces when he makes the understanding of meanings continuous with the acceptance of their validity ("appropriation") and hence their applicability to the interpreters' life-context. To borrow terms used by Ricoeur, there is a tension in the hermeneutical process between *participatory belonging* and *alienating distantiation*—as regards a text's belonging to or distantiation from a tradition and as regards interpreters' participation in or distantiation from tradition and text. The question when and how it is justifiable to overcome such distantiation and appropriate a text into a constructed tradition or into the reconstruction of cultural heritages; or, conversely, when and how it is justifiable to estrange ourselves from a text or tradition, negating the participatory belonging that has linked us to it—these questions too are always open. And their resolution, moreover, will always have a relatively ad hoc standing, situationally dependent on the interpreters' commitments to "the struggles and wishes of the age" and on the level of self-clarification that those struggles and wishes have been able to achieve.

The life-context to which validated meanings are "applied" and against which other meanings are invalidated or criticized is precisely our own society, understood now as a configuration of social struggles over the institutionalized forms of domination and the evolving forms of contestation, critique, and opposition. Whether viewed as the reception-context in which cultural heritages are preserved-transmitted or as the life-context to which interpretations are applied, the social site of interpretation is an arena of politically relevant conflicts of interpretation.

Index

Library of Congress Cataloging-in-Publication Data
Brenkman, John.
    Culture and domination.
    Includes index.
    1. Culture. 2. Sociology—Philosophy. I. Title.
HM101.B74 1987   306   87-47543
ISBN 0-8014-1457-1 (alk. paper)